The Modern Muslim World

Series Editor
Dietrich Jung, Centre for Contemporary Middle East Studies, University of Southern Denmark, Odense, Denmark

The modern Muslim world is an integral part of global society. In transcending the confines of area studies, this series encompasses scholarly work on political, economic, and cultural issues in modern Muslim history, taking a global perspective. Focusing on the period from the early nineteenth century to the present, it combines studies of Muslim majority regions, such as the Middle East and in Africa and Asia, with the analysis of Muslim minority communities in Europe and the Americas. Emphasizing the global connectedness of Muslims, the series seeks to promote and encourage the understanding of contemporary Muslim life in a comparative perspective and as an inseparable part of modern globality.

Dietrich Jung · Florian Zemmin
Editors

Postcolonialism and Social Theory in Arabic

Intellectual Traditions and Historical Entanglements

palgrave
macmillan

Editors
Dietrich Jung
Center for Modern Middle East
and Muslim Studies
University of Southern Denmark
Odense, Denmark

Florian Zemmin
Freie Universität Berlin
Berlin, Germany

ISSN 2945-6134 ISSN 2945-6142 (electronic)
The Modern Muslim World
ISBN 978-3-031-63648-6 ISBN 978-3-031-63649-3 (eBook)
https://doi.org/10.1007/978-3-031-63649-3

Cover credit: imageBROKER.com GmbH & Co. KG/Alamy Stock Photo

This Palgrave Macmillan imprint is published by the registered company Springer Nature Switzerland AG
The registered company address is: Gewerbestrasse 11, 6330 Cham, Switzerland

Acknowledgements

This volume evolved from a workshop on "Writing Social Theory in Arabic" that was organized by Dietrich Jung, Sari Hanafi, and Florian Zemmin and held at Freie Universität Berlin in November 2022. The workshop and the later editing of the book manuscript was funded by the Danish Institute in Damascus. We are grateful to the Institute and its director for making this project possible. For their help in organizing and conducting the workshop, we thank Elisabeth Kanarachou and Rosa van Dorp. For very much improving the language of all chapters, far beyond mere formalities, the editors are most grateful to Catherine Schwerin. Aram Abu-Salah was of great help in checking the transliteration of Arabic terms. Above all, we thank all the authors of this volume for contributing their scholarship and for their excellent collaboration. We also once again thank those participants in the workshop whose papers for one reason or another did not come to be included in this publication, but nonetheless contributed significantly to our discussions.

Contents

1 Beyond Deconstruction: An Introduction to Writing Social Theory in Arabic 1
Dietrich Jung and Florian Zemmin

Part I Social Theory in Academic Disciplines

2 (Post-)Colonialism, Authoritarianism, and Authenticity: Sociology in Arab Countries 17
Florian Zemmin

3 Who Counts as a Theorist? Locating Maghrebi Sociologists in the Intellectual History of Decolonization 47
Florian Keller

4 Decentering First World War History: Arabic Perspectives on a Global Event 69
Ahmed Abou El Zalaf

5 The Islamization of Knowledge: Critique and Alternative 93
Sari Hanafi

Part II Social Theory Beyond Academic Disciplines

6 Liquid Modernity in Arabic 121
Haggag Ali

7 **Crisis and Creativity: Tradition and Revolution in Arab Social Theory** 145
Mohammed A. Bamyeh

8 **The Road Out of Marxism: Entangled Thought in 1970s Lebanon** 165
Sune Haugbolle

9 **Arabic Social Theory in Japanese and Indonesian: Transregional Ideoscapes of the Long 1960s** 187
Claudia Derichs

List of Contributors

Haggag Ali Academy of Arts, Giza, Egypt

Mohammed A. Bamyeh University of Pittsburgh, Pittsburgh, PA, USA

Claudia Derichs Humboldt University, Berlin, Germany

Sari Hanafi Department of Sociology, Anthropology and Media Studies, American University Beirut, Beirut, Lebanon

Sune Haugbolle Department for Social Sciences and Business, Roskilde University, Roskilde, Denmark

Dietrich Jung University of Southern Denmark, Odense, Denmark

Florian Keller Graduate School for Global Intellectual History (GIH), Freie Universität Berlin, Berlin, Germany

Ahmed Abou El Zalaf Copenhagen, Denmark

Florian Zemmin Freie Universität Berlin, Berlin, Germany

CHAPTER 1

Beyond Deconstruction: An Introduction to Writing Social Theory in Arabic

Dietrich Jung and Florian Zemmin

This book engages in a scholarly endeavor that Dipesh Chakrabarty once described as the provincialization of Europe. Taking his point of departure in the Indian *Subaltern Studies* project, in *Provincializing Europe* Chakrabarty aimed at decentering the imaginary of a Europe whose post-Enlightenment history was authoritative in the construction of the conceptual world of "political modernity" (Chakrabarty, 2000).[1] According to him, the overwhelming majority of contemporary social scientists applied Eurocentric conceptual tools in researching European and non-European histories alike. Even more significant, the study of non-European histories has been informed by a historical philosophy of evolutionary progress according to which modernity appeared first in Europe and then elsewhere. With respect to political modernity, so

D. Jung (✉)
University of Southern Denmark, Odense, Denmark
e-mail: jung@sdu.dk

F. Zemmin
Freie Universität Berlin, Berlin, Germany

D. Jung and F. Zemmin (eds.), *Postcolonialism and Social Theory in Arabic*, The Modern Muslim World,
https://doi.org/10.1007/978-3-031-63649-3_1

Chakrabarty's argument, non-European peoples have been placed in an "imaginary waiting room of history." In the end, this philosophy of history served the European great powers in their legitimation of colonial domination as a "civilizing mission" (2000: 8). Within these historical and conceptual contexts, Chakrabarty considered European thought to be both "indispensable and inadequate" in the historical and political study of the various life practices outside Europe (2000: 6).

Dipesh Chakrabarty and other scholars in the field of postcolonial studies have raised justified criticism when it comes to the taken-for-granted universal analytical validity of contemporary and classical social science concepts. At the center of this criticism is the above-described Eurocentric nature of this conceptual apparatus. There is certainly no doubt that most of the concepts and categories of modern social theory almost exclusively rely on abstractions from European and North American histories and societies. In the context of the Middle East area studies debate in the USA, for instance, Timothy Mitchell heavily criticized this Eurocentric character of the social sciences. In his call for provincializing American social science, Mitchell echoed the critique by theorists in the field of postcolonial studies such as Dipesh Chakrabarty (Mitchell, 2003). Regarding contemporary research on the Middle East, to mention another example, Steve Heydemann claimed—basically in line with Mitchell and Chakrabarty—"that European experiences should not be seen as offering an automatic starting point" for the analysis of Middle Eastern history (Heydemann, 2000: 9).

There is no going back behind this criticism and its valuable points. Indeed, the historical background knowledge in contemporary debates on social theory largely represents the historical experiences of Western Europe and North America. The conceptual world of classical historical sociology—Norbert Elias, Charles Tilly, Max Weber—is inseparably linked to modern state formation in Europe (cf. Jung, 2017). In this sense, the categories and concepts of the social sciences have a Eurocentric bias. Some sociologists with a postcolonial orientation, therefore, advocate that the teaching of sociology should incorporate a critical discussion of the Eurocentric character of classical authors such as Emile Durkheim, Karl Marx, or Max Weber. Moreover, they urge for the incorporation of non-European and female thinkers in an expanded *Sociology beyond the Canon* (Alatas & Sinha, 2017). European sociology is indeed in need of such a critique with respect to its all-too-long unquestioned hegemonic

European premises. Yet, what are the alternatives that could replace Eurocentric conceptual frameworks? Unfortunately, the literature in the field of postcolonial studies does not offer many concrete answers to this question. All too often the postcolonial critique of Eurocentric social science finds rest in the deconstruction of so-called Western thought alone.

This focus on deconstruction was already apparent when it came to one of the foundational contributions to postcolonial studies. In 1985, Gayatri Chakravorty Spivak, a scholarly icon of postcolonial critique, published her landmark article "Subaltern Studies: Deconstructing Historiography." In this article, in volume IV of the Subaltern Studies project, Spivak deals with the attempt of the scholarly project to return agency to the suppressed and dispossessed people of India. Yet in referring to more than twenty "Western" philosophers, the article reads like a who's who of the philosophy of modernity from German Idealism to French Poststructuralism, rather than an account of the voices of the suppressed peoples of the Global South.[2] Spivak's pilot article in this way clearly underlines Chakrabarty's opinion that the study of non-European histories cannot neglect the Eurocentric legacy in global social thought. As a consequence, the critique of Western social theory by proponents of postcolonial studies has often taken place within the discursive frameworks of precisely those scholarly works against which their critique has been directed. Even more significant, the analysis of postcolonial studies rests predominantly on literature in English and French. References to non-English primary sources such as in Hindi, Urdu, or Arabic have been rather rare in this debate (Hassan, 2002: 2).[3] Somehow ironically, most postcolonial attempts within the English-speaking academy often remain on the rather abstract level of criticizing the Eurocentric formation of modern social thought based on texts in English language. Postcolonial approaches tend to not really investigate the construction of social theories in other linguistic settings. Instead, they are continuously engaged in the deconstruction of so-called Western hegemonies.

Due to this constant engagement with Western philosophy, postcolonial theory has meanwhile itself become the target of critique by more radical approaches from scholars operating under the concept of "decoloniality." Constituting a specific intellectual movement calling for more fundamental changes in social thought, scholars representing this kind of decolonialization studies today demand a radical departure from Western epistemologies. According to this more recent trend,[4] scholars in postcolonial studies are still working within epistemological frames of reference that are characterized by core elements of coloniality (see, e.g., Rodríguez, 2010; cf. Gu, 2020). When calling for a radical departure from Eurocentric epistemologies, decolonization studies want to entirely do away with the European legacy in social science research. They basically rebut Dipesh Chakrabarty's claim that in contemporary social theory, European thought is both indispensable and inadequate. Scholars who represent this theoretical approach of decolonization demand a complete "delinking" from all dictates of "coloniality." Instead of dealing with epistemological contradictions and ambiguities, they advocate that scholars extricate themselves from the all-encompassing "colonial matrix of power" (Mignolo, 2020: 613). Unlike Dipesh Chakrabarty, they do not regard the European heritage of the social sciences as an indispensable part of contemporary social theory, but rather as ballast that needs to be cast off.

The present anthology addresses this discussion with respect to work on social theory in the Arab Middle East and North Africa, decidedly aiming to go beyond deconstruction. Instead of endorsing the radical position of decoloniality, we share Chakrabarty's claim that we should keep the European conceptual and historical legacy in mind. On the one hand, the studies collected here all show the indispensable role of European legacies in the writing of social theory in Arabic. The works of Arab scholars referenced in this volume clearly contain those signs of ambiguity which Dipesh Chakrabarty identified in the social sciences more generally. On the other hand, this book underpins Raewyn Connell's argument that scholars from the previously colonized regions of the world have constantly produced original social thoughts about the modern world (Connell, 2007: xii). Consequently, this book aims to contribute to a discussion of social theory from a perspective that does not forget Europe, but embeds it in a global context of intellectual thought (cf. Schlichte, 2023: 9). Arab authors, in reflecting on social relations and developments, draw on both local intellectual traditions and European thought. Their reflections are relevant for the construction of this kind of global social theory and deserve greater consideration therein. In doing so, this volume aims to go beyond the deconstruction of established Eurocentric theory and thus to make a contribution to a more globally oriented discussion about the construction of entangled social theories.

In this discussion, the concept of entanglement helps to liberate non-European social actors from sitting in the waiting room of history. It draws our attention to historical processes of interdependence, interactions, and exchange in the emergence of the modern world. The concept of entanglement is predicated on the idea of a mutual construction of modernity in a global dimension. In the rise of global modernity, diverse cultural traditions have played formative roles in the construction of the present (Randeria, 2002: 308). The analytical prism of entanglement emphasizes complex processes of historical exchange without denying the asymmetric power relations of colonialism. It is these processes of asymmetric exchange that we have to take into consideration in our efforts at contemporary social theory building (Bhambra, 2014).[5] European and later also US-American social theories form hegemonic metropolitan centers on both institutional and theoretical levels. Consequently, they influenced and continue to influence the formation and practice of social thought in Arab countries. Social theory in Arabic, however, is shaped by other factors, too. It has its own specific characteristics, traditions, and contributions, and it is therefore a clear expression of the general ambiguity in contemporary social thought.

Against this background, we suggest not only critically reflecting upon the concepts of so-called Western social science but also thoroughly engaging with Arabic contributions to social theory at the same time. In so doing, the authors of this book apply the concept of social theory in a broad sense. Social theory in this anthology includes different subcategories and strands, such as political theory, sociology, social history, social philosophy, normative social theories, and political ideologies. In short, we consider social theory here as an umbrella for various forms of contemporary thinking about the social in the modern world. The authors of this book take a close look at works on social theory in the Arabic language in this sense. Consequently, the chapters of this anthology present both unity and difference. They are united in the effort to present contributions to social theory perhaps unknown to readers not familiar with Arabic.

Thereby, the red thread running through its chapters is a specific gaze at the global entanglements which took place in the construction of these contributions in Arabic. Yet the individual chapters differ in the kind of social theory and literature they address. By purpose, the chapters present rather diverse forms of social thought, however, guided by some of the following common questions.[6] What are the concepts, themes, and historical narratives in contemporary Arabic social theory? In which ways do

Arab social theorists provide us with alternatives to the conceptual apparatuses employed by so-called Western social theory? To what extent are Arab and Western sociologies entangled with each other? Do their works confront us with wholesale alternatives to European thought? Can we indeed observe an epistemological change in social theory in Arabic? The authors of this book respond to these questions from a variety of angles, and we have organized the book into two parts. The first part takes a closer look at disciplinary formations in Arab social sciences, whereas the second part widens our view to include forms of literary critique and political ideology.

In the first part, the authors address social theory in terms of sociology, and social history, and attempt to establish social sciences in a specifically Islamic perspective. In Chapter One, Florian Zemmin gives an overview of both institutional and theoretical developments of sociology in Arab countries since the early twentieth century. The emphasis in his study is on sociology in Egypt and Morocco, while alluding to the broader Arab environment. In taking the discipline of sociology as his reference to social theory, Zemmin looks at entanglements between specifically Arab themes and structural characteristics with global frames of reference in sociological theory building. In the following chapter, Florian Keller takes up the theme of the relationship of Arab sociologists with the postcolonial state. Keller sheds light on the paradoxical situation of Arab social scientists who represent both the results and the critics of the various modernizing projects of Arab state regimes. The chapter focuses on sociologists from the Maghreb, in particular from Algeria and Tunisia, placing them in conversation with the Italian philosopher Antonio Gramsci. Keller addresses our common point of reference, the issue of global intellectual entanglements, regarding the ways in which this sociological critique was directed against the application of theoretical elements of Western social thought in the political ideologies that informed the modernization policies of Arab regimes.

Sari Hanafi presents in Chapter Three the more recent attempts at "Islamically grounding" the social sciences. The chapter delivers a content analysis of books, journal articles, and MA and PhD theses in Arabic that claim to work with an Islamic perspective. Hanafi's chapter is guided by the question of whether this kind of social theory writing represents a necessary alternative to Eurocentric approaches or rather an instance of contemporary identity politics. Following this view on sociology, Ahmed Abou El Zalaf provides in the fourth chapter an overview of the scholarly production of Arab historians. The focus of his chapter is on the historiography of the First World War. As there is no systematic study in English on the ways in which historiographical works in Arabic have presented the Great War to Arab readers, this chapter is a first attempt in this direction and provides a brief overview on the subject, including two case studies focusing on Algeria and Tunisia respectively.

In the first part of this book, thus, social theory appears in terms of different forms of academic disciplines. The second part opens up to a broader understanding of the concept of social theory, including in particular political ideologies and the role of public intellectuals in contemporary social thought. In Chapter Five, Haggag Ali discusses the role of metaphors in social theory in putting two intellectuals center stage. Focusing on the metaphor of "liquid modernity," Ali's contribution discusses its usage by the Egyptian intellectual Abdelwahab Elmessiri and the Polish-British sociologist Zygmunt Bauman, analyzing the close entanglement of European and Arab discourses about liquid modernity. In Chapter Six, then, Mohammed Bamyeh analyzes two genres of Arab intellectual thought in terms of being ideological precursors to the uprisings of 2011. These genres are, namely, heritage studies and the historical novel, which both served Arab public intellectuals to approach questions of radical social change. With this study, Bamyeh not least provides insights into the social role of intellectuals in the complex relationship between societal crises and creativity.

In Sune Haugbolle's chapter on the historical development of Marxism in Lebanon, the ideological character of certain social theories comes further to the fore. Haugbolle argues in Chapter Seven that the transformation of Marxist intellectual thought had already taken place in the 1970s. Rather than being a mere result of the collapse of Soviet Communism, this transformation should be understood as the product of internal criticism. Haugbolle's chapter articulates the concept of entanglement by looking at the specific contextual developments that accompanied the transformation of Marxism in Lebanon and its impact on the Left in Europe. Finally, Chapter Eight brings us beyond the boundaries of social thought in Arabic. Claudia Derichs argues that social theory in Arabic has also informed intellectual thought in South-East and East Asia. This final chapter, therefore, is an expression of global entanglement in its ultimate form. Derichs presents the readers with a transregional perspective in the construction of contemporary social theory that connects the Middle East with Southeast Asia on the one hand and with Japan on the other.

Taken together, the chapters of this volume highlight the relevance and fruitfulness of considering Arabic contributions to the construction of a more global understanding and practice of social theory. The various chapters show that studies in Arabic can play a crucial role in tackling the "impasse of postcolonial studies" which results from their strong reliance on the discussion of postcolonial literature that has been written in English and French (Hassan, 2002: 60). The collection of articles in this book mark steps toward going beyond the mere deconstruction of earlier Eurocentric formations. In addition, the authors of this anthology also suggest several directions in which to expand future endeavors of the theorization of social life and which aspects to keep in mind.

One aspect that turns up frequently and should continue to be borne in mind is the distinction between social theory and social thought. The question of who counts as a theorist is decisive when it comes to global social theory beyond its hegemonic core. As Omnia El Shakry (2019) argued, Arab intellectual production is too often considered as mere thought, valid in its local context only. In sharp contrast, European intellectual production is often perceived as "real" social theory with universal reach. However, there is no clear-cut distinction between social theory and social thought. This is apparent, for instance, in Mohammad Bamyeh's contribution, which deals with concepts of the social in historical novels instead of academic disciplines. Bamyeh argues that prompted by social crises intellectual activity produces new knowledge. In the Arab context, he thereby identifies two genres for this knowledge production: Social theory emerged specifically in the critical heritage school and the panoramic historical novel. The broad notion of social theory applied in this book is able to accommodate these different genres and even includes the reasoning about the social as part of political ideologies. Then again, under the aim of constructing a globally entangled and integrated social theory, not all thoughts about life in common is includable. Future endeavors should explicate their criteria based on which particular thinkers and types of thought are included as part of social theory.

Several of the chapters make the distinction between theory and ideology. The boundaries between these two concepts are definitely not easy to draw. On the one hand, social theories can hardly claim to be objective, neutral, and free of value judgments and normative assumptions. The formulation of social theories always takes place from a certain position. On the other hand, the construction of political ideologies necessarily implies the incorporation of elements of social theories. The modernization policies of post-independence Arab regimes and their critique by Tunisian sociologists as presented in Florian Keller's chapter is a case in point. Florian Zemmin's contribution further underlines the role of sociological thought in the postcolonial state- and nation-building in Arab countries. Consequently, in the political practice of the postcolonial Arab state, we can identify the role of social theory in the formulation of state ideologies and national modernization projects. In this context, Islamist movements have increasingly advocated alternative projects of "Islamic modernities." These Islamic projects of modernity draw on religious traditions and are directed against state policies informed by classical modernization theories. They represent not only a critique of postcolonial Arab regimes but also a struggle against the hegemonic ideas of Western modernities (cf. Majid, 1995; Thurfjell, 2008). Sari Hanafi's contribution clearly brings out these ideological motivations behind the attempts to construct Islamic theories of society and to Islamize the social sciences.

In public debate, ascription of the status of "ideology" to social thought is often an attempt to deny their theoretical validity. Tellingly, thinkers from the Global South who are considered social theorists by postcolonial authors (e.g., Byrd & Miri, 2018; Connell, 2007) have frequently been dismissed by others as mere ideologists. The contributions to this volume, however, underline the close and often almost inseparable intersection of theory and ideology for strands of social thought, such as those of Marxist (Derichs, Haugbolle) and Islamist (Hanafi) provenience. The boundaries between social theory and political ideologies are often fluent. Social theories and ideologies seem to be at the ends of a continuum, leading from heuristic to legitimizing purposes. Even more importantly, as Claudia Derichs argues, there is a circular relationship between experiences, social practices, and theoretical reflections. Derichs aptly shows this in her examples of the Japanese–Palestinian solidarity movement and the faith-based relations between Muslims in Southeast Asia and the Middle East. Therefore, it is difficult to draw definite or universally valid lines between social theory and ideology, making it the task of individual research projects to reflect on their specific understanding of the relationship between both.

A further characteristic of the collection of articles presented here is the fact that social theory in Arabic builds decisively on global entanglements. These entanglements, too, combine theoretical thought, historical social experience, and local cultural traditions. Ahmed El Zalaf's chapter on historiographic works on the First World War delivers proof for this close entanglement of European and non-European thought and experience regarding a global event. The majority of concepts and themes of Arab historians seem familiar to European readers. More significantly, Zalaf argues that the growing body of historiographical research in Arabic is an inherent part of the global growth in World War I studies. Zalaf's contribution shows that historiography in Arabic may not rely on alternative concepts and themes, but it tells its readers local alternative narratives about mutually experienced global events. The combination of local social and political contexts with more general conceptual frames, which is the lesson of his chapter, results in alternative interpretations rather than in a rejection of all elements of hegemonic European thought. However, this hegemony is not uncontested. When it comes to the origin of the metaphor of liquid modernity, Haggag Ali points to the fact that the Egyptian intellectual Elmessiri apparently used it before it was found in the work of Zygmunt Bauman. Ali furthermore provides Arabic and Egyptian examples for how the globalized metaphor of liquid modernity came to be used in the reflection upon and the evaluation of societal conditions and developments. Sune Haugbolle's contribution, to take another example, describes the influence which the Palestinian Mounir Shafiq had on the ideological formation of the Norwegian student movement for Palestine and of related Maoist groups in Oslo. Despite the asymmetric power relations of colonialism, from the perspective of entanglement, we can see that concepts and social thought more generally do not only travel in one direction. The period of the "long 1960s"—the central time frame of both Haugbolle's and Derichs's contributions—gives ample proof for this observation.

Finally, new theorizing is also constituted through various forms of social practice. The role of social practices in contemporary theory building is highlighted in several case studies (Ali, Haugbolle, Derichs). This is also true for the global knowledge production in which we are involved. In this endeavor, the conceptual world of the social sciences still relies too heavily on the practices of Europe and North America. Idealized types of "Western" social practices become the heuristic tools for understanding the "Other." Consequently, historical processes of the Global South have often been narrated in terms of "dysfunctionality, deviance, or pathology" (Schlichte, 2023: 5). These narratives clearly show that power asymmetries continue to shape contemporary theorizing on a political, economic, and institutional level. These asymmetries also imply language. In order to assume a global reach, social theory has been narrated almost exclusively in English. Any attempt at provincializing Europe or North America for this sake must go along with breaking this linguistic hegemony in social theory (Mamdani, 2019: 25). Albeit indirectly, this book may also contribute to this task.

In the end, a number of questions remain against the background of the above power asymmetries: Who has the ability to research on whom? Who has access to literature and the means for publishing? Who has the funds and the right passport to be able to travel for academic purposes? As scholars based in the Global North, we can hardly work on, let alone resolve, all these questions. We should, however, be conscious of our privileged means for shaping knowledge production. Cooperating with colleagues from less-privileged settings and making visible global contributions to knowledge production is the least we can do. In this endeavor, we can only hope that colleagues from the Global South might consider us as cooperating partners, too. It is our contention that constructive contributions to future global social theory will have to come from a variety of perspectives and actors who share this common interest.

Notes

1. The Subaltern Studies project is documented in the five volumes *Subaltern Studies. Writings on South Asian History and Society*, edited by Ranajit Guha and published by Oxford University Press between 1982 and 1989. Dipesh Chakrabarty also contributed chapters to three of these anthologies. Besides Edward Said's *Orientalism*, the writings of this project played a fundamental role in the development of postcolonial studies.
2. Spivak's approach is anchored in French poststructuralism and introduced the category of gender into postcolonial studies (Hassan 2002: 48). Her later works also count among those studies with a broad and diverse set of empirical sources.
3. A notable exemption is the work of Sheldon Pollock (2003a, 2006), who aims to offer insights for the scholars of postcoloniality through his work on the "literary precoloniality" of South Asia (2003b: 32). In his works, he draws on literature in Sanskrit and "premodern" South Asian vernacular languages.
4. Earlier programmatic calls for decolonizing sociology tellingly came from intellectuals in Morocco, a country in which sociology before

independence in 1956 was most closely linked to French colonialist interests (see Ben Jelloun 1977 and especially Khatibi 1985).

5. In the field of historiography, the concept of entanglement is an aspect of the approaches of historians, such as Bayly (2004) and Conrad (2016), who promote the concept of "Global History."
6. Given the intended diversity of the contributions to this book, this introduction does not contain a discussion of a mutually shared state of the art. The authors of the individual chapters, therefore, acquaint the readers with the essential discussions in their respective fields of specialization.

References

Alatas, S. F., & Sinha, V. (Eds.). (2017). *Sociological Theory Beyond the Canon*. Palgrave.

Bayly, C. A. (2004). *The Birth of the Modern World 1780–1914*. Blackwell Publishing.

Ben Jelloun, T. (1977). Decolonizing Sociology in the Maghreb: Usefulness and Risks of a Critical Function. In S. E. Ibrahim & N. S. Hopkins (Eds.), *Arab Society: Social Science Perspectives* (pp. 70–75). American University of Cairo Press.

Bhambra, G. K. (2014). *Connected Sociologies*. Bloomsbury Publishing.

Byrd, D., & Miri, S. J. (2018). *Ali Shariati and the Future of Social Theory: Religion, Revolution, and the Role of the Intellectual*. Studies in Critical Social Sciences. Brill.

Chakrabarty, D. (2000). *Provincializing Europe*. Princeton University Press.

Connell, R. (2007). *Southern Theory. The Global Dynamics of Knowledge in Social Science*. Polity Press.

Conrad, S. (2016). *What is Global History?* Princeton University Press.

El Shakry, O. (2019). Rethinking Arab Intellectual History: Epistemology, Historicism, Secularism. *Modern Intellectual History, 18*(2), 547–572. https://doi.org/10.1017/S1479244319000337

Gu, M. D. (2020). What is "Decoloniality"? A Postcolonial Critique. *Postcolonial Studies, 23*(4), 596–600.

Hassan, W. S. (2002). Postcolonial Theory and Modern Arabic Literature: Horizons of Application. *Journal of Arabic Literature, 33*(1), 45–64.

Heydemann, S. (2000). *War, Institutions and Social Change in the Middle East*. University of California Press.

Jung, D. (2017). War and State in the Middle East. Reassessing Charles Tilly in a Regional Context. In L. B. Kaspersen & J. Strandsbjerg (Eds.), *Does*

War Make States? Critical Investigations of Charles Tilly's Historical Sociology (pp. 221–242). Cambridge University Press.

Khatibi, A. (1985). Double Criticism: The Decolonization of Arab Sociology. In H. Barakat (Ed.), *Contemporary North Africa: Issues of Development and Integration* (pp. 9–19). Center for Contemporary Arab Studies, Georgetown University.

Majid, A. (1995). Can the Postcolonial Critic Speak? Orientalism and the Rushdie Affair. *Cultural Critique, 32*(Winter 1995–96), 5–42.

Mamdani, M. (2019). Decolonising Universities. In J. Jansen (Ed.), *Decolonising in Universities* (pp. 15–29). Wits University Press.

Mignolo, W. D. (2020). On Decoloniality: Second Thoughts. *Postcolonial Studies, 23*(4), 612–618.

Mitchell, T. (2003). The Middle East in the Past and Future of Social Science. In D. L. Szanton (Ed.), *The Politics of Knowledge: Area Studies and the Disciplines*. Global, Area, and International Archive 3, University of California Press: International and Area Studies Digital Collection.

Pollock, S. (Ed.). (2003a). *Literary Cultures in History: Reconstructions from South Asia*. University of California Press.

Pollock, S. (Ed.). (2003b). Introduction. In *Literary Cultures in History: Reconstructions from South Asia* (pp. 1–36). University of California Press.

Pollock, S. (2006). *The Language of the Gods in the World of Men. Sanskrit, Culture, and Power in Premodern India*. University of California.

Randeria, S. (2002). Entangled Histories of Uneven Modernities: Civil Society, Caste Solidarities and Legal Pluralism in Post-Colonial India. In Y. Elkana, I. Kratev, E. Malcamo, & S. Randeria (Eds.), *Unravelling Ties—From Social Cohesion to New Practices of Connectedness* (pp. 284–311). Campus.

Rodríguez, E. G. (2010). Decolonizing Postcolonial Rhetoric. In E. G. Rodríguez, M. Boatcă, & S. Costa (Eds.), *Decolonizing European Sociology: Transdisciplinary Approaches* (pp. 49–67). Routledge.

Schlichte, K. (2023). Indien gibt es nicht. Die Vernachlässigung Osteuropas steht für ein größeres Problem der deutschen Sozialwissenschaften. *Soziologie, 52*(4), 415–424.

Spivak, G. C. (1985). Subaltern Studies: Deconstructing Historiography. In R. Guha (Ed.), *Subaltern Studies IV: Writings on South Asian History and Society* (pp. 330–363). Oxford University Press.

Thurfjell, D. (2008). Is the Islamist Voice Subaltern? In K. W. Shands (Ed.), *Neither East nor West: Postcolonial Essays on Literature, Culture, and Religion* (pp. 157–162). Södertörn högskola.

PART I

Social Theory in Academic Disciplines

CHAPTER 2

(Post-)Colonialism, Authoritarianism, and Authenticity: Sociology in Arab Countries

Florian Zemmin

2.1 Introduction

The only Arab thinker who has been included in broader introductory works on sociology, and partly in the sociological canon, is Ibn Khaldūn. The extent to which Ibn Khaldūn's theory of communal life shares the basic assumptions of modern sociology is, of course, a matter of mixed opinion: Some commentators ahistorically equate Ibn Khaldūn's concepts with modern sociology, while others modernistically deny him any relevance for sociology. However, there are also more nuanced commentaries reflecting aspects of both camps (e.g., Alatas, 2014; Irwin, 2018). In any case, the fact is that Ibn Khaldūn died in 1406. Thus, the only significant Arab contribution to sociology is over 600 years old. Modern sociology, in turn, appears to have originated exclusively in European societies. The

F. Zemmin (✉)
Freie Universität Berlin, Berlin, Germany
e-mail: forian.zemmin@fu-berlin.de

D. Jung and F. Zemmin (eds.), *Postcolonialism and Social Theory in Arabic*, The Modern Muslim World,
https://doi.org/10.1007/978-3-031-63649-3_2

institutionalization and current practice of sociology in Arab countries remains barely known to a European readership.

This chapter provides an overview of the entangled institutional and theoretical development of sociology in Arab countries since the beginning of the twentieth century. Central aspects are the impact of the mostly authoritarian state, of colonial heritage, and of European sociology on the formation and development of sociology in Arab countries. Propositions of an "Arab" or "Islamic sociology" are discussed separately. Against particularist and universalist claims alike, it will become clear that a common sociology can be legitimized and shaped differently in the global present. As part of global theories, sociology in Arab countries nevertheless exhibits its own structural characteristics and thematic emphases.

The disciplinary history of sociology goes back almost as far in Arab countries as in Europe: the first chair of sociology was established at Cairo University in 1925, and sociological perspectives and debates manifested themselves in the Arab public sphere as early as the end of the nineteenth century. Practices of social engineering can be considered even earlier precursors. Nonetheless, institutional beginnings remained limited in colonial modernity. A broader establishment of the discipline occurred in the independent nation-states of the 1950s and 1960s. A renewed push for expansion occurred from around the 1990s, accompanied by the general development of the education system. Today, sociology is established as an independent subject at roughly half of the Arab universities (Bamyeh, 2015: 18–21). This chapter will focus on the formation and development of sociology as an academic discipline, alluding to broader forms of social theorizing inasmuch as these appear as precursors or in the immediate context of this disciplinary history.

Differences between the formation and shaping of sociology in different Arab countries are no surprise. They result, among other things, from the following factors: how long the history of sociology and, more generally, of modern universities goes back; what role colonial influence played in its formation; what political influence nation-states exert on education and, in particular, on sociology; what economic resources individual countries make available to institutional sociology; and what role foreign funding institutions play. To illustrate the range: in the populous states of Egypt and Morocco, sociology was established as early as the beginning of the twentieth century, but the former predominantly under national reformist interests, and the latter in the service of French colonial power; the United Arab Emirates and Qatar, which are sparsely populated but rich in oil and gas, recently established satellite campuses of Anglosphere and French universities; in the likewise small, scientifically liberal Jordan, foreign research sponsors, and thus foreign interests, play a central role.

The greatest commonality among Arab countries results from the colonial imprint of sociology under European—or, more precisely, French and English—hegemony. This colonial imprint, and with it the question of a distinct sociological tradition, has remained a longstanding point of discussion, even in postcolonial states and to the present. It involves the broader question of canon and genealogy, but, under (post)colonial auspices, also one of the identity and authenticity of sociology and its contribution to social reform and national sovereignty. The related, overarching question of the universality and particularity of sociology has relevance for sociology beyond Arab countries, most evidently so since the reception of postcolonial criticism in the social sciences.

With regard to the role of the state, the connection between sociology and socialism was central in the first decades of the independent nation-states. This connection could be encouraged and demanded by the government, as in socialist Egypt, or it could lead to tensions with the government, as in monarchical Morocco. More fundamentally, and despite noticeable differences between Arab countries in this regard as well, Arab sociologists have for some time criticized political obstacles to the exercise and development of sociological theory and practice. The problem here, in short, is one of authoritarianism.

Taking political and also economic aspects into account, Sect. 2 outlines the institutional and theoretical development of sociology in Arab countries. Under the question of universality and particularity central to this volume, Sect. 3 discusses attempts to establish an independent "Arab" or "Islamic sociology." It will become clear that a separation into "Arab" and "European" theories is ultimately impossible in view of the entanglement of the two. Sociology in Arab countries was and is exposed to specific structural conditions, both historical and current, that contribute to its formation; however, in theoretical terms, there is no independent Arab sociology, but instead it is part of global sociological knowledge production. Building on this finding, Sect. 4 briefly identifies topics that have received especial attention in contemporary Arab sociology. The chapter ends with a conclusion that summarizes the main findings and suggests the writing of a global history of sociology as a next step (Sect. 5).

2.2 The Historical Development of Sociology in Arab Countries

While the history of sociology goes back almost as far in Arab countries as it does in Europe, institutional beginnings remained limited in colonial modernity (2.1). A broader establishment of the discipline occurred in the independent nation-states of the 1950s and 1960s (2.2). A renewed push for expansion occurred from around the 1990s, accompanied by the general development of the education system. Today, sociology is established as an independent subject at roughly half of the Arab universities (2.3).

2.2.1 The Beginnings in Colonial Modernity

2.2.1.1 Egypt: French Sociology in the Service of National Sovereignty

The year 1925 marks a decisive date in the history of sociology in two respects. First, an Institute of Sociology was established at Cairo University in the Faculty of Philosophy. The Egyptian University, as it was then known, had been founded in 1908 as a private institution and was nationalized in 1925, shortly after Egypt gained formal independence from the British and the protectorate was abolished. In 1940, the institution was renamed "King Fuʾad I University," and since 1953, in the aftermath of the 1952 revolution, it has been called "Cairo University." Second, the first Arabic monograph on sociology (*ʿilm al-ijtimāʿ*) appeared in Cairo in 1924/1925, written by the Syrian-born, socialist intellectual Niqūlā Ḥaddād (al-Ḥaddād, 1925).

Both the founding of the Institute of Sociology at the Egyptian University and Ḥaddād's book are characterized by the creative appropriation of hegemonic modern European models and ideas. The university was founded as a modern, secular educational institution based on European models. However, this should not be seen unilaterally as a sign of dependence, since the Egyptian intellectuals, entrepreneurs, and politicians who promoted its foundation were aiming precisely at the attainment of sovereignty as a modern nation. Social sciences, such as politics and economics, were established early on at the university as part of this national project, in a sense even at its "heart" (Roussillon, 1991: 364). There had been individual courses in sociology since 1913, namely in the sociology of crime (Zayid, 1995: 42). The hegemony of European ideas is clearly evident afterward: The holder of the chair established in 1925 was the Belgian statistician Hostelet (Roussillon, 1991: 358, 2003: 456), and Ḥaddād's book was a mixture of his own account and paraphrases of mainly English sociologists and social philosophers.

The presence of sociology as a university subject came to a temporary end as early as 1934. The reasons for this are not entirely clear (Roussillon, 1991: 367–368). A sociological institute was not reestablished in Egypt until 1947 in Alexandria; sociology was only reconstituted in Cairo after the Egyptian Revolution of 1952, now as an institute independent of philosophy (Zayid, 1995: 42–44). Nevertheless, the first half of the twentieth century saw the consolidation of a basic trait that would initially help shape the situation and form of sociology even after 1952. What is meant here is the difference between, on the one hand, a largely theoretical sociology in the universities, which—despite the work of the English social anthropologist Evans-Pritchard at the University of Cairo in the early 1930s—was for a long time noticeably influenced by Comte and above all Durkheim, and, on the other hand, a decidedly empirical and practically oriented form of social science, which was supported by non-university institutes and associations and drew more heavily on Anglo-Saxon approaches (Roussillon, 1991: esp. 382f.).

On the university side, it was in Paris that Egyptian students first wrote doctoral theses in sociology. The dissertation of Manṣūr Fahmī (1886–1959), supervised by Claude Levy-Brühl and submitted in 1913, caused a scandal. In it, Fahmī argued that the status of women had deteriorated as a result of the Prophet Muhammad's message. When Cairo University, which had sent Fahmī to Paris on a scholarship, caught wind of this, it tried in vain to prevent Fahmī from receiving his doctorate (Reid, 1987: 64–66). The great literary figure, first Egyptian dean of Cairo University, and later minister of education Ṭaha Ḥusayn (1889–1973) wrote his doctoral dissertation on the social philosophy of Ibn Khaldūn, completed in 1917, under Durkheim's supervision. It was translated from French into Arabic in 1925 (Ḥusayn, 1917, 1925). Ḥusayn, who emphasized similarities between modern Egyptian and European culture, argued in the process that Ibn Khaldūn could ultimately not be considered the founder of sociology as the science of modern society. This position was also held by the socialist intellectual Niqūlā Ḥaddād, according to whom sociology first became known to Arabs through translations of Gustave Le Bon (1925: 3–4).

The contrary claim that Ibn Khaldūn was very much the founder of sociology was made at the turn of the twentieth century by intellectuals who emphasized more strongly the Arab or Islamic character of society. Several Egyptian sociologists between the 1930s and early 1950s devoted their doctoral dissertations to a synopsis of Ibn Khaldūn and Comte or Durkheim (Roussillon, 2002: 203f.; Zayid, 1995: 53). In doing so, they increasingly intertwined a Durkheimian reading of Ibn Khaldūn with a Khaldūnian reading of Durkheim (Roussillon, 2002: 204).

Alain Roussillon (1952–2007), who presented the most thorough research on early sociology in Egypt, attributes Durkheim's attractiveness to his putting the question of what holds modern society together in center position, with Egyptian sociologists focusing particularly on the importance of morality in their reading of Durkheim (Roussillon, 1991: 365–366). This question was also central in the Arab public sphere from the second half of the nineteenth century. One crucial point was the significance of religion and science in reforms and the desired social order. Several Egyptian sociologists cite Arab-Islamic reformers as precursors of their own discipline (Roussillon, 1991: 359–362). Indeed, these reformers spoke positively about sociology as necessary and useful knowledge on modern society. However, discussions of sociology remained rather superficial, for instance in the famous Islamic journal *al-Manār* (Zemmin, 2018: 367–372). Journals published by Syrian-Lebanese Christians in Cairo played a more important role in the early dissemination of European social philosophy, above all the journal *al-Muqtaṭaf*. It also published the first Arabic article on sociology (Birbārī, 1897), a paraphrased translation of excerpts from the writings of Herbert Spencer, who was received more widely by Arab intellectuals in the late nineteenth and early twentieth centuries (Elshakry, 2015).

A number of non-university institutions, including charitable ones, were concerned with practical answers to "the social question" using scientific methods (Roussillon, 1991: 368–380). To this end, empirically oriented Anglosphere approaches were more attractive than the more theoretical Francophone contributions. Empirical fieldwork in sociology or social anthropology (the boundaries here are not sharp) seems to have remained limited to the American University in Cairo (Zayid, 1995: 65–66). Empirical analyses of society outside of the university refer in their epistemic assumptions to the formation of sociological perspectives beyond their academic establishment. Social science institutions in this sense can be traced back to at least the founding of the Egyptian Geographical Society in 1875 (El Shakry, 2007). And already in the first half of the nineteenth century, the ruling household of Muḥammad ʿAlī (then still part of the Ottoman Empire, but largely autonomous) had made use of social engineering practices. French Saint-Simonists were among the European experts he drew on (ʿĪsā, 1957).

2.2.1.2 *Morocco: "Sociologie Musulmane" in the Service of French Colonial Power*

The work of Saint Simon's followers is also documented for Algeria: There they saw a particularly fertile ground for the implementation of their reform program, which they then wanted to bring to maturity in France as well (Abi-Mershed, 2010). In this respect, there was also a transfer of ideas and practices from the colonial periphery to the metropolis. More characteristic of the French-colonized Maghrib, however, is the fact that sociology was introduced and practiced decidedly for the direct benefit of the colonial exercise of power. The goal was clear:

> If sociology enjoyed a special favor in the Maghreb during the colonial period, this is [...] because the colonial administration needed to know perfectly the society it had decided to dominate. Sociology was thus part of the colonial strategy of penetration and pacification; it was organized to be useful and to be applied. (Ben Jelloun, 1977: 70)

The collection of data on the social realities of the colonized society was pursued even more extensively in Morocco than in Algeria and Tunisia, and functioned there under the title of a "sociologie musulmane" (Roussillon, 2002: 196–200). Central to the endeavor was the Mission Scientifique founded by Alfred Le Chatelier in Tangier in 1904 (al-Ẓāhī, 2011: 14). The concept "sociologie musulmane"—also the title of Le Chatelier's chair in Paris—did not refer to a delineated discipline of sociology, but rather the bundling of all social science and historical research, some of which was also carried out by bureaucrats and military functionaries. The connection between research and the exercise of political power can be seen, for example, in the supposed differences between

Amazigh and Arabs, which were politically and legally codified in the "Berber Decree" of 1930.

How directly sociological studies in Morocco contributed to colonial policies, or were even mandated by them, varied. An early critic of colonial sociology, even before Moroccan independence in 1956, was Jacques Berque (1910–1995) (Madoui, 2015: 102–103; Roussillon, 2003: 454). Nevertheless, sociology in colonized Morocco, as in the Maghrib more generally, remained an exclusively French project, without significant participation of the population to be dominated. Admittedly, there were Moroccan collaborators in the colonial administration who also contributed to studies (Roussillon, 2002: 200). However, the constitutive place of Muslims in the "sociologie musulmane" remained that of a pure object of research. It is therefore not surprising that after the attainment of national independence, the question of decolonization and how to deal with the colonial legacy of sociology arose in Morocco with particular urgency, as we will see below.

2.2.2 *The Broader Establishment of Sociology in Independent Nation-States*

2.2.2.1 *Egypt: Regional Importance, Socialism, and Increasing US-American Influence*

As shown above, Egypt had a historical pioneering role in the establishment of a modern university as well as in sociological works and institutions that were European in character but, unlike in the Maghrib, served not only colonial power but decidedly also national sovereignty. Through its pioneering role, Egypt functioned as a model for other Arab states. After the independence of Iraq (1930) and Syria (1946), universities were established in Baghdad and Damascus following the example of Cairo (Ibrahim, 1997: 548–549). In Iraq (al-Qazzaz, 1972: 93; Al Hashimi, 2013: 252) and at the American University in Beirut (Ibrahim, 1997: 548), there had already been individual courses in sociology in the interwar period. In Syria, sociology remained relatively marginal (Ibrahim, 2014: 69–70). Its broader establishment as an independent discipline in other Arab countries occurred only in the postcolonial states. Egyptian teachers were sent to a number of other Arab countries, especially from the 1970s, and Egyptian textbooks were widely used (Bagader, 1997: 63–64).

In Egypt itself, sociology was established more widely after the 1952 revolution, which ended the monarchy and led to Gamal Abdel Nasser's pan-Arab and socialist rule, which lasted until 1970. By the 1970s sociology was on offer at universities in all Egyptian governorates (Zayid, 1995: 43–45). Abdel Nasser himself spoke of "revolution" as "the science of complete social change" (quoted in Roussillon, 1996: 95). Sociologists were expected to help with this change scientifically, or at least not to criticize it. Some retreated to apolitical positions (Roussillon, 1996: 120), while others adopted a decidedly ideological, state-serving understanding of sociology (Ibrahim, 1997: 550; Zayid, 1995: 67–68). The latter was reflected in prominent themes of the 1960s, namely the analysis of social development and the identification of obstacles on this path. Concrete topics were, for example, the shaping of industrialization and urbanization (Zayid, 1995: 67–68) or the use of mass media, again in the interest of the socialist state (Roussillon, 1996: 127).

However, the revolution did not immediately constitute an absolute break. A combination of Durkheim and Ibn Khaldūn was continued not least by ᶜAlī ᶜAbd al-Wāfī (1901–1991), who became the first Egyptian chair of sociology at Cairo University after studying in Paris. Continuity on the side of practically oriented social sciences can be seen in the fact that some of their leading representatives became ministers in Abdel Nasser's government (Roussillon, 1996: 106–107). This made for a certain paradox: on the one hand, the state was interested in a unified science that served its needs; on the other hand, it promoted contradictory tendencies that were reinforced by a lack of connections between different sites of sociology (Roussillon, 1996: 107–109). This diversification was reflected in the coexistence of different schools of theory from the 1970s onwards. The Durkheimian school was now joined by British functionalism and Marxism. The latter was more strongly represented outside the universities, as were the equally persisting empirical and application-oriented Anglosphere social sciences (Roussillon, 2003: 458). English theories found their way into universities primarily through the increasing number of sociologists who had studied in Great Britain since the 1950s, instead of in France as before (Ibrahim, 2014: 63–64; Roussillon, 2002: 214). Probably the best-known recipient of German sociology—which was far less influential than French and English—is Muḥammad al-Jawharī, who worked mainly on popular culture and folklore (Ibrahim, 2014: 66). Tönnies, Simmel, and Weber seem to be the German sociologists most extensively received (on the latter, although not comprehensively and not yet reflecting the noticeably increased reception of Weber recently: Leder, 2014). Under Abdel Nasser's successor Anwar al-Sadat, an economically liberal policy turned toward the USA took hold under the slogan *infitāḥ* (opening). The influence of American sociology had already increased from the 1960s through students returning from the USA (Ibrahim, 1997: 549). Now more and more US research institutions and funds were coming to the country, which influenced research topics and also fueled conflicts of political loyalty among sociologists (Roussillon, 1996: 133).

The growing influence of US-American sociology as well as American and European research funds appears in other Arab countries from the 1980s, too. In Jordan, for example, the majority of sociological research by foreigners takes place at foreign-funded institutes (ʿAbd al-Ḥakīm, 2014). Oil-rich Saudi Arabia based its institutionalization of sociology, which began in the 1970s, on the expertise of both US-American sociologists and those from other Arab countries (al-Khalīfa, 2014). As another case, in socialist Algeria, the state tasked sociology with supporting the construction of institutions and the intended modernization of the country (Madoui, 2007: 151). Until 1967, Algeria, which became independent in 1962, only had a university in the capital Algiers. Sociology became more widely established from the 1970s onwards. Then, in addition to technocratic sociology in the service of the state, other directions can be discerned, such as liberal and Islamist versions (Ramʿūn, 2014).

2.2.2.2 Morocco: Activist Sociology and Double Criticism Under Postcolonial Auspices

In Morocco, the relationship of socialist sociology to the monarchical state was noticeably tense and led to the temporary end of institutionalized sociology barely fifteen years after independence in 1956. The central figures of the first generation of sociologists in independent Morocco combined Marxist convictions with their analytical work. This is particularly true of Paul Pascon, who promoted an "activist sociology" (*sociologie d'action*). Pascon, who was born in Fez in 1932 and of French origin, turned sympathetically to local society at an early age, campaigned for independence, and took Moroccan citizenship in 1964. He decidedly wanted an engaged sociology that had to be independent of the state. He contended that a certain distance from social conflicts ought to be maintained, but without taking these conflicts on and giving them orientation, sociology was sterile and pointless. In this sense, Pascon's circle focused on socially disadvantaged or oppressed groups, primarily peasants and women. Every sociologist was expected to have a concrete sphere of activity that included practical action. Pascon founded a "cabinet of cooperative studies" in 1960 and, in cooperation with trade unions, participated in the elaboration of a five-year plan (for the entire paragraph up to here: al-Zāhī, 2011: 20, 67–71; Madoui, 2015: 103; Tozy, 2013). The politically left orientation of sociology was additionally fueled by the student protests of 1968. In Morocco, the radicalizing sociology met a state that was once again increasingly conservative and authoritarian. As a result, the fledgling institution of sociology at universities came to a rapid end. The *Institut de Sociologie*, founded in 1960 in a cooperation between UNESCO and the University of Rabat, was closed again as early as 1970 (al-Zāhī, 2011: 21; Madoui, 2015: 105; Roussillon, 2003: 458–460).

Sociology was not institutionalized again until the end of the 1980s. Under the rule of the current Moroccan king, Muhammad VI, the social sciences have been in better shape since the 2000s. This is also related to the political interest in analyzing Islamist groups that emerged in the 1980s as well as the social change promoted by the economic opening (Madoui, 2015: 101). The state viewed sociologists mainly as experts and advisors who could help with economic liberalization through their understanding of social problems such as poverty, exclusion, and migration (Madoui, 2015: 112). The analysis of Islamic groups was added to the still prominent research on the social position and role of Moroccan women, which had already been prominently addressed by Pascon's group. Among Moroccan sociologists who tackled the latter topic, Rahma Bourquia (b. 1949) should be mentioned alongside the internationally renowned feminist Fatima Mernissi (1940–2015) (Madoui, 2015: 106).

Criticism of colonial sociology was shared more widely in Morocco early on, including by Marxist sociologists. Explicit demands for "decolonization" were made in the Maghrib by sociologists and intellectuals in the 1970s (Zghal & Karoui, 1973; Ben Jelloun, 1977). The formulation of a "double criticism" by Abdelkabir Khatibi (1938–2009) was particularly succinct.

> Like any sociology of decolonization (although one may ask what is 'decolonization'), that of the Arab world would consist of carrying out two tasks: (1) A deconstruction of 'logocentrism' and of ethnocentrism, that speech of self-sufficiency par excellence which the West, in the course of its expansion, has imposed on the world. [...] (2) [...] a criticism of the

knowledge and the discourses developed by the different societies of the Arab world about themselves. (Khatibi, 1985: 9; for the earlier French coinage of "double critique": Khatibi, 1975)

Khatibi thus regarded self-critique of Arab societies and Arab sociology as equally important as the critique of the colonial and Eurocentric aspects of sociology. He moreover noted that colonialist sociology had collected useful information and produced insights that were still useful. After all, he made extensive use of theories of French philosophy himself, not least that of Derrida. Khatibi, who was director of the *Institut de Sociologie* from 1966 until its closure in 1970, continued to work primarily as a philosopher and author of literary works. His relatively early reflections on decolonization remain groundbreaking and, as part of his life's work, have recently been appreciated more extensively (Hiddleston & Lyamlahy, 2020).

Jaques Berque's criticism of colonial sociology, which he formulated even before Morocco's independence, was taken up in particular by Anglosphere social anthropologists who were increasingly active in Morocco from the 1960s onwards. Anthropology tends to have a negative reputation in Arab countries because of its colonial influence, and it is noticeably less represented at universities than other social sciences (Bamyeh, 2015: 21). In comparison with French anthropology, however, Anglosphere anthropology was not as negatively marked in Morocco. One critical question of Berque that Anglosphere social anthropologists took up was what actually constituted a "North African tribe," a concept of colonial analysis and practice (Madoui, 2015: 103; Roussillon, 2002: 199–200).

2.2.2.3 ʿAlī al-Wardī: An Iraqi School of Sociology, US Theory, and Ibn Khaldūn

ʿAlī al-Wardī (1913–1995), the founding figure of sociology in Iraq stands for a detailed connection between Ibn Khaldūn's theories and contemporary sociology. Al-Wardī had studied in the USA and was the first chair of sociology at Baghdad University after his return to Iraq in 1950. He shaped an entire generation of Iraqi sociologists, whom he advised to study in Paris, London, or, most importantly, the USA, at the same time urging them to be aware of the particularities of Iraqi society (Ibrāhīm, 2014: 66–68). While some speak of "an Iraqi school of sociology" (Ibrāhīm, 2014: 68), a recent survey of sociology students in Baghdad points to little knowledge of earlier Iraqi sociologists (ʿAbd al-Ḥusayn, 2014: 140). In this context, the institutional discontinuity fostered by the Iran–Iraq war and the two Gulf wars must be taken into account. Nevertheless, al-Wardī is still considered the central figure of sociology in Iraq (Al Hashimi, 2013). For the Iraqi sociologist Maʿn Khalīl ʿUmar, al-Wardī was the only one of the five protagonists of sociology in Iraq to have his own theoretical framework (ʿUmar, 1990: 191).

Most prominent are al-Wardī's concept of an "Iraqi personality" (*shakhṣiyya ʿirāqiyya*) and his comparison of nomadic and urban culture, formulated with reference to Ibn Khaldūn. According to al-Wardī, it was not least tensions between the traditional nomadic life of the Bedouin and modern urban culture that led to a "split personality," a concept he adopted from MacIver (ʿUmar, 1990: 50). The themes of Bedouin society and the Iraqi personality marked by contradictions between tradition and modernity were also prominently treated by other Iraqi sociologists, mainly using conflict-theoretical approaches (ʿUmar, 1990: 199). Al-Wardī emphasized that the peculiarities of Iraqi and Arab society had to be taken into account on a methodological level, too. For example, he rejected statistical methods and the collection of data through interviews and surveys: unlike in the USA, researchers in Iraq could not simply approach female citizens, as distance and skepticism were too great; instead, al-Wardī also quoted verses from the Koran to support his assessments (Al Hashimi, 2013: 255, 257).

Maʿn Khalīl ʿUmar criticizes—in a remarkable debate that he had with al-Wardī in a journal—that al-Wardī ultimately did not develop a refined theory: al-Wardī's statements on the relationship between Bedouin and urban culture remained hypotheses even after more than 40 years, and no actual modification of Ibn Khaldūn's concepts in the light of contemporary theories was discernible (ʿUmar, 1990: 79). To this criticism must be added the culturalist premises underlying al-Wardī's theoretical considerations. Such culturalist assumptions were more widely shared in postulates of an "Arab sociology," not least by Maʿn Khalīl ʿUmar himself, as will be shown in the third section.

2.2.3 Expansion and Current Status of Sociology: Structural Problems

In the last three decades or so, there has been a noticeable expansion of sociology. This goes hand in hand with the general expansion of higher education, but is also reflected in an increase in the number of research institutes: before 1980, there were only 43 research institutes in the social sciences—including sociology, but mainly political science and economics—but by 2015, there were over 430, most of them in Algeria, Egypt, Lebanon, Saudi Arabia, Jordan, and Iraq (Bamyeh, 2015: 19, 34); and 97% of the 597 universities in Arab countries studied in one report were founded after 1970, with 70% founded even after 1990 (Bamyeh, 2015: 18). This was accompanied by a significant increase in the number of students, especially in the humanities and social sciences. These subjects are less lucrative in terms of career prospects, but have easier admission requirements than natural sciences, medicine, or engineering. Quantitative expansion, however, was not automatically accompanied by qualitative development.

In some cases, it even had the opposite effect, insofar as the increasing number of students was not accompanied by an adequate increase in resources. With regard to financial resources, there are differences between public and private universities (for an example from Lebanon: Kriener, 2015: 125–127). Many research institutions and programs continue to be (co-)financed to a noticeable extent by foreign donors, and are thus also dependent on them. The influence of research funding on social issues can be seen, for example, in the fact that in Jordan, the European Union's funding of research on historical heritage contributed to the broader significance of heritage in society (ʿAbd al-Ḥakīm, 2014: 239). The dependence on foreign research funding is particularly pronounced in Palestine, for example (Hanafi, 2010), while the rich Gulf states determine for themselves which science they bring into the country.

Alongside a lack of economic resources, political restrictions are the most serious of the structural problems that Arab sociologists have been criticizing for some time. The continuity of central problems is reflected in the fact that a recent critical survey (Ḥamzāwī & Kawāshī, 2017) consists largely of quotations from a conference in the 1980s (Markaz Dirāsāt al-Waḥda al-ʿArabiyya, 1986). A discussion of the noticeable differences between individual countries or specific cases lies outside the scope of this overview. It requires little explanation that authoritarian governments strive to limit or even prevent sociological research on politically sensitive and socially taboo topics. This affects foreign social scientists working in Arab countries, too (Eickelman, 2012), albeit with less serious potential consequences.

In addition, there are a number of other obstacles to the qualitative development of sociology in Arab countries. Students are not only demotivated by low career prospects, but often have to make do with outdated teaching material (for Egypt, succinctly: Badawī, 2012: 135–136). A particularly striking example is the recent reprinting of an Egyptian textbook from the 1960s (al-Khashshāb, 2017). This does not contain any updates, explanations, or historical classifications. Accordingly, it reflects not only the state of theory from half a century ago, but also the contemporaneous examples and concerns of the socialist republic at the time. But even newer textbooks often make no reference to recent theoretical developments (e.g., Ghazwī et al., 2006; ʿUthmān, 2008). Furthermore, most of the references, and thus the range of theories represented, consist of European, especially French and English, works or translations of the same, which points to the relatively low establishment of Arabic-language contributions to sociological theories. What is also striking is the extremely low average publication activity in some countries. In Morocco, according to one survey, 55% of university teachers in sociology had not yet published a single paper (al-Zāhī, 2011: 39; Madoui, 2015: 109).

In addition, there is the problem of linguistic fragmentation, not only of literature, but also of training and teaching. In Morocco (as in Algeria and Tunisia), there has been a project of "Arabization" of the education system since the 1980s. Even today, however, French is still heavily represented in the social sciences, especially at the master's and doctoral level. The use of English is generally increasing, but noticeably more at the universities in Casablanca and Rabat than at other locations. Mastery of these languages on a level allowing independent research is obviously a high demand—too high for most students and also some lecturers. The most highly qualified Arab sociologists, in turn, often find more favorable working conditions in Europe and the USA and emigrate (*brain drain*). In addition to publishing in French and English, they continue to participate in Arabic debates, which are increasingly facilitated by the possibilities of digital communication. Nevertheless, they are confronted with a dilemma that has been formulated as follows: "publish globally and perish locally vs. publish locally and perish globally" (Hanafi, 2011).

The problems mentioned—which have been identified by Arab sociologists themselves—are also counterbalanced by positive tendencies. The most important concrete initiative is the Arab Council for the Social Sciences, founded in 2012. This network organization, which is supported by social scientists in Arab countries, but also from outside, has its headquarters in Beirut and is largely financed by the Swedish government. It contributes to the further development of the social sciences, including sociology, primarily through documentation and networking (see: www.acss.org). As a broader trend, the increasing interweaving of Arabic and English-language debates can be observed, not least under the auspices of postcolonial criticism and globally oriented research contexts. Since the 1990s, there has also been a stronger presence of the social sciences in the media, more so in cultural magazines than in daily newspapers (Bamyeh, 2015: 84–126).

The focus on structural difficulties in this section pursued one main purpose: From a sociological point of view, these structural conditions are central factors for the (impeded) development of sociology in Arab countries, both in terms of its social relevance and with regard to the development of its own range of theories. This should be remembered when we now turn to formulations of a specifically "Arab" or "Islamic" sociology, which attributes the perceived weakness of sociology in Arab countries predominantly to the fact that it is dependent on European theories and concepts.

2.3 A Separate Sociology? On the Question of Universality and Particularity

As shown above, there was already a creative combination of French and Arabic reference ideas in the early days of sociology in Egypt: Ibn Khaldūn was read through Durkheim and vice versa. The positioning toward European sociology on the one hand and the Arab heritage on the other was thus an almost universal characteristic of sociology in Egypt (Zayid, 1995), but also beyond. The late sociologist, human rights activist, and former director of the Ibn Khaldun Center for Strategic Studies in Cairo, Saʿd al-Dīn Ibrāhīm (1938–2023), coined the term "cross-eyed sociology" for this dual orientation (Ibrahim, 1997). The question of a specifically Arab sociology in distinction from European or Western sociology became virulent under postcolonial auspices in the independent nation-state. Programmatic efforts to indigenize sociology noticeably intensified from the 1980s onwards (Sabagh & Ghazalla, 1986; al-Ghālī, 1999; on social anthropology: Morsy et al., 1991; Lange, 2005).

Most significant here are conceptions of an "Arab" or an "Islamic sociology." Formulations of national sociologies hardly play a role, despite the factual importance of the nation-state for the formation and function of sociology (an exception is al-Baraydī, 2018). Aspirations for an "Arab sociology" figure on the background of pan-Arab political tendencies and the notion of an Arab society. ᶜAbd al-ᶜAzīz ᶜIzzat—among the first generation of sociologists at Egyptian universities after independence—authored an early formulation of a common Arab society (ᶜIzzat, 1960). Its most significant expression at the academic level is the Centre for Arab Unity Studies (Markaz Dirasāt al-Waḥda al-ᶜArabiyya), founded in 1975 and still very active, based in Beirut. The sociopolitical context for attempts at an "Islamic sociology" is formed by the increasing influence of political and cultural Islamic currents after the heyday of socialism. On the intellectual level, they tie in with global efforts to Islamize science, put forward in Malaysia (Keim, 2015), the USA, and Iran (Stenberg, 1996), but also in Saudi Arabia and Egypt (Abaza, 2000). Connections between these can be seen, for example, in Arabic publications by the International Institute for Islamic Thought in Virginia, founded in 1981 in Herndon, Virginia (e.g., Mahwar Bāsha, 2018). Mutual references between Islamic and Christian critiques of the secularity of the social sciences (e.g., Milbank, 1991) seem not to play a role.

It should be noted in advance that attempts to establish an independent, even self-sufficient sociology were not successful, as Sari Hanafi discusses at greater length in this volume. Nevertheless, they remain informative for our question of Arabic contributions to sociological theory. In particular, they point to the possibilities of making Eurocentric sociology more inclusive, but also to certain limits in this regard. They are thus also an occasion for European or American sociologists to reflect on the particularities, implicit assumptions, and excluding mechanisms of their discipline.

2.3.1 *The Outline of an "Arab (Theory of) Sociology"*

Discussions on the development of "Arab sociology" in the 1980s started from diagnosing a crisis (Khalīfa & Suhair, 1984; Markaz Dirāsāt al-Waḥda al-ᶜArabiyya, 1986; Roussillon, 1996: 135). Like more recent contributions (Ḥanafī et al., 2014), they focused on the state of sociology in Arab countries, challenges, and possible solutions. Programmatic formulations of an Arab theory of sociology, on the other hand, are rarer. One attempt in German (Irabi, 1989) was rightly critically reviewed (Ende, 1991) and does not seem to have found any significant resonance. Insofar as the construction of one's own sociological tradition plays a central role, engagements with one's own "heritage" could be added (e.g., Maᶜtūq, 2007). The circle of relevant literature would be wider still if sociological conceptions of an "Arab society" or even the widespread references to Ibn Khaldūn were included.

Here, however, the focus is on a monograph whose aim is the development of an "Arab theory of sociology" *(naẓariyya ᶜarabiyya fī ᶜilm al-ijtimāᶜ)* or, as it is called in an alternative title of the same work, an "Arab sociology" (*ᶜilm ijtimāᶜ ᶜarabī*) (ᶜUmar, 1991, 1992). The author, Maᶜn Khalīl ᶜUmar was already mentioned above when discussing Iraqi sociology. ᶜUmar was born in 1939 and received his doctorate in the USA in 1976. He subsequently worked at universities in various Arab countries and was extremely prolific in writing introductory works on various subfields of sociology (ᶜUmar 2021).

In the book of interest to us here, ᶜUmar emphasizes that he is not striving for a particular "Arab sociology." For Arab societies do not differ fundamentally from other societies, but show differences as well as similarities to them. He was therefore interested in highlighting Arab contributions to sociology. Classical Arab thinkers' reflections on their societies are of particular interest to sociology because, unlike modern European and American sociologists, they referred not only to their own societies, but more generally to human society (ᶜUmar, 1991: 5–6).

This ostensibly universalist understanding of sociological thought receives a culturalist twist: Arab sociological heritage is in ᶜUmar's view still relevant today because Arab society has deep roots and unalterable characteristics. Unlike European sociologists, Arab sociologists could therefore actually fall back on their own heritage. However, the majority of them do not do so, but instead orient themselves toward modern Western theories. One trait of Arab society, which has already been dealt with by classical thinkers and is still relevant, is that of kinship relations. For ᶜUmar, activating one's own heritage, which has remained alive in the subconscious, is a way both to better understand contemporary Arab society and to reform it. Ultimately, ᶜUmar brings together the universalist and culturalist features of his argument when he emphasizes that returning to Arab heritage contributes to supporting general sociological theories (ᶜUmar, 1991: 7–11).

Accordingly, ᶜUmar attempts to demonstrate that the themes and theories of modern sociology had already been convincingly dealt with by Arab "sociologists," predominantly those of the eighth to fourteenth centuries, with the high point and conclusion being Ibn Khaldūn. This equation obviously has apologetic and ahistorical features. But it can also be understood as a particular form of legitimizing and indigenizing sociology. At a time when the idea of an "Arab society" was in vogue, ᶜUmar formulated a sociology for this imagined society. In addition to his culturalist assumptions, he postulated an "Arab personality" (*shakhṣiyya ᶜarabiyya*), which allegedly bore the characteristics of this society. Islam is one of these characteristics and has also promoted the unity of Arab society, whose roots, however, go back to pre-Islamic times, according to ᶜUmar.

Tellingly, ᶜUmar's book was reprinted a good twenty years later as "Islamic Sociology" (*ᶜilm al-ijtimāᶜ al-islāmī*). As in the title, in the text, characterizations as "Arab" were simply changed to "Muslim" or "Islamic" (ᶜUmar, 2013). The renaming of ᶜUmar's book may be due to its new place of publication, Saudi Arabia, as well as to better marketability. In any case, it points to the now greater prominence of the idea of an Islamic society and thus of an "Islamic sociology."

2.3.2 *"Islamic Sociology": Confrontational or Complementary to "Western Sociology"*

Drafts of an "Islamic sociology" are more numerous and more persistent than those of an "Arab sociology." Examples can be found in both Arab and non-Arab contexts, including in English (Ba-Yunus & Ahmad, 1985). In Arabic, more than twenty monographs are dedicated to the development of an "Islamic sociology" (*ᶜilm al-ijtimāᶜ al-islāmī*). One could add sociological analyses and thus constructions of an "Islamic society," as well as criticism of (Western) sociology from an Islamic perspective. Islamizing features can moreover be discerned in social science works with innocuous titles in this regard (Ḥamūdī, 2018: 23). I focus here on two early and markedly different explicit drafts of an "Islamic sociology": Nabīl al-Samālūṭī's work is ostensibly formulated in contrast to "Western sociology" and may strike readers more as social theology than sociology; Sāmiya al-Khashshāb's book conceives of Islamic sociology as a branch of general sociology and lends itself not least to reflection on sociology's secular self-understanding.

2.3.2.1 The Confrontational Type: Nabīl al-Samālūṭī

Nabīl al-Samālūṭī is professor emeritus of sociology et al.-Azhar University in Cairo. He has published continuously on Islamic sociology since the 1970s and has been active in national and international debates. His publications overlap noticeably in terms of content, and his position on Islamic sociology can basically be considered constant. We focus here on his book "The Structure of Islamic Society and its Institutions: A Study in Islamic Sociology" (*Binā᾽ al-mujtamaᶜ al-islāmī wa-nuẓumuhu: dirāsa fī ᶜilm al-ijtimāᶜ al-islāmī*), from 1981.

Despite its self-designation as "sociology," al-Samālūṭī's book reads predominantly like an Islamic program for the shaping of society. He posits the scientific goal of sociology as recognizing social and historical laws—and equates these with laws established by God. Orientation toward these laws and their implementation for the benefit of humanity is a social goal to which sociology contributes. In pursuit of this goal, so his argument, Arab-Muslim sociologists should turn away from ostensibly positivist European theories and return to the Qur'an. Only by referring to the divine source can sociology produce true knowledge and realize social values. For the good of all humanity, Islamic sociology must therefore prevail over (Western) positivist sociology. When al-Samālūṭī asks God for victory over the unbelievers, it seems that the opposition to hegemonic sociology could hardly be more fundamental, both epistemologically and normatively (al-Samālūṭī, 1981: 8–9).

And yet, the borrowings from established sociological theories and shared basic assumptions of a functionally differentiated society are too clear. Al-Samālūṭī postulates that the shariᶜa set out the perfect structure of social orders, including the institutions of the family, the economy, politics, administration, education, and so on. All too clearly, he projects a modern view of society back into the Qur'an and early Islamic times. The introduction of English-language concepts makes the orientation toward the supposedly fundamentally rejected Western sociology even clearer. Moreover, al-Samālūṭi does not address actual historical or social conditions, nor does he suggest how their analysis from an Islamic perspective would practically differ from other approaches. One thus searches in vain for a specifically Islamic theory or method of sociology, let alone its practical application.

2.3.2.2 The Complementary Type: Sāmiya al-Khashshāb

The latter is also true of Sāmiya al-Khashshāb's work, which nevertheless differs noticeably from al-Samālūṭī's and here represents a conception of Islamic sociology that is complementary rather than confrontational to Western sociology. When publishing her book in 1980, al-Khashshāb was an assistant professor at Cairo University. Given the low proportion of women among the professoriate, it may be assumed that her attainment of this position was at least favored by her kinship with the formative Egyptian sociologists Aḥmad and Muṣṭafā al-Khashshāb. Sāmiya Muṣṭafā al-Khashshāb's book was cited extensively, though largely unmarked, by a later work on "Islamic sociology" (al-Shamarī, 2011); this too is evidence of a certain visibility and continuing relevance.

Al-Khashshāb argues for the establishment of Islamic sociology as a separate branch of general sociology. This is appropriate, she argues, because Islamic sociology has its own topics (such as social thought in Islam) and goals (such as highlighting Islamic sociological heritage) and also has different approaches (al-Khashshāb, 1980: 5–6). One of al-Khashshāb's premises is that Islam is a social religion. Not unlike al-Samālūṭī, she names parts of modern society as addressed by Islam. However, she emphasizes parallels rather than differences and highlights contemporary values such as freedom of belief and expression. Moreover, al-Khashshāb (1980: 37) emphasizes that Islamic sociology is a descriptive, not a normative science (*ʿilm taqrīrī yadrus mā huwa kāʾin wa-lā yataṣṣadā li-mā yanbaghī an yakūn*). Admittedly, her own account is not free of value judgments, for example, when she wants to ascertain whether Sufism had a positive or negative influence on society (al-Khashshāb, 1980: 47, 50).

It is clear, however, that al-Khashshāb, unlike al-Samālūṭī, positions Islam not only as subjecting society to historical and social factors, but also as itself subject to such factors (esp. al-Khashshāb, 1980: 49–50, 57, 63). This is reflected on the level of references: while al-Samālūṭī refers almost exclusively to the Qur'an, this hardly plays a role in al-Khashshāb's book. Instead, she constructs an Islamic sociological tradition that can be found similarly in ʿUmar's "Arab sociology," one which culminates in Ibn Khaldūn's ostensibly strictly empirical and positivist approach. For al-Khashshāb, the transcendental truth of religion forms a framework and background for Islamic sociology, but is not used to analyze or shape society.

Al-Khashshāb's work can thus be considered a particular—not particularist—contribution to a universal—not universalist—understanding of sociology. It shows the possibility of justifying sociology via an Islamic tradition and genealogy, similar to Maʿn Khalīl ʿUmar's Arab variant. And it points to the possibility of a secular, empirical analysis of society also within a religious, metaphysical framework. The inclusion of this Islamic variant and non-Islamic variants of sociology touches the level of justification and framing of sociology more than questions of theory and methodology. In the latter respect, Eurocentric imprints of sociological theories and concepts still need to be criticized and revised. However, this critique and revision should be conducted under the premises and within the framework of sociology itself. Arab sociologists, too, have long been critical of identity-motivated efforts to create a particulate sociology (Abaza, 2000) or even consider it a failure (Ḥanafī, 2016, and this volume). According to Sari Hanafi, this failure is increasingly being recognized, and there are signs of sociologists overcoming the juxtaposition of universalist and particularist positions (Hanafi, 2021).

2.4 Themes of Arab Sociology as Part of Global Sociology

Indeed, what is at stake today are Arab contributions to the increasingly global sociological production of knowledge, in which Arab and non-Arab contributions cannot be stringently separated. From the perspective of Arab sociologists, who have been familiar with European sociology since the establishment of the discipline, this is not a novelty; European sociologists have some catching up to do here. According to the findings of the second and third sections, the lack of recognition of Arab contributions depends more on structural, sociopolitical, and economic imbalances than on various theoretical or even epistemic premises, although there are also "text-immanent" reasons for the appropriation or rejection of social science knowledge production (Keim, 2016). In principle, however, Arab sociologists participate in the range of theory that has been used, and largely formulated, by European and American sociologists. In this sense, this section provides an insight into prominent topics of Arab sociology, as part of global sociology, which is nevertheless shaped by local conditions and questions.

One of the structural local conditions, as described above, is that the possibility of sociologically researching social issues is partly restricted by sociocultural and political obstacles and taboos, while other topics are encouraged by the state. One example is that poverty in Saudi Arabia only really became a subject of research after it was officially recognized as a social problem by the King in 2000, while crime received outsized attention, measured by the actually low rate of everyday crime (Bamyeh, 2015: 27–28).

An overarching paradigm of research in the 1960s and 1970s was that of modernization and development. In the 1980s, the question shifted to why development or even the state had failed. In this context, greater attention was paid to social tensions and protest movements. In the 1990s, questions of civil society, democratization, population growth, economic reform, and globalization were added (Ibrahim, 1997: 550–551). A central issue is that of migration, initially predominantly the intra-Arab migration of labor to the oil-rich Gulf states, and then also migration to Europe. In connection with the latter and drastic demographic change, the research field of youth has emerged in the last two decades. Specific topics in individual countries are, for example, the position and integration of Palestinians in Jordanian society (who arrived as refugees after the founding of the state of Israel and now make up around half of the Jordanian population) or the social causes and consequences of the civil war from 1975 to 1990 in Lebanon.

Among the few detailed, representative studies on sociological knowledge production in individual Arab countries is an analysis of study programs and publications in Saudi Arabia between 1973 and 2013 (al-Khalīfa, 2014). Among the publications, 12 of the 40 identified fields of sociology are responsible for 69% of the publications. These are, first and foremost, crime, family, women, and sociology of religion (*ʿilm al-ijtimāʿ al-dīnī*), the latter including works on "Islamic sociology." Economy, population, and development follow; sociology of language and technology, but also sociological theory, are responsible for only one title each among 1037 publications (al-Khalīfa, 2014: 181–183). Almost all topics have seen a noticeable increase in the last two decades, which is due to the fact that the proportion of Saudi sociologists, on whose publications the analysis is limited, has increased significantly since then. An exception to this increase is the sociology of religion, which saw most publications in the 1980s and 1990s, both because of the prominence of an Islamization of sociology at the time and because of the threat that Islamists posed to the state (al-Khalīfa, 2014: 185–186). Overall, al-Khalīfa (2014: 192) identifies a trend toward applied, pragmatic sociology, which also takes place outside academic institutions and is increasingly accepted by society.

The second report of the Arab Council for the Social Sciences (Ḥamūdī, 2018) is insightful for recent trends in several Arab countries, even if it is necessarily less detailed. According to this report, prominent themes of Arabic-language books in the Maghrib (Morocco, Algeria, Tunisia) in the period from 2000 to 2016 are values, religiosity (*tadayyun*), and culture (Ḥamūdī, 2018: 13–14). In countries of the Mashriq (Palestine, Lebanon, Jordan, Syria, Iraq), political sociology, cultural sociology, and also gender sociology are identified as the most prominent fields (Ḥamūdī, 2018: 30). In Egypt, prominent topics are cultural heritage, social change, crime and deviance, poverty, social movements, and violence and globalization (Ḥamūdī, 2018: 43–44). In contrast to the Maghrib, Egypt has seen a decline in book publications, due to declining government funding for monographs, but at the same time sociologists have become increasingly involved in field studies and government projects (Ḥamūdī, 2018: 41–42). The prominence of women and youth as topics in social science journals published between 2010 and 2014 (Ḥamūdī, 2018: 88) is confirmed by an earlier study of the Arab Council for the Social Sciences, which, however, identifies the Arab Spring and Revolution, as well as individual biographies, as even more prominent topics (Bamyeh, 2015: 66–68). The identification of central themes—despite overarching trends—seems thus more coherent for individual Arab countries or at best journals (Hanafi, 2013) than for the sociological landscape in the Arab world as a whole.

2.5 Conclusion

The last aspect, as we have seen, applies more generally to sociology in Arab countries. Attempts to develop a particular "Arab" or "Islamic" sociology were not successful. The entanglement with sociological knowledge production in other regional and linguistic contexts is too close, initially primarily with French sources, and since the 1950s increasingly and now dominantly with the Anglosphere. At the same time, the formation and shaping of sociology is affected by the conditions of the nation-states.

The complexity of the formation and development of sociology in Arab countries is further enhanced by the significance of colonial influence and ongoing European and US-American hegemony in the understanding and shaping of sociology, especially sociological theories. In Arab countries, sociology was developed with almost inevitable reference to European imprints of modern society, while in European countries an ostensibly self-sufficient understanding of modern society—and modernity at large—prevailed for a long time. Both understandings have since been corrected: in Arab countries, modern society is not only the result of importing external developments, and in European countries it did not develop on its own. For European sociology, the colonial context of its emergence has been taken into account (Steinmetz, 2013, 2023).

This chapter has aimed to advance a greater awareness of modern and contemporary Arabic contributions to global sociology, while also sketching the formation and development of sociology in Arab countries as part of the global history of sociology. While broader forms of Arabic social theorizing were alluded to only as context to the formation and development of sociology as an academic discipline, these, too, should fruitfully be viewed as part of global social theory. Further overcoming the divide between social sciences and area studies, a next step would be to integrate in a common frame of observation histories of sociology or social theory in different locations, including European and Arab countries.

References

Abaza, M. (2000). The Islamization of Knowledge between Particularism and Globalization: Malaysia and Egypt. In C. Nelson & S. Rouse (Eds.), *Situating Globalization: Views from Egypt* (pp. 53–95). Transcript.

ʿAbd al-Ḥakīm, Khālid al-Ḥisbān. (2014). al-Dirāsāt al-Sūsiyūlūjiyya wa-l-Anthrūbulūjiyya fī al-Urdun: al-Ishkāliyyāt al-Ībīstīmūlujiyya [Sociological and Anthropological Studies in Jordan: Epistemological Challenges]. In Sārī Ḥanafī, Nūriya bin Ghabrīṭ-Ramʿūn & Majāhidī Muṣṭafā (Eds.), *Mustaqbal al-ʿUlūm al-Ijtimāʿiyya fī al-Waṭan al-ʿArabī* [The Future of Social Sciences in the Arab World] (pp. 219–241). Markaz Dirāsāt al-Waḥda al-ʿArabiyya.

ʿAbd al-Ḥusayn, Lāhay. (2014). Tawajjuhāt ʿIlm al-Ijtimāʿ fī al-ʿIrāq: al-Māḍī wa-l-Ḥāḍir [Directions of Sociology in Iraq: Past and Present]. In Sārī Ḥanafī, Nūriya bin Ghabrīṭ-Ramʿūn, & Majāhidī Muṣṭafā (Eds.), *Mustaqbal al-ʿUlūm al-Ijtimāʿiyya fī al-Waṭan al-ʿArabī* [The Future of Social Sciences in the Arab World] (pp. 131–152). Markaz Dirāsāt al-Waḥda al-ʿArabiyya.

Abi-Mershed, O. (2010). *Apostles of Modernity: Saint-Simonians and the Civilizing Mission in Algeria*. Stanford University Press.

al-Baraydī, ᶜAbdallāh. (2018). ᶜIlm al-Ijtimāᶜ 'al-Saᶜūdī': al-Manshūd wa-l-Mafqūd ["Saudi Arabian" Sociology: Aspirations and Losses]. *Iḍāfat, 43–44*, 9–32.

Alatas, S. F. (2014). *Applying Ibn Khaldūn: The Recovery of a Lost Tradition in Sociology*. Routledge.

al-Ghālī, Balqāsim. (1999). Muḥawalāt fī Taʾṣīl ᶜIlm al-Ijtimāᶜ [Attempts to Indigenize Sociology]. *Shuʾūn Ijtimāᶜiyya, 63*, 9–40.

al-Ghazwī, Fahmī Salīm et al. (2006). *al-Madkhal ilā ᶜIlm al-Ijtimāᶜ* [Introduction to Sociology]. Dār al-Shurūq.

Al-Ḥaddād, N. (1924/1925). *ᶜIlm al-ijtimāᶜ: Ḥayāt al-Hayʾa al-Ijtimāᶜiyya wa-Taṭawwuruhā* [Sociology: The Life and Development of the Social Body], 2 vols. al-Maṭbaᶜa al-ᶜAṣriyya.

Al Hashimi, Hamied G. M. (2013). Iraqi sociology and Al Wardi's contributions. *Journal of Contemporary Arab Affairs, 6*(2), 251–259.

al-Khalīfa, ᶜAbdallāh bin Ḥusayn. (2014). al-Takwīn al-ᶜIlmī fī ᶜIlm al-Ijtimāᶜ: al-Saᶜūdiyya [Academic Formation in Sociology: The Case of Saudi Arabia]. In Sārī Ḥanafī, Nūriya bin Ghabrīṭ-Ramᶜūn, & Majāhidī Muṣṭafā (Eds.), *Mustaqbal al-ᶜUlūm al-Ijtimāᶜiyya fī al-Waṭan al-ᶜArabī* [The Future of Social Sciences in the Arab World] (pp. 153–189). Markaz Dirāsāt al-Waḥda al-ᶜArabiyya.

al-Khashshāb, M. (2017 [1965]). *'Ilm al-Ijtimāᶜ wa-Madārisuhu, vol. 2: al-Madkhal ilā ᶜIlm al-Ijtimāᶜ* [Sociology and Sociological Schools, vol. 2: Introduction to Sociology]. Maktabat al-Anjilū al-Miṣriyya.

Al-Khashshāb, S. M. (1980). *ᶜIlm al-Ijtimāᶜ al-Islāmī* [Islamic Sociology]. Dār al-Māᶜarif.

al-Qazzaz, A. (1972). Sociology in Underdeveloped Countries: A Case Study of Iraq. *The Sociological Review, 20*, 93–103.

Ba-Yunus, I., & Ahmad, F. (1985). *Islamic Sociology: An Introduction*. Hodder & Stoughton.

Badawī, A. M. (2012). at-Takwīn al-ᶜIlmī al-Sūsijūlūjī fī al-Mashriq al-ᶜArabī: ᶜIlm al-Ijtimāᶜ Baḥthan wa-Tadrīsan fī Miṣr wa-l-Sūdān [Academic Formation in Sociology in the Arab East: Sociological Research and Teaching in Egypt and the Sudan]. *al-Mustaqbal al-ᶜArabī, 400*, 121–152.

Bagader, A. A. (1997). The State of Arab Sociology as seen by an Arab Sociologist. In A. Zghal & A. L. Ouedern (Eds.), *Questions from Arab Societies; Proceedings of the ISA Arab Regional Conference, International Studies Association, Hammamet, Tunisia* (pp. 61–72). International Sociological Association.

Bamyeh, M. (2015). *Social Sciences in the Arab World: Forms of Presence [First Report of the Arab Social Science Monitor]*. Arab Council for the Social Sciences.

Jelloun, T. B. (1977). Decolonizing Sociology in the Maghreb: Usefulness and Risks of a Critical Function. In S. E. Ibrahim & N. S. Hopkins (Eds.), *Arab Society: Social Science Perspectives* (pp. 70–75). American University of Cairo Press.

Birbārī, N. E. (1897). al-Sūsiyūlūjiyā ay ʿIlm al-Ijtimāʿ al-Insānī [Sociology, i.e. the Science of Human Society]. *al-Muqtaṭaf, 21*(8, 9, 11), 574–579, 674–679, 825–830.

Eickelman, D. F. (2012). Social Science under Siege: The Middle East. In H. Hazan & E. Herzog (Eds.), *Serendipity in Anthropological Research: The Nomadic Turn* (pp. 213–227). Ashgate.

El Shakry, O. (2007). *The Great Social Laboratory: Subjects of Knowledge in Colonial and Postcolonial Egypt*. Stanford University Press.

El Shakry, M. (2015). Spencer's Arabic Readers. In B. Lightman (Ed.), *Global Spencerism: The Communication and Appropriation of a British Evolutionist* (pp. 35–55). Brill.

Ende, W. (1991). [Rezension zu] Arabische Soziologie. Studien zur Geschichte und Gesellschaft des Islam von Abdulkader Irabi. *Die Welt des Islams, 31*(2), 277–278.

Ḥamūdī, ʿA. (2018). al-ʿUlūm al-Ijtimāʿiyya fī al-ʿĀlam al-ʿArabī: Muqāriba li-l-Intājāt al-Ṣādira bi-l-Lugha al-ʿArabiyya (2000–2016) [Social Sciences in the Arab World: Assessing the Output in Arabic Language (2000–2016)]. *al-Marṣad al-ʿArabī li-l-ʿUlūm al-Ijtimāʿiyya: al-Taqrīr al-Thānī*. ACSS.

Ḥamzāwī, S., & Kawāshī, S. (2017). Ishkālāt ʿIlm al-Ijtimāʿ fī al-Waṭan al-ʿArabī: Qirāʾāt Taḥlīliyya li-Iʿtirāfāt baʿḍ ʿUlamāʾ al-Ijtimāʿ al-ʿArab [Problems of Sociology in the Arab World: Analytical Readings of Statements by some Arab Sociologists]. *Majallat Al-ʿulūm Al-Insāniyya Wa-l-Ijtimāʿiyya, 28*, 91–100.

Hanafi, S. (2010). Palestinian Sociological Production: Funding and National Considerations. In S. Patel (Ed.), *The ISA Handbook of Diverse Sociological Traditions* (pp. 257–267). SAGE.

Hanafi, S. (2011). University systems in the Arab East: Publish globally and perish locally vs publish locally and perish globally. *Current Sociology, 59*(3), 291–309.

Hanafi, S. (2013). Writing Sociology in the Arab world: Knowledge Production through Idafat, the Arab Journal of Sociology. *Contemporary Arab Affairs, 6*(2), 220–236.

Ḥanafī, S. (2016). Aslamat wa-Taʾṣīl al-ʿUlūm al Ijtimāʿiyya: Dirāsa fī baʿḍ al-Ishkāliyyāt [Islamizing and Indigenizing the Social Sciences: Investigation of some Problems]. *al-Mustaqbal al-ʿArabī, 451*, 45–64.

Hanafi, S. (2021). A Cognitive Arab Uprising?: Paradigm Shifts in Arab Social Sciences. In A. Salvatore, S. Hanafi, & K. Obuse (Eds.), *The Oxford Handbook of the Sociology of the Middle East* (Oxford Handbooks Online).

Oxford University Press. https://doi.org/10.1093/oxfordhb/9780190087470.013.4.

Ḥanafī, Sārī, Nūriya Bin Ghabrīṭ-Ramᶜūn, & Mijahdī Muṣṭafā. (2014): *Mustaqbal al-ᶜUlūm al-Ijtimāᶜiyya fī al-Waṭan al-ᶜArabī* [The Future of Social Sciences in the Arab World]. Markaz Dirāsāt al-Waḥda al-ᶜArabiyya.

Hiddleston, J., & Lyamlahy, K. (2020). *Abdelkébir Khatibi: Postcolonialism, Transnationalism, and Culture in the Maghreb and Beyond*. Liverpool University Press.

Husayn, T. (1917). *La philosophie sociale d'Ibn-Khaldoun*. A. Pedone.

Ḥusayn, Ṭ. (1925). *Falsafat Ibn Khaldūn al-Ijtimāᶜiyya: Taḥlīl wa-Naqd* [The Social Philosophy of Ibn Khaldun: Analysis and Critique], trans. M. ᶜAbdallāh ᶜAnān. Maṭbaᶜat al-Iᶜtimād.

Ibrahim, S. E. (1997). Cross-Eyed Sociology in Egypt and the Arab World. *Contemporary Sociology, 26*(5), 547–551.

Ibrāhīm, Saᶜd al-Dīn. (2014). al-Murjiᶜyāt al-Gharbiyya li-l-ᶜUlūm al-Ijtimāᶜiyya fī al-Waṭan al-ᶜArabī [Western Sources for Social Sciences in the Arab World]. In Sārī Ḥanafī, Nūriya bin Ghabrīṭ-Ramᶜūn, & Majāhidī Muṣṭafā (Eds.), *Mustaqbal al-ᶜUlūm al-Ijtimāᶜiyya fī al-Waṭan al-ᶜArabī* [The Future of Social Sciences in the Arab World], (pp. 59–73). Markaz Dirāsāt al-Waḥda al-ᶜArabiyya.

Irabi, A. (1989). *Arabische Soziologie: Studien zur Geschichte und Gesellschaft des Islam*. WBG.

Irwin, R. (2018). *Ibn Khaldun: An Intellectual Biography*. Princeton University Press.

ᶜĪsā, Muḥammad (1957): *Atbāᶜ Saint-Simon: Falsafatuhum al-Ijtimāᶜiyya wa-Taṭbīquhā fī Miṣr* [The Followers of Saint-Simon: Their Social Philosophy and Its Application in Egypt]. Maṭbaᶜat Jāmiᶜat al-Qāhira.

ᶜIzzat, ᶜAbd al-ᶜAziz. (1960). al-Idīyūlūjiyya al-ᶜarabiyya wa-l-mujtamaᶜ al-ᶜarabī. Maṭbaᶜat al-Waḥda.

Keim, W. (2015). Islamization of Knowledge: Symptom of the Failed Globalization of the Social Sciences? *Method(e)s African Review of Social Sciences Methodology, 2*(1–2), 127–154.

Keim, W. (2016). The International Circulation of Social Science Knowledge: Relevant Factors for Acceptance and Rejection of Travelling Texts. *Revue d'anthropologie des connaissances, 10*(1), a–aj.

Khalīfa, A., & Suhair, L. (1984). *Ishkāliyyāt al-ᶜUlūm al-Ijtimāᶜiyya fī al-Waṭan al-ᶜArabī* [Problems of the Social Sciences in the Arab World]. Dār al-Tanwīr.

Khatibi, A. (1975). Sociologie du monde arabe. *Positions, BESM, 126*(1), 13–26.

Khatibi, A. (1985). Double Criticism: The Decolonization of Arab Sociology. In H. Barakat (Ed.), *Contemporary North Africa: Issues of Development and Integration* (pp. 9–19). Center for Contemporary Arab Studies, Georgetown University.

Kriener, J. (2015). Like on Different Planets? Lebanese Social Scientists in Their Scientific Communities. *Middle East—Topics & Arguments, 4*, 122–136.

Lange, K. (2005). *Zurückholen, was uns gehört: Indigenisierungstendenzen in der arabischen Ethnologie*. Transcript.

Leder, S. (2014). Max Weber in der arabischen Welt. In M. W. Stiftung, M. Kaiser, & H. Rosenbach (Eds.), *Max Weber in der Welt: Rezeption und Wirkung* (pp. 23–32). Mohr Siebeck.

Madoui, M. (2007). Les sciences sociales en Algérie: Regards sur les usages de la sociologie. *Sociologies Pratiques, 2*(15), 149–160.

Madoui, M. (2015). La Sociologie marocaine: Du déni à la rehabilitation. *Sociologies Pratiques, 1*(30), 99–113.

Mahwar Bāsha, ʿAbd al-Ḥalīm. (2018). *ʿIlm al-Ijtimāʿ fī al-ʿĀlam al-ʿArabī min al-Naqd ilā al-Taʾsīs: Naḥwa ʿIlm al-ʿUmrān al-Islāmī* [Sociology in the Arab World from Critique to Establishment: Towards the Science of Islamic Civilization]. International Institute for Islamic Thought.

Markaz Dirāsāt al-Waḥda al-ʿArabiyya. (1986). *Naḥwa ʿIlm Ijtimāʿ ʿArabī: ʿIlm al-Ijtimāʿ wa-l-Mushkilāt al-ʿArabiyya al-Rāhina* [Towards an Arab Sociology: Sociology and Current Arab Problems]. Markaz Dirāsāt al-Waḥda al-ʿArabiyya.

Maʿtūq, F. (2007). *Madkhal ilā Sūsiyūlujiyā al-Turāth* [Introduction to the Sociology of Heritage]. Dār al-Ḥadātha.

Milbank, J. (1991). *Theology and Social Theory: Beyond Secular Reason*. B. Blackwell.

Morsy, S., Nelson, C., Saad, R., & Sholkamy, H. (1991). Anthropology and the Call for Indigenization of Social Science in the Arab World. In E. L. Sullivan & J. S. Ismael (Eds.), *The Contemporary Study of the Arab World* (pp. 81–111). University of Alberta Press.

Ramʿūn, Ḥ. (2014). Mumārisat al-ʿUlūm al-Ijtimāʿiyya fī al-Jazāʾir [Practicing the Social Sciences in Algeria]. In S. Ḥanafī, N. B. Ghabrīṭ-Ramʿūn, & M. Muṣṭafā (Eds.), *Mustaqbal al-ʿUlūm al-Ijtimāʿiyya fī al-Waṭan al-ʿArabī* [The Future of Social Sciences in the Arab World] (pp. 289–300). Markaz Dirāsāt al-Waḥda al-ʿArabiyya.

Reid, D. M. (1987). Cairo University and the Orientalists. *International Journal of Middle East Studies, 19*(1), 51–75.

Roussillon, A. (1991). Projet colonial et traditions scientifiques: aux origines de la sociologie égyptienne. In CEDEJ (Ed.), *D'un Orient l'autre: les métamorphoses successives des perceptions et connaissances, vol. 2: identifications* (pp. 347–388). Editions du CNRS.

Roussillon, A. (1996). Sociologie et société en Egypte: Le contournement des intellectuels par l'Etat. In T. Al-Bishri (Ed.), *Les intellectuels et le pouvoir* (pp. 3–138). CEDEJ.

Roussillon, A. (2002). Sociologie et identité en Égypte et au Maroc: Le travail de deuil de La colonisation. *Revue D'histoire Des Sciences Humaines, 2*(7), 193–221.
Roussillon, A. (2003). Sociology in Egypt and Morocco. In T. M. Porter & D. Ross (Eds.), *The Cambridge History of Science vol. 7: The Modern Social Sciences* (pp. 450–465). Cambridge University Press.
Sabagh, G., & Ghazalla, I. (1986). Arab Sociology Today: A View from Within. *Annual Review of Sociology, 12*, 373–399.
al-Samālūṭī, N. (1981). *Binā' al-Mujtamaᶜ al-Islāmī wa-Nuẓumuhu: Dirāsa fī ᶜIlm al-Ijtimāᶜ al-Islāmī* [The Structure of Islamic Society and Its Institutions: A Study in Islamic Sociology]. Dār al-Shurūq.
al-Shamarī, H. (2011). *Mabāḥith fī ᶜIlm al-Ijtimāᶜ al-Islāmī: Islamic Sociology* [Studies in Islamic Sociology: Islamic Sociology]. Dār al-Manāhij.
Steinmetz, G. (2013). *Sociology and Empire: The Imperial Entanglements of a Discipline*. Duke University Press.
Steinmetz, G. (2023). *The Colonial Origins of Social Thought: French Sociology and the Overseas Empire*. Princeton University Press.
Stenberg, L. (1996). *The Islamization of Science: Four Muslim Positions Developing an Islamic Modernity*. Novapress.
Tozy, M. (2013, February 20). Paul Pascon: un pionnier de la sociologie marocaine, *SociologieS*, Discoveries/rediscoveries. https://journals.openedition.org/sociologies/4322 (last accessed May 2, 2021).
ᶜUmar, Maᶜn Khalīl. (1990). *Ruwwād ᶜIlm al-Ijtimāᶜ fī al-ᶜIrāq* [Leaders of Sociology in Iraq]. Dār al-Shu'ūn al-Thaqāfiyya al-ᶜĀmma.
ᶜUmar, Maᶜn Khalīl. (1991 [1989]). *Naḥwa Naẓariyya ᶜArabiyya fī ᶜIlm al-Ijtimāᶜ* [Towards an Arab Theory of Sociology]. Dār Majdalāwī.
ᶜUmar, Maᶜn Khalīl. (1992 [1984]). *Naḥwa ᶜIlm Ijtimāᶜ ᶜArabī* [Towards an Arab Sociology]. Dār Majdalāwī.
ᶜUmar, Maᶜn Khalīl. (2013). *ᶜIlm al-Ijtimāᶜ al-Islāmī* [Islamic Sociology]. Dār al-Zahra.
ᶜUmar, Maᶜn Khalīl (2021): Homepage of Maᶜn Khalīl al-ᶜUmar. https://drmaanalomar.com (Accessed on 8 May 2021).
ᶜUthmān, Ibrāhīm ᶜĪsā. (2008). *Muqaddima fī ᶜIlm al-Ijtimāᶜ* [Introduction to Sociology]. Dār al-Shurūq.
al-Zāhī, Nūr al-Dīn. (2011). *al-Madkhal li-ᶜIlm al-Ijtimāᶜ al-Maghribī* [Introduction to Moroccan Sociology]. Dafātir Wijhat Naẓar.
Zayid, A. (1995). Seventy Years of Sociology in Egypt. *Cairo Papers in Social Science, 18*(3), 41–71.
Zemmin, F. (2018). *Modernity in Islamic Tradition. The Concept of 'Society' in the Journal al-Manar (Cairo, 1898–1940)*. De Gruyter.
Zghal, A., & Karoui, H. (1973). Decolonization and Social Science Research: The Case of Tunisia. *Middle East Studies Association Bulletin, 7*(3), 11–27.

CHAPTER 3

Who Counts as a Theorist? Locating Maghrebi Sociologists in the Intellectual History of Decolonization

Florian Keller

3.1 Introduction

In 2019, Tunisian sociologist Hamdi Ounaina organized a series of seminars titled "Being a sociologist in Tunisia" focusing on the first generation of social scientists in Tunisia after the country achieved independence in 1956. In the introduction to a publication that followed the seminar, titled *Ecrire L'Histoire Sociale de la Sociologie en Tunisie* (Write the Social History of Sociology in Tunisia), Ounaina diagnosed the absence of an intellectual history of Tunisian social science (Ounaina, 2021: 16).

To take up Ounaina's question, what would an intellectual history of sociology in Arab societies look like? This raises questions regarding the universality or particularity of social theory. As Omnia El-Shakry asks,

F. Keller (✉)
Graduate School for Global Intellectual History (GIH), Freie Universität Berlin, Berlin, Germany
e-mail: f.keller@fu-berlin.de

D. Jung and F. Zemmin (eds.), *Postcolonialism and Social Theory in Arabic*, The Modern Muslim World,
https://doi.org/10.1007/978-3-031-63649-3_3

what "makes one intellectual the originator of theoretical models and another [merely] an object of study and a producer of thought," rather than theory? (El-Shakry, 2021: 550). In the growing field of Arab intellectual history, scholars have questioned the "compositional logic" that overemphasizes thinkers such as Frantz Fanon, who played a major role for European and American academics and activists, but whose influence in Arab societies was relatively marginal, while leading Arab thinkers do not appear in the global, primarily Anglophone archive of Arab intellectual history (El-Shakry, 2015: 921). The historian becomes a gatekeeper who decides who will be included in Arab intellectual history, consequently, historian Fadi Bardawil asks, "*Who* counts as an Arab intellectual in the genealogies constructed by intellectual historians?" (Bardawil, 2018: 179).

Therefore, in this chapter, I focus on how Maghribi intellectuals such as Abdelkader Zghal (1931–2015), Ali El-Kenz (1946–2020), and Tahar Labib (b. 1942) understood themselves and critiqued their own relationship to political power in the form of the independent postcolonial state.[1] To that end, these thinkers analyzed how colonial subjugation at once ruptured the production of knowledge in Arab societies and created new possibilities for it. As historian Hosam Aboul-Ela has shown, projects to historicize thought had been undertaken in the Arab region as early as the 1980s—not least by the Moroccan philosopher Muhammad Abed al-Jabiri (Aboul-Ela, 2018). Building upon this work, I argue that the debates among Maghrebi sociologists in the 1980s represent pioneering efforts to develop an "intellectual history," albeit without labeling itself as such.

The following investigation is divided into five parts. In the second section, I begin by exploring how debates about the role of the intellectual were sparked by the crisis of political legitimacy that shook post-independence Arab states from the early 1970s. Arab sociologists trace the roots of this crisis back to the paradoxical impact of colonial regimes, which had founded the educational framework for a new, bilingual class, leading to a division into francophone and arabophone "intellectuals." These deliberations were inseparable from a critical revision of the social sciences in the Arab region. For a better understanding of the social sciences in the Maghreb, I will provide some historical context for the Tunisian case in the third section and then introduce Tunisian social science research, which was more advanced compared to Algeria and Morocco. In the fourth section, I show how the criticisms and reflections among Arab sociologists were part of a larger debate on theory and methods. The central question within those debates was how existing sociological methods, which had evolved mostly in Europe, could be used in or adapted to an Arab context. In line with this question, I will demonstrate, in the fifth section, how particularly the approach of a "developmentalist" sociology that understands society only through the analysis of positive data at the expense of a more holistic understanding of society was criticized by the sociologists themselves. Finally, in the sixth section, I will demonstrate how the search for "tools" to understand society led sociologists to explore concepts of the Italian thinker Antonio Gramsci, who, facing an economic division between Northern and Southern Italy, sought to redefine the conditions of the "formation" of intellectuals. I conclude that these efforts by the Maghrebi sociologists were an attempt to reflect and historicize the conditions of their own existence. In this process, they actively sought to advance the "process" of decolonization. My aim in this chapter is not to evaluate whether Maghrebi sociologists were "public," "organic," "revolutionary," or "regime" intellectuals. Rather, my aim is to demonstrate how these concepts were used, and what this usage reveals about the intellectual history of the Arab Maghreb at the beginning of the 1980s, particularly in Tunisia and Algeria.

3.2 Intellectuals and the State

In 1983, an interview with the Algerian sociologist Abdelkader Jaghlul under the title *Intelligentsia or Intellectuals in Algeria?* (Intilijansiyya am Muthaqqafun fi al-Jazaʾir?),[2] triggered a fierce debate in the weekly francophone cultural newspaper *Algerie-Actualité*. The debate that the sociologist from the University of Oran initiated and the questions raised were an attempt to find answers to the social conflicts in Algeria that had accompanied the country since its independence from French colonialism in 1962 and had reached a temporary peak at the end of the 1970s. Algerian sociologist Ammar Belhassan suggests that, from 1980 onward, the discourse around "culture" and "intellectuals" resurfaced and became a common intellectual "battleground" in Algeria. As the newspaper *Algerie-Actualité* was known for its loyalty to the regime, the editor's willingness to publish a discussion critical of the regime, accompanied by a call for the formation of a "critical intelligentsia," was a significant event and reveals the urgency of these questions (ʿAmmar Belhassan, 1983: 1). Because scholars from many different backgrounds participated in the debate, including academics, artists, and journalists, it is an excellent example of the contemporaneous cultural discourse around the question of identity of Algerian intellectuals. As Amar Belhassan argues, the debate in *Algerie-Actualité* was a decisive moment in the course of advancing and formulating the question of culture in Algeria and offered a profound opportunity to grasp and restore intellectuals' awareness of their own situation and positions and the historical and social conditions for the existence of the intellectuals themselves (ᶜAmmar Belhassan, 1983: 1).[3]

However, the issue was not just limited to Algeria but had implications for the entire Arab region. In June 1984, the Egyptian sociologist Saad Eddin Ibrahim (1938–2013) published an article titled "Tajsir al-Fajuda baina al-Mufakkir wa-Saniᶜi al-Qarrarat fi al-Watan al-ᶜArabi" (Bridging the Gap between Thinkers and Decision-makers in the Arab World) in the scholarly journal *al-Mustaqbal al-ʿArabi* (The Arab Future). This article sparked a larger debate in the journal that brought together thinkers from different Arab countries, scholars such as Tahar Labib, the Moroccan writer Mohammed Berrada (b. 1938), and the Egyptian sociologist Nader Ferjani (b. 1944). One of the main questions addressed was the relationship of the "intellectual" to "authority" in the Arab region at the beginning of the 1980s, which—as Ferjani suggests—had witnessed a crisis that is well accepted and no longer needs further documentation or evidence (Ferjani, 1984; Ibrahim, 1984). The debate was moderated by the Center for Arab Unity Studies (Markaz al-Dirasat al-Wahda al-ᶜArabiyya [CAUS]), an organization established in Beirut in 1975 by a number of independent scholars and thinkers to facilitate debate on various topics in the Arab region by sponsoring studies and publications and organizing conferences. The CAUS journal, *The Arab Future*, appeared monthly starting in 1978 and quickly became a lively forum for debate and contributions from all parts of the Arab region (Kassab, 2010: 150). For the April 1985 issue, the contributors were tasked with diagnosing and overcoming this crisis by starting with themselves, that is, "to consider their own conditions" (Ferjani et al., 1985: 128). The participating sociologists from Egypt and the Maghreb mainly asked conceptual questions about the social category of the figure of the intellectual. Unlike previous forums, which had discussed the "Arab intellectual," all contributors directly or indirectly referenced ideas on the "formation" of intellectuals by the Italian Marxist thinker Antonio Gramsci.

The debates in *Algerié-Actualité* and *The Arab Future* marked the beginning of a series of congresses and symposia throughout the 1980s dealing with the question of the past and present of the "intellectuals" in the Arab region in general and in the Maghreb in particular.[4] I argue that these debates were inseparable from an intense re-evaluation of the state and the development of Arab sociology. Simultaneously, during conferences in Cairo and Abu Dhabi conceptual and methodological questions had become a pressing topic among Arab sociologists.[5]

In 1985, the Arab Sociology Association (*al-Jamᶜiyya al-ᶜArabiyya li-ᶜIlm al-Ijtimaᶜ)* was founded in Tunis, significantly driven forward by Maghrebi sociologists, such as Tahar Labib—who served as the first general secretary. Consequently, the Association organized a conference under the title "The Arab Intelligentsia" (*al-Intilijansiyya al-ʿArabiyya*) in Cairo in 1987 (the conference was in 1987 and some conrtibutions were published in 1989). The reference is the one that follows. For Labib, the conference in Cairo was a "request and expectation" that the participants take a more scientific approach: to transition from the classification of writings, texts, and speeches to the social classification of the drafters themselves (Labib, 1989: 5).[6] Central questions of the debate affected all participants equally, but as Algerian sociologist Ali El-Kenz suggests, particularly the issue of whether an Arab intelligentsia existed and, if so, in what form had raised the question of the specificities of the Maghreb and the Mashreq as two subregions (El-Kenz, 1997: 38). As Ali El-Kenz reflected, the foundational meeting in Tunis in 1985 took inventory of the then-current situation of Arab sociology (El-Kenz, 1997: 31). One faction of the participants, following a Marxist framework, rejected the idea of an "ontological" specificity of Arab societies that could justify the existence of a uniquely Arab sociology (El-Kenz, 1997: 33). In El-Kenz's words, the second faction "quite eclectically brought together 'Durkheimians,' in the broad sense of the French 'model,' associated with 'critical sociology'; this mainly concerned North Africans whose region was colonized by France" (El-Kenz, 1997: 33). This current, he continues, had also included "functionalists," an Anglosphere type of descriptive and quantitative sociology that was especially prevalent in the Mashriq. The two currents found themselves united, but from different and even opposed political positions, and thus not without friction (El-Kenz, 1997: 33).

3.3 The State of Sociology in Tunisia and the Maghreb by the 1980s

In order to understand the development of Tunisian social science institutions as well as the topics and debates that were researched and discussed, some historical background is necessary. In 1958, two years after Tunisia achieved independence from France, the Tunisian minister of education, Mahmoud Messadi (1911–2004), released a ten-year plan to modernize the education system in order to provide the state with a skilled and specialized labor force. The success was remarkable: within ten years, by 1968, the number of university graduates had tripled (Krichen, 1994: 61–68). Education was the "crown jewel" of the state's reform agenda (Jebari, 2022: 107). However, in the process of rebuilding the education system in the wake of French colonialism, Tunisia, as well as other French-colonized countries of the Maghreb, such as Algeria and Morocco, confronted the legacy of a bilingual colonial education that had prioritized French over Arabic. Before France officially made Tunisia a protectorate in 1881, the education system had been embedded in religious institutions, such as the Zaytuna Mosque, for many centuries. As the Tunisian sociologist Aziz Krichen writes, institutions such as the bilingual Sadiqi College formed a "buffer" between the almost exclusively Arabic "Zaytunian" education and the francophone private schools that almost exclusively served the children of the colonists. While the Zaytuna primarily provided education for the lower classes, the Sadiqi College produced a new generation of bilingual, middle-class Tunisians. Graduates of Sadiqi College constituted the core of the Neo Destour party that led the fight for independence, and included the later president of Tunisia, Habib Bourguiba himself (Krichen, 1987: 300). The restoration of national culture, including the project of Arabizing the education system, formed an integral part of the Neo Destour party's program. However, after the party came to power under Bourguiba, its Arabization project came under intense criticism for being nothing more than rhetorical lip service. Critics argued that, instead of an Arabization of the education system, the ruling party had instituted a static hierarchical bilingualism in which French served as the language of the elite and arabophone education remained marginalized and underfunded. In Krichen's words, a bilingual "modern intelligentsia" victoriously defeated French domination on the political level, yet, ironically, became the best guarantor of the perpetuation of "French hegemony" in the linguistic and cultural spheres after political independence (Krichen, 1987: 301). Moreover, at the beginning of the 1960s, Bourguiba's administration adopted socialist policies, as reflected in the ruling party's name change from the Neo Destour to the Socialist Destour party in 1964. This undertaking involved a radical restructuring of the economy, primarily through the creation of agricultural cooperatives, as part of a larger project to transform not only the modes of production but also social issues such as family planning (Dakhli, 2021: 53).

The Centre des Études et de Recherches Économiques et Sociales (CERES) was a prestigious education and research project within the efforts to reconstruct the education system. The institute organized colloquia to allow researchers to present their work and provided opportunities for discussion with scholars working on similar projects. In the words of one historian, CERES was part of Tunisia's "global interface," its "researchers participating in collaborative and interdisciplinary conversations at international, national, and local levels" (Kallander, 2021: 129). Two important publications were issued by the center from 1964 onwards: The *Revue tunisienne de sciences sociales* (Tunisian Social Science Review [*RTSS*]) and *Cahiers du CERES* (Notebooks from CERES). The sociological paradigm that had dominated CERES in the aftermath of independence, according to the Tunisian sociologist Imed Melliti, was a "developmentalist agenda" establishing an "alliance between a modernizing state and sociologists of modernization" (Melliti, 2014: 167). Moreover, he suggests that Tunisian sociology was founded on the rejection of colonial science and topics privileged by colonial ethnographers, such as tribalism and religious rites. The first generation of Tunisian sociologists focused on the "analysis of social change, perceived as a progressive and irreversible entry into modernity," as Melliti describes it (Melliti & Mahfoudh-Draoui, 2014: 273).

While researchers at CERES, such as Abdelkader Zghal (1931–2015), a sociologist who belonged to the first generation of the institute, were partly involved in opposition movements and union activism, the directors of the center were expected to have an impeccable reputation and a pedigree outside of the orbit of the ruling Destour party. Abdelwahab Boudhiba (1932–2020), who served as the director of CERES from 1972 to 1992, was trained at Sadiqi College in the 1940s and holds a philosophy degree from the Sorbonne in Paris. In an article titled "La sociologie du développement africain" (The sociology of African development), Boudhiba situates Tunisia—in the spirit of the Bandung

Conference of 1955—within a huge development project that includes the entire continent of Africa. Boudhiba argues that the time had finally come for Tunisians to hold their heads high and break the chains that colonialism had placed on Tunisia under the cover of colonial science. In particular, the division of scientific labor, that is to say, the separation of economics, sociological studies, and political science had led to a fragmented vision of social reality, alongside the reductive binary between "primitive" and "civilized" (Bouhdiba, 1970: 7–8). The sociology of Africa, Boudhiba claims, can therefore only be a sociology of development, to "illuminate the opacity of the present, to demythologize African consciousness" (Bouhdiba: 21). One of the main tasks of development sociology, according to Boudhiba, was to address the "rural question," that is, the role of the African peasantry. This required an evaluation of whether Lenin's analysis of the Russian peasantry could also apply to Africa. Boudhiba asks: "Is the Revolution agrarian reform along with the electrification of the countryside?" (Bouhdiba: 17). However, the answer to the Tunisian "peasant question," which was to engage in efforts to collectivize agriculture and create big cooperatives, met with little approval from the "peasants" themselves and was, in the end, unsuccessful. The failure of the cooperatives marked the end of the "socialist experiment" of the Tunisian government in 1969.

At the same time, Abdelkader Zghal published a survey asking *why* the government's plans for collectivization met with resistance from Tunisian farmers (Zghal, 1969). Doubts regarding the relevance of the developmentalist paradigm emerged at the end of the 1960s in the face of the failure of agrarian reforms and attempts to centrally plan the development of the national economy. However, criticism from within the institute was not a tolerated practice, with the government persecuting and punishing open criticism and dissent. As a former colleague of Zghal's later reported, criticizing government policies was a "brave and controversial thing to do" (Michalak, 2017: 121).

Criticism from within the institute became increasingly loud and directed against the official agent of decolonization, the Tunisian state. In 1973, Abdelkader Zghal and Hachimi Karoui stated in their report "Decolonization and Social Science Research: The Case of Tunisia" that the government's developmentalist agenda ignored a comprehensive understanding of the real problem that Tunisia faced. They called for intellectual sovereignty and analyzed the capacity of political regimes in "third world countries" to tolerate criticism. Without a minimum of tolerance, they concluded, "no real research is possible, even if there are researchers of unquestionable scientific skill available" (Zghal & Karoui, 1973: 17). Thus, their call for decolonization encompassed a critique of the state and its organs.

At the beginning of the 1970s, other sociologists and thinkers from the Maghreb region in particular called for decolonization of the social sciences too (Ben Jelloun, 1974; Khatibi, 1985). The post-independence history of social science research and the establishment of its institutional framework in Algeria, Morocco, and Tunisia were an inherent part of education policies. In Morocco, the Institute of Sociology, established by the Moroccan government in 1960, was already closed down again in 1971. The institutional framework was marginal in Algeria as well. El-Kenz suggests that the first notion the sociologists had of themselves as a group emerged by the middle of the 1970s. Prior to 1971, when sociology was included as an autonomous discipline at the University of Algiers, students had been trained in departments of philosophy or anthropology (El-Kenz & Beaud, 1998: 130). Unlike Algeria and Morocco, the institutionalization of the social sciences was most advanced in Tunisia. Roughly twenty-five years after the founding of the Tunisian social science research institute CERES in 1962, Tunisian social scientists could look back on research experiences and debates and were therefore quite self-confident (Ben Salem, 2009: 129).[7] At the time of the foundation of the Arab Sociology Association in 1985, the state of social sciences was highly uneven across different Arab countries, and discussions were developed to various degrees and had different emphases (Zemmin, 2022: 8–11). For example, Egypt and Tunisia were among the countries that had already seen a heated discussion at the beginning of the 1980s about the methods and orientation of the social sciences. Despite such local variations, thinkers from these different Arab countries came together because they had a common goal. Decolonization, especially of the social sciences, had become a project that had to be carried out against the state, or in defiance of the state.

3.4 Methodological and Epistemological Stakes

In the introduction to an edition of selected contributions to the foundational meeting of the Arab Sociology Association in 1985, Egyptian sociologist Muhammad ʿIzzat Hijazi outlined some of the severe problems Arab sociology faced: Arab sociology had arisen and developed in the Arab region, but it was still weak and proved unable to provide fertile theoretical categories capable of suggesting ideas that would aid development, renewal, and effective results with a solid scientific foundation. Moreover, it was isolated and alienated from the living social reality (Hijazi, 2002: 13). For Hijazi, the main reason for the crisis of the social sciences in the Arab region was that they were not able to produce their "own" knowledge, but rather theory and methods were mostly imported from French sociology. Algerian sociologist Ali El-Kenz made a similar claim: Western social theory had been imported and applied without paying attention to the particular historical circumstances and the field of knowledge that these theories had grown and developed (El-Kenz, 2002: 100). The question of how Arab social science should deal with Western European social theory and methods was the subject of a controversial debate. The contribution of the Egyptian economist (and former Marxist) Adil Husayn titled "Al-Nazariyyat al-Ijtimaᶜiyya al-Gharbiyya: Qasira wa-Maᶜdiyya" (Western Social Theories: Inadequate and Hostile) was particularly polarizing (Hijazi, 2002: 37).[8] The main argument of Husayn's paper, as Hijazi highlights, was twofold: Western social theories were not able to account for the realities of the Arab region, and therefore their universalist claims and secular worldview have to be rejected. Husayn called for a process of self-renewal by returning to Islamic values and metaphysics, where God is the center of the universe (Hijazi, 2002: 38). In discussing Husayns's claims, Hijazi outlines the program of the Arab Sociology Association: Dealing with Western European social thought needs to be problematized and scrutinized for its adaptability to Arab reality. However, Hijazi clarifies that the assessment of Arab specificity cannot necessarily be solved through an approach of Islamization and Arabization. On the contrary, Arabization bears the danger of an "Arabocentrism" (*Markaziyya ᶜArabiyya*) similar to Eurocentrism. Western social schools were involved in colonial domination and carry a Eurocentric worldview, but Hijazi holds that "they are not necessarily hostile to us" (Hijazi, 2002: 38). The problem that Hijazi addresses here, I suggest, refers to the general question for non-European thinkers of whether the categorical rejection of a certain (European) theoretical tradition is feasible. What Hijazi tries to avoid is a short-cut Arabization of concepts that necessarily bears the danger of a simple conceptual reproduction, rather than a shift in the epistemological perspective.[9] In the following section, I discuss a criticism of "developmentalism" that some thinkers identified as the leading paradigm of post-independence sociology in Tunisia and other parts of the Arab region.

3.5 The Developmentalist Paradigm

The "developmentalist paradigm," as Zghal emphasizes in a later reflection, was limited neither to Tunisia nor to the field of the emerging social sciences in the Arab region. Rather, it was ubiquitous in the postcolonial governments of the formerly colonized "Third World." To define the character of the developmentalist paradigm, Zghal refers to the Moroccan historian Abdallah Laroui (b. 1933). Why, despite all efforts, had postcolonial utopias not become a reality? "Why," as Laroui puts it, "are we facing the same difficulties as our parents and grandparents faced?" (Laroui, 1976: viii). Laroui published a famous essay "L'ideologie arabe contemporaine" (Contemporary Arab Ideology), in 1967.[10] In the essay, he grappled with the severe crisis of modernizing projects in the Arab region. In his diagnosis of the prevailing mindset, Laroui criticized the paradigm that he called "Objective Marxism" (*marxisme objectif*). Objective Marxism, according to Laroui, is an approach that consists of an "unsystematised set of ideas, notions, theories, each of which can be linked in one way or another to Marxism" (Laroui, 1967: 10), and it is this approach that has been implicitly adopted by the "modernist Arab intelligentsia." Laroui, who worked with Marxist methodology himself, did not intend to reject Marxism in general. On the contrary, the focus of his criticism was a vulgar reading of Marxist theory that reduced the political-economic analysis of society to an empiricist model based on positive data. Thus, according to Laroui, Objective Marxism is essentially no different than the positivism of Auguste Comte and Herbert Spencer (Laroui, 1967: 153–154).

Zghal uses the terms "Objective Marxism" and "developmentalist paradigm" interchangeably. Thus, Tunisian post-independence sociology may serve as an example of a form of Objective Marxism. According to Zghal, positivism was not so much a proper school established in post-independence Tunisia, but rather a simplistic derivative of a concept dating back to early nineteenth-century Europe. In Zghal's view, followers of Objective Marxism as a positivist paradigm held that "the management of the positive state can only be the work of the holders of positive knowledge, represented by the model of the engineer" (Zghal,

1989: 221). Thus, in Zghal's reflections, the position of the sociologist—his own position—toward the state becomes a central question. Zghal contends that statolatry[11]—worship of the state—is the "secular religion of positivism and developmentalist ideology" (Zghal, 1989: 221). Consequently, the young sociologists of CERES ought to be the executers of this very ideology. He writes:

The result was that we were well programmed for "objective Marxism," which is really only positivist empiricism driven by a critical but fundamentally pro-state attitude. We were positivists without having read Auguste Comte, and Objective Marxists with an often superficial knowledge of Marx's work (Abdelkader Zghal, 1989: 222).

Interpreting Zghal's statement, I suggest that "Objective Marxism" cannot necessarily be derived solely from French sociology. Rather, it is an amalgam of a wide variety of theories, including elements of the work of the American sociologist Talcott Parson (1902–1979). While he formulated his evolutionist ideas of social development in opposition to Marxist theory, Parson repeatedly invoked Marx and Engel's controversial models of economic evolution. In practice, for Zghal, the ubiquitous focus on positive data and the "rule" of conducting fieldwork within an administrative discourse in which the object of research was determined and limited resulted from the fact that researchers lacked theory and a proper hypothesis. In addition to a rigorous focus on economics, the sociologists of CERES attempted to explain social and political phenomena exclusively on the basis of competing economic interests (Zghal, 1989: 223). What becomes clear in Zghal's reflections, I suggest, is the contradicting atmosphere in which the young sociologists of the first generation work and theorize. On the one hand, their scope as "academic suppliers" to state modernization programs is very narrow. On the other hand, they themselves benefited from, and were products of, the state's extensive investments into the modernization of the Tunisian education system. In particular, the success of the extensive educational reforms emphasized by the accessibility of higher education and the associated social mobility explains the fascination of young sociologists with the modernization program of the state.

3.6 Between Ibn Khaldun and Gramsci

In search of an Arab thinker to use as a reference point for an independent Arab tradition of social thought, many Arab social scientists and historians drew on the scholar Ibn Khaldun (1332–1406), Some of them saw him as an early sociologist (Mohamed, 1991; Zemmin, 2022). At the 1985 convention in Tunis, Tahar Labib summarized the state of sociology in the Maghreb and particularly that of Tunisia throughout the 1960s and 1970s. He showed that Ibn Khaldun had a continuous presence through references in sociological works in Tunisia since the 1970s (Labib, 1985). The growing popularity of Ibn Khaldun is an important example of the attempts within Maghrebi sociology to establish an alternative body of literature that could serve as a "toolbox" for a "decolonized" post-independence sociology. Another thinker whose ideas became important for the Maghrebi sociologists was the Italian Marxist Antonio Gramsci (1891–1937).[12] As Zghal suggests, Antonio Gramsci—who coined the term hegemony—faced similar problems to the Arab sociologists insofar as Gramsci was posing new questions while being caught within an old paradigm. Zghal unfortunately does not develop this particular point further, but it is not difficult to see what he is aiming at. I suggest that Gramsci's comprehensive project to adopt a theoretical corpus of theory—in his case, Marxist theory—in a different political, economic, and religious context led scholars like Zghal to draw on his work. In the early twentieth century, Italy was sharply divided into the industrially developed North and the rural South, which still had a predominantly peasant society. Moreover, Italy occupied a peripheral position within Europe, and leading Italian intellectuals, including many secular Marxists, considered the southern Catholic peasantry to be particularly religiously and ethnically backward. Thus, one of the most pressing questions in Gramsci's work is how revolutionary Marxist theory could be translated to the southern Italian context. Gramsci aimed to further develop Marxist theory. He strove to overcome a simplified base–superstructure scheme, i.e. the idea that all social life is totally determined by the economic base and can only be understood in economic terms. A major theme in Gramsci's work, as Roger Simon suggests, is that the nature of the state cannot be understood without a thorough understanding of *civil society* (Simon, 1982: 68). According to Gramsci, civil society is a space structured by private, non-governmental institutions that struggle for cultural and ideological hegemony, whereas political society is used for the various institutions of the state, such as the armed forces, law enforcement, and administration. Civil society is the sphere of political and ideological struggles and where political parties, trade unions, religious bodies, and a great variety of other organizations come into existence. It is not only the sphere of class struggles; it is also the sphere of all the popular-democratic struggles which arise out of the different ways in which people are grouped together [...] (Simon, 1982: 69).

But how is the state to be understood through the concept of civil society in a rural society such as southern Italy in the 1920s, where the "state" and its various institutions were rather underdeveloped in contrast to the industrial North? Gramsci analyzed this dilemma in a 1926-essay titled "Some Aspects of the Southern Question." Gramsci drew a parallel between southern Italy, which was subjugated by the northern Italian bourgeoisie, and an exploited colony. For Gramsci, the proletariat and the peasantry were the bearers of the future. In order for them to exercise this function, Gramsci saw it as necessary for these two social forces to form an alliance.

Gramsci's "Southern question" was a key text for many Maghrebi sociologists, including the Algerian sociologist Ali El-Kenz and the Tunisian sociologist Tahar Labib, who was one of the first "Maghribis" to discuss Gramscian concepts and introduce his ideas to a broader readership at the beginning of the 1980s. As Labib writes, "the thirty pages written by Gramsci on the Southern question are perhaps [...] among his richest and densest texts" (Labib, 1981: 117). Ali El-Kenz argues that Gramsci's thought was an important asset because Gramsci had reached a comprehensive understanding of the unequal level of the social experience in Italy in the early twentieth century. Italy had fallen far behind its neighboring countries, and the process of building a modern nation state through industrialization and political unification was ongoing and far from complete. Moreover, southern Italy was "backward compared to the north," an unequal development of capitalism leading to different forms of struggles, and therefore requiring its own political strategies and offering new possibilities (El-Kenz, 1994: 57–58).Moreover, El-Kenz emphasizes another aspect that goes beyond a mere conceptual reading: particularly in the Arab cultural context, where the intellectual, even of the left, identified himself with the elite, a specific Gramscian "ethic" of the (committed and imprisoned militant) was a real revolution (El-Kenz, 1994: 56).

For Abdelkader Zghal the Tunisian "Southern question"—as reflected in the agricultural reforms of the Tunisian state—is the project of "collectivization" and land reform. He is concerned with the intellectuals who implement social change and seek to modernize the country's agriculture. Even if they had revolutionary goals, Zghal contends that the "new" intellectuals could not free themselves from inherited structures, for they could not escape the ideology of the old regime (Zghal, 1981: 232). For Zghal, the main question—drawing on the Gramscian concept of political and civil society—is how a potential class alliance could be possible in the first place within the realm of civil society, where the hegemonic struggle for intellectual, ideological, and cultural leadership takes place. What has been significant to many readers of Gramsci—not only in the Arab context—is his analysis that the "independence" of "free-floating" intellectuals is a myth. Intellectuals are not a distinct "independent" social group and are therefore not free of social and economic realities. Each intellectual has distinctive qualities of mind, and each intellectual or group of intellectuals has a distinctive relation to the social world. Thus, Zghal's main argument shifts the focus to the structures that post-independence governments inherited from the colonial state. Decolonization demands a critical confrontation with the structures of the state and, above all, with the role of its intellectuals. The task of sociology is, therefore, the self-consciousness and radical self-critique of this structural inheritance of colonialism. However, as Tahar Labib aptly analyzes, there can be no "outside" position of the thinker, theorist, sociologist, or intellectual: Any image that intellectuals draw of themselves as an antithesis to power does not prove right: The majority of "people of knowledge" can only exist within the institutions of power that they "are born in, live from, and die in" (Labib, 1985: 33).

3.7 Conclusion

Posing new questions within an old paradigm, as Zghal suggests, compelled sociologists to rethink their own social position relative to the institutions of the state. The debates at the beginning of the 1980s were characterized by a new perspective on the "intellectual." This perspective was informed by a highly sociological view that was able to help explain the "social being" of the "intellectuals" and their relation to power.[13] This view led Maghrebi sociologists to question a functional, positivist understanding of society, and, at the same time, further develop the unfinished process of decolonization. The search for analytical tools led leading sociologists to draw on Gramscian concepts. I suggest that Maghribi sociologists drew on the Gramscian notion of an "untimely" development in Italy in order to rethink the role of the intellectual, while also "provincializing" the history of Europe.

The debates around intellectuals and power in academic journals and at conferences demonstrate that Maghrebi sociologists engaged in an urgent project to establish sociology as a relatively new discipline for describing and analyzing social change. However, in order to do so, they held that it was first and foremost necessary to overcome the deep social and political crisis that had arisen roughly twenty-five years after independence. Ultimately, this crisis revealed that political independence was not the end of the decolonization process, but only the beginning. Furthermore, the relevance of the debates seemingly extended beyond the Maghreb and the Arab region. As Tahar Labib has suggested, the place of intellectuals in post-independence states was a question that could similarly be found in Latin America and other parts of the "Third World" (Labib, 1985: 29).

Overall, this chapter highlighted the process of self-reflection from within Maghrebi post-independence sociology. Thereby, I seek to contribute to what Ounaina has called an "intellectual history of Tunisian sociology." That is, I suggest, an intellectual history of the important debates that belong to the process of decolonization. Sociology and the sociologists who practiced it—through the lenses of Zghal, Labib, and El-Kenz—were explicitly political. What remains an open question, however, is a more comprehensive examination of Tunisian, Algerian, and Moroccan sociology and its actors. As historian Idriss Jebari suggests, intellectuals in the Maghreb engaged in radical and vivid acts of intervention; caught between being co-opted by the state apparatus or facing repression and marginalization, some pursued "a third option: subversion of the state" (Jebari, 2018: 61). The call for decolonization and reorganization of the social sciences demonstrates this practice of "subversion" and invites us to consider decolonization in the sense of Omnia El-Shakry as an "ongoing process and a series of struggles" that is far from being over (El-Shakry, 2015: 925).

Notes

1. A "homage" to the life and work of Abdelkader Zghal including contributions from friends and colleagues was edited by the Tunisian sociologist Mohamed & Abdelkader (2017).
2. I work with an Arabic edition (ʿAmmar Belhassan, 1983) that includes an introduction, the interview with Abdelkader Jaghlul, and a collection of all contributions to the debate in *Algerie-Actualité*.
3. Idriss Jebari speaks of a "turning point" for the Maghribi states at the end of the 1970s in which it "looked possible that the regimes might be opening in new ways" (Jebari, 2018: 66).
4. Thus, for example, the debate in *Algerié-Actualité* was followed by a congress at the University of Oran by Abdelkader Jaghloul under the title "The Intelligentsia in the Arab Maghreb" (Abdelkader Jaghlul, 1984). A congress was held at the University of Rabat under the title "The Arab Intellectual, his Role and Relationship with Power and Society" (1985). The participants at the various conferences, colloquia, and symposia throughout the 1980s came from all over the Arab region. Subsequent to the events, the large number of contributions were generally compiled in the form of—more or less—well-edited conference publications. Rarely, as in the case of the Rabat gathering, was a real discussion documented. In general, the contributions were compiled relatively unconnected to each other, sometimes grouped by different topics.
5. Abu Dhabi, April 15–30, 1983, and Cairo, February 26–28, 1983 (Hijazi, 2002).
6. All translations, unless otherwise noted, are mine.
7. Belonging to the Faculty of Humanities and Social Sciences, the sociology department was created in 1960, four years after Tunisia's independence from French colonialism.
8. I borrow the citation of the article from Hijazi. I could not access the original document. For a discussion of Adil Husayn's controversial work see also Abaza (2006: 27).
9. This question was extensively discussed by the Indian Historian Chakrarbarty in his essay "Provincialising Europe." He suggests: "The phenomenon of "political modernity" [...] is impossible to think of anywhere in the world without invoking certain categories

and concepts, the genealogies of which go deep into the intellectual and even theological traditions of Europe" (Chakrabarty, 2009: Introduction).

10. For an introduction into Laroui's comprehensive œuvre see particularly the work of Nils Riecken. Riecken brought Laroui and Chakrarbarty in dialogue with each other. To discuss Laroui's and Chakrarbarty's constant dealings with the *Universal* versus the *Particular*, Riecken suggests the term "situated Universalism" (Riecken, 2016).
11. The term "statolatry" was not coined but used by Antonio Gramsci to describe a period in "backward countries" without a strong civil society where it can be necessary to heavily rely on the state (cf. Simon, 1982: 77–78).
12. Gramscian thought in the Arab region has recently gained broader scholarly attention. On the occasion of the 80th anniversary of Gramsci's death in 2017, scholars organized a conference in Bari (Italy) under the title "Gramsci in the Arab world." See particularly the work of Alessandra Marchi, Patrizia Manduchi (Manduchi et al., 2017). Manduchi (2020: 232) speaks of a "Gramscian moment" in the Arab region after 1990. Furthermore, two journals, *Middle East Critique* and *The Journal of Northern African Studies* have published special issues on "Gramsci in the Arab World" and "Gramsci and the Uprisings in North Africa." An excellent introduction and overview comes from Gennaro Gervasio and Patrizia Manduchi (2021). For the influence of Gramsci particularly in the Arab East, see Michaelle Browers (2021: 25–40). On the civil society debate in the Arab region, see also Browers (2006).
13. According to Labib, new about this debate was its approach. The figure of the intellectual was not seen as a producer of discourse alone, but rather as a social category (Brondino & Labib, 1994: 31).

References

Abaza, M. (2006). *Debates on Islam and Knowledge in Malaysia and Egypt: Shifting Worlds*. Routledge.

Aboul-Ela, H. (2018). The Specificities of Arab Thought in Morocco since the Liberal Age. In J. Hanssen & M. Weiss (Eds.), *Arabic Thought against the*

Authoritarian Age towards an Intellectual History of the Present (pp. 143–162). Cambridge University Press.

ʿAmmar Belhassan (1983). *Intilijansiyya am Muthqqafun fi Al-Jazaʾir [Intelligentsia or Intelectuais in Algeria]*. Markaz al-Buhuth wa-l-Iʿlam al-Wathaʾiqa.

Bardawil, F. A. (2018). Sidelining Ideology: Arab Theory in the Metropole, circa 1977. In J. Hanssen & M. Weiss (Eds.), *Arabic Thought against the Authoritarian Age: Towards an Intellectual History of the Present* (1st ed., 139–232). Cambridge University Press. https://doi.org/10.1017/9781108147781

Ben Jelloun, T. (1974). Décolonisation de la sociologie au Maghreb. *Le Monde diplomatique, 245*, 18.

Ben Salem, L. (2009). Propos sur la sociologie en Tunisie: Entretien avec Sylvie Mazzella. *Genèses, 75*(2), 125–142. https://doi.org/10.3917/gen.075.0125

Bouhdiba, A. (1970). La Sociologie Du Développement Africain. *Current Sociology, 18*(2), 5–21. https://doi.org/10.1177/001139217001800201

Brondino, M., & Labib, T. (Eds.). (1994). *Gramsci dans le monde arabe*. Alif-les Éd. de la Méditerranée.

Browers, M. (2006). *Democracy and Civil Society in Arab Political Thought: Transcultural Possibilities* (1st ed.) (Modern Intellectual and Political History of the Middle East). Syracuse University Press.

Browers, M. (2021). Beginnings, Continuities and Revivals: An Inventory of the New Arab Left and an Ongoing Arab Left Tradition. *Middle East Critique, 30*(1), 25–40. https://doi.org/10.1080/19436149.2021.1875174

Chakrabarty, D. (2009). *Provincializing Europe: Postcolonial Thought and Historical Difference–New Edition*, new edition with a new preface by the author. Princeton University Press.

Dakhli, L. (2021). The Fair Value of Bread: Tunisia, 28 December 1983–6 January 1984. *International Review of Social History, 66*(S29), 41–68. https://doi.org/10.1017/S0020859021000110

El-Shakry, O. (2015). History Without Documents: The Vexed Archives of Decolonization in the Middle East. *American Historical Review, 120*(3), 920–934.

El-Shakry, O. (2021). Rethinking Arab Intellectual History: Epistemology, Historicism, Secularism. *Modern Intellectual History, 18*(2), 547–572. https://doi.org/10.1017/S1479244319000337

El-Kenz, A. (1994). Gramsci et les Arabes: Une rencontre tardive? In M. Brondino & T. Labib (Eds.), *Gramsci dans le monde arabe*. Alif-les Éd. de la Méditerranée.

El-Kenz, A. (1997, May 16–18). Réflexions autour d'une expérience collective. In A. Zghal & A. I. Ouederni (Eds.), *Social Knowledge: Heritage, Challenges, Perspectives. Questions from Arab Societies*, Proceedings of the ISA Arab Regional Conference (pp. 31–46).

El-Kenz, A. (2002). Al-Mas'ala al-Nazariyya wa-l-Siyasiyya li-ᶜIlm al-Ijtimaᶜi al-ᶜArabi [The Theoretical and Political Issue of Arab Sociology]. In Hijazi et al., *,Nahwa ᶜIlm Ijtimaᶜ ᶜArabi: ᶜIlm al-Ijtimaᶜ wa-l-Mushkilat al-ᶜArabiyya al-Rahina*, (pp. 99–106). Markaz Dirasat al-Wahda al-ᶜArabiyya.

El-Kenz, A., & Beaud, S. (1998). *Regards Sur La Sociologie En Algérie et Dans Le Monde Arabe: Entrien Avec Ali El-Kenz*. Genèses, no. 32

Ferjani, N. (1984). Muthaqqaf al-Amir am Muthaqqaf al-Jamahir? [An Intellectual of the Prince or an Intellectual of the Masses?[. *Al-Mustaqbal Al-ᶜArabi, 68*(October), 120–127.

Ferjani et al. (1985). al-Muthaqqaf wa-l-Sulta Fi al-Watan al-'Arabi [The Intellectual and Power in the Arab Homeland]. *Al-Mustaqbal al-'Arabi, 74*(April), 127–145.

Gervasio, G., & Manduchi, P. (2021). Introduction: Reading the Revolutionary Process in North Africa with Gramsci. *The Journal of North African Studies, 26*(6), 1051–1056. https://doi.org/10.1080/13629387.2020.1801264

Ibrahim, S. E. (1984). Tajisir al-Fajuda beina al-Mufakkir wa Sanᶜay al-Qararat fi al-Watan al-ᶜArabi [Bridging the Gap between Thinkers and Decision-makers in the Arab World]. *al-Mustaqbal al-'Arabi*, 64(June), 4–30.

Jaghlul, A. (1984). *Al-Intilijansiyya fi al-Maghrib al-ᶜArabi* [The Intelligentsia in the Arab Maghreb]. Dar al-Hadatha.

Jebari, I. (2018). Rethinking the Maghreb and the Post-Colonial Intellectual in Khatibi's *Les Temps Modernes* Issue in 1977. *The Journal of North African Studies, 23*(1–2), 53–70. https://doi.org/10.1080/13629387.2018.1400239

Jebari, I. (2022). Illegitimate Children: The Tunisian New Left and the Student Question, 1963–1975. *International Journal of Middle East Studies, 54*(1), 100–123. https://doi.org/10.1017/S0020743821001057

Kallander, A. A. (2021). *Tunisia's Modern Woman: Nation-Building and State Feminism in the Global 1960s* (1st ed.). Cambridge University Press. https://doi.org/10.1017/9781108961264

Kassab, E. S. (2010). *Contemporary Arab Thought: Cultural Critique in Comparative Perspective*. Columbia University Press.

Khatibi, A. (1985). The Decolonization of Arab Sociology. In H. Barakat (Ed.), *Contemporary North Africa: Issues of Development and Integration* (pp. 9–20). Croom Helm.

Krichen, A. (1987). La Fracture de l'Intelligentsia: Problèmes de la Langue et de la Culture Nationales. In M. Camau (Ed.), *Tunisie au présent: Une modernité au-dessus de tout soupçon?* (pp. 297–341). Institut de recherches et d'études sur les mondes arabes et musulmans. https://doi.org/10.4000/books.iremam.2539

Krichen, A. (1994). Formation d'intelligentsia, formation de la culture, édification de l'Etat, construction de la nation en Tunisie. In M. Brondino & T.

Labib (Eds.), *Gramsci dans le monde arabe* (pp. 61–68). Alif-les Éd. de la Méditerranée.
Labib, T. (1981). Dars Ghramshi [Gramsci Lesson]. *Al-Karmel, 2*, 115–121.
Labib, T. (1985). Tasawwulat hawla al-Muthaqqaf wa-l-Sulta [Questions around the Intellectual and Power]. In *Al-Muthaqqaf al-ᶜArabi Dawruhu waᶜAlaqatuhu bi-l-Sulta wa-l-Mujtamaᶜ* (pp. 29–36). Al-Majlis al-Qawmi li-l-Thaqafa al-ᶜArabiyya.
Labib, T., & al-Jamiyya al-ᶜArabiyya li-ᶜIlm al-Ijtimaᶜ. (1989). *Al-Intilijansiyya al-Arabiyya* [The Arab Intelligentsia]. Al-Dar al-ᶜArabiyya li-l-Kitab.
Laroui, A. (1967). *L'Ideologie Arabe Contemporaine*. Maspero.
Laroui, A. (1976). *The Crisis of the Arab Intellectual: Traditionalism or Historicism?* [Translated from French by Diarmid Cammell]. University of California Press.
Manduchi, P. (2020). Gramsci in the Arab World. In R. M. Dainotto & F. Jameson (Eds.), *Gramsci in the World* (pp. 224–239). Duke University Press.
Manduchi, P., et al. (2017). *Studi gramsciani nel mondo: Gramsci nel mondo arabo*. Società editrice Il mulino.
Melliti, I. (2014). Sociologie et francophonie en Tunisie. *Sociologies pratiques, HS 1*(Supplément), 167–170. https://doi.org/10.3917/sopr.hs01.0167
Melliti, I., & Mahfoudh-Draoui, D. (2014). Les sciences sociales en Tunisie: histoire et enjeux actuels. *Sociologies pratiques, HS 1*(Supplément), 271–280. https://doi.org/10.3917/sopr.hs01.0271
Michalak, L. (2017). Abdelkader Zghal. A guide to Tunisian society. In M. Kerrou (Ed.), *Abdelkader Zghal: l'homme des questions: hommage à Abdelkader Zghal, 5 avril 1931–22 Fevrier 2015* (pp. 118–128). CERES Éditions.
Mohamed, K. (1991). Etre Sociologue Dans Le Monde Arabe Ou Le Savant Epouse La Politique. *Peuples Mediterraneens* (pp. 54–55, 247–268).
Mohamed, K., & Abdelkader, Z. (Eds.). (2017). Abdelkader Zghal: l'homme des questions: hommage à Abdelkader Zghal, 5 avril 1931–22 Fevrier 2015. Tunis: Ceres Éditions
Muhammad ᶜIzzat Hijazi. (2002). Al-Azma al-Rahina li-ᶜIlm al-Ijtimaᶜ fi al-Watan al-'Arabi [The Current Crisis of the Social Sciences in the Arab Homeland]. In Hijazi et al. (Eds.), *Nahwa ᶜIlm Ijtimaᶜ ᶜArabi: ᶜIlm al-Ijtimaᶜ wa-l-Mushkilat al-ᶜArabiyya al-Rahina* (pp. 13–44). Markaz Dirasat al-Wahda al-ᶜArabiyya.
Ounaina, H. (2021). *Ecrire L'Histoire Sociale de La Sociologie En Tunisie*. Med Ali Editions.
Riecken, N. (2016). Relational Difference and the Grounds of Comparison: Abdallah Laroui's Critique of Centrism. *ReOrient*, *2*, 1.
Simon, R. (1982). *Gramsci's Political Thought: An Introduction* (1st ed.). Lawrence and Wishart.

Zemmin, F. (2022). (Post-)Kolonialismus, Autoritarismus und Authentizität: Soziologie in arabischen Gesellschaften. In Heike Delitz, Julian Müller, and Robert Seyfert (Eds.). *Handbuch Theorien der Soziologie*, 1–27. Springer.

Zghal, A. (1969). Modernisation de l'agriculture et Populations Semi-Nomades. *Revue Tiers Monde, 10*(38), 444–445.

Zghal, A. (1981). Peasants and National Integration in the Maghreb: Why Does Agrarian Reform Not Mobilize the Peasants of Maghreb? In C. Agüero (Ed.). *Peasantry and National Integration* (1st ed., 215–236). El Colegio de México. https://doi.org/10.2307/j.ctv233p1r

Zghal, A. (1989). Le Concept de Société Civile et La Transition Vers Le Multipartisme. *Annuaire De L'afrique Du Nord, 28*, 207–228.

Zghal, A., & Karoui, H. (1973). Decolonization and Social Science Research: The Case of Tunisia. *Review of Middle East Studies, 7*(3), 11–27. https://doi.org/10.1017/S2151348100058687

CHAPTER 4

Decentering First World War History: Arabic Perspectives on a Global Event

Ahmed Abou El Zalaf

4.1 Introduction: History Writing in Arabic

As a monumental event of deep consequences for the entire globe, the Great War[1] reshaped the modern world in penetrating and lasting ways. Its repercussions did not end at the confines of great empires but pervaded the smallest village and made its implications felt on almost every individual in one way or another. Consequently, a large body of research pertaining to the war and its outcomes has been produced. In large part, however, this research has been dominated by Euro-centric/Western-centric frames that take Europe as the main point of departure (Fromkin, 2009; Koller, 2014; Liebau et al., 2010: 1, 20; McMeekin, 2011; Rogan, 2015: xvi; Ulrichsen, 2014: 2).[2] Furthermore, even accounts that specifically address non-European/Western areas and aspects of the war are written in European languages and from a Western perspective, thus primarily reaching audiences in Europe and America.

A. A. E. Zalaf (✉)
Copenhagen, Denmark
e-mail: Zalaf_5@hotmail.com

D. Jung and F. Zemmin (eds.), *Postcolonialism and Social Theory in Arabic*, The Modern Muslim World,
https://doi.org/10.1007/978-3-031-63649-3_4

The emphasis of these studies is time and again put on European and Western personalities and power structures, thus leaving out actors of the Global South. This also characterizes those studies dealing with the war's impact on the Middle East. David Fromkin's excellent book, first published in 1989, is a case in point. Describing the focus of his book, Fromkin underlines:

> As you will see when you read the book, Middle Eastern personalities, circumstances, and political cultures do not figure a great deal in the narrative that follows, except when I suggest the outlines and dimensions of what European politicians were ignoring when they made their decisions. (Fromkin, 2009: 9)

In turn, literature written in non-Western languages hardly makes it into Western academic communities. As a result, a dichotomy of sorts has occurred in which most studies in "non-Western" languages remain isolated from the dominant field of research as well as from conceptual debates in social theory.

This situation, however, has been rectified to a certain extent in recent years. The shift in historical interpretation by scholars of global history, leading away from parochialism toward "connected history," has given rise to a field of study devoted to examining and presenting historical events in a global framework (Bayly, 2004, 2018; Werner & Zimmermann, 2006). Understood broadly, global history is an attempt to challenge the widespread tendency to study history as events exclusively formed within isolated national or regional confines. Instead, it argues that history takes place across national and regional borders, and we must therefore study it in light of such historical entanglements. The study of history must transcend national "containers."

In order to overcome this "fragmentation," global historians employ a method that focuses on "mobility and exchange, with processes that transcend borders and boundaries" (Conrad, 2016: 2, 5). The "methodological nationalism," as termed by Sebastian Conrad, that has dominated the historical enterprise so far, obscured the role of entanglements across borders and made national history the most dominant game in town (Conrad, 2016: 3). This resulted in fragmented histories and unbalanced discourses within the historical framework, generally with Europe's history as the dominant paradigm (Gran, 1996: 13). Consequently,

"Eurocentrism influences nearly all established historical writing, especially that in world history" (Gran, 1996: 2). Even more important, when it comes to social theory, European experiences and European concepts were transformed into universal concepts and imposed everywhere and on "everybody else's past," thus rendering "all other societies colonies of Europe." Europe was, according to this critique of the historical enterprise, placed in the foreground of global history and came to be considered as the driving force of world history (Conrad, 2016: 4).

For Sebastian Conrad, this entrenched kind of Eurocentrism was one of the "birth defects" inherent to the modern humanities and global history attempts to do away with it (Conrad, 2016: 3). Thus, the "old continent" became the locomotive of world history, reducing the rest of the world to being more or less passive passengers in Europe's tracks (see Gran, 1996: 336).

Against the background of this critique, a number of studies have meanwhile been published that deal more systematically with the implications of the First World War beyond Europe/the West. These studies made a shift in focus in order to better grasp the "long-term consequences" of the War on larger parts of the world (Bayly, 2018: 21).[3] Nevertheless, while "peripheral" areas and groups have been introduced to the domain of World War I studies, they are mostly analyzed with respect to their "'contribution' to metropolitan 'war efforts', i.e. from an unabashedly Eurocentric angle" (Liebau et al., 2010: 1). We still observe historiographic production *from* the "periphery" being starkly overlooked, resulting in "segregated history writing" in which Western historians base their studies of the Middle East first and foremost on Western sources, seconded sometimes by a few references to sources in Arabic. To state it boldly, most research written in Arabic remains uncharted territory for the wider academic public.

This chapter, therefore, is an attempt to shed some light on such studies in Arabic. Inspired by the work of global history proponents, it aims to get beyond Eurocentrism in contemporary history writing on the First World War. The chapter takes up their call for an inclusive and polycentric perception of history as overlapping and crisscrossing webs of events, often presented by diverging and competing narratives. It is the multiplicity of these narratives and voices that we should take into consideration in our efforts to reach a global presentation of history (Conrad, 2016: 2). The awareness of the existence of other pasts and the value of including those other pasts in our historical perception should guide our research. I therefore look at ways in which Arab historians studied the First World War. In which kind of framework do they present this global event to their readers? What are the narratives and arguments they employ when studying the Great War?

Answering these questions will help us in moving toward a better comprehension of how non-Western studies have viewed and rendered the Great War as a global event. For this purpose, I will examine a number of studies in Arabic dealing with the war in a non-Western academic context. Rather than understanding it as exclusively destructive and hence entirely harmful, some of these studies ascribed to the war's originative effects that brought forth new ideas and gave rise to ingenious reactions and developments. By being pulled into it, facing its tremendous and deadly effects but also interacting with modern European concepts and ideas, the Arab communities developed embryonic but clear-cut national identities, leading subsequently to nationalist, anti-colonial movements. These are the arguments put forward by, among others, Noureddine Teniou (2016) and Halima Moulai (2019). In this way, the chapter is a study of the historiographical depictions of this war as provided by so far un-applauded historians rather than a study of the First World War in Arab regions.

4.2 The First World War in the Middle East

In her book on the Middle East in the First World War, Leila T. Fawaz argued that everyone in the region remembers the Great War far more than World War II (Fawaz, 2014: 5). The reason for this preponderance of the Great War in the collective memory of the Middle East can be found in its long-term consequences on the region's geopolitical landscape and on the lives and destinies of millions of Middle Easterners (Murphy, 2022: 84). Within a few years, millions of people went from being subjects of the Ottoman Empire and its sultan-caliph to becoming dwellers in camouflaged colonies dubbed "mandates" in the Fertile Crescent.[4] From the remnants of the defeated and dismembered Ottoman Empire, new states were carved out by the victorious European powers and a new reality was constructed.

Whereas Europe suffered the lion's share of destruction and endured the largest numbers of casualties, urban and rural dwellers of the Arab world[5] were not spared similar torments. As a case in point, men in large numbers were recruited from across the Ottoman Empire and from the colonies in North Africa to fight on both sides of the conflict. By way of illustration, more than 170,000 Algerian men were enlisted in the French army, with about 120,000–125,000 facing frontline action. Of those young Algerian men, around 26,000–28,000 were killed or went missing while 72,000 were injured. Concurrently, nearly 120,000 Moroccan and Tunisian men were recruited to the French army, taking part on both the Ottoman and Western fronts (al-Yazidi, 2016: 239 Rogan, 2015: 65; Shamsi, 2019; Teniou, 2016: 310, 320; Vince, 2020: 21). Furthermore, and adding to the torments of the locals, from 1916–1918 a war-related famine claimed the lives of between 300,000 and 500,000 civilians in Syria and Lebanon (Fawaz, 2014: 100; Rogan, 2015: 291) At around the same time, Mesopotamia and Egypt were suffering from food scarcities, making the war and its impact an anguishing reality for urban and rural dwellers alike (McMeekin, 2016: 143–144; Rogan, 2015: xviii, 393). Finally, and as a more lasting and monumental outcome, historic cities and former caliphal seats such as Damascus and Baghdad were seized by Allied forces in the wake of the war, heralding an era of colonization and direct European control in the hinterland of the Arab world. The "World of yesterday," to borrow Stefan Zweig's phrase, was all at once changed and replaced by a new and troubling reality (Zweig, 2011). Once the dust settled, it became painfully obvious that the region had changed in lasting ways (Goldschmidt & Al-Marashi, 2019: 181). In the words of David Fromkin, "Ottoman entry into the war marked the first step on the road to a remaking of the Middle East: to the creation, indeed, of the modern Middle East" (Fromkin, 2009: 76).

In what follows, I will proceed with a short review of this historiography in Arabic as it has developed in recent years. Offering a succinct account of the circulation of these studies and their authors' backgrounds and trajectories. Then a section on the topics and themes of these studies follows. With these two sections, I seek to offer a general outline of this body of research in Arabic in order to illuminate how this corpus has developed during the recent years. This general discussion, then, will be continued by zooming in on two case studies, presenting work from Algeria and Tunisia respectively.

4.3 Arab Historiography: The Search for a Non-Western Understanding of the War

In view of the historic consequences of the war, it comes as no surprise that a growing number of historians have turned their attention to studying the history of the Great War in the region. This growing interest is part of a global trend that has seen an increasing production of research on World War I by historians in general.[6] Shedding light on the quotidian experiences in war zones, areas of recruitment, prisoner-of-war camps, and societies that were affected by the war, these approaches contribute to a deeper understanding of the dynamics during World War I. They center their attention on mass populations, the average soldier, and non-combatants, thus transforming what had hitherto been peripheral into the center of attention (see, for example, Hart, 2015; Olusoga, 2019). I argue that the growing body of research in Arabic is part and parcel of this global growth in World War I studies. Arab historians, like their Indian, Philippine, and Danish counterparts, have come to grasp the importance of understanding the history of World War I as a vehicle to reach a broader and more comprehensive perception of their national histories. In this section, I will provide some general data on this body of research in Arabic.

Coming from a variety of national, generational, and disciplinary backgrounds, Arab historians publish in Arabic-language journals such as the *Dawriyat Kan al-Tārīkhiyya* (Historical Kan Periodical) and *Majallat Dirāsāt - al-ᶜUlūm al-Insāniyya wal-Ijtimāᶜiyya* (Dirasat: Human and Social Sciences), reaching a variety of readers. By way of illustration, while Halima Moulai's, 2019 article has been downloaded 1656 times,[7] Ahmad Fawzi Shamsi's article from the same year was downloaded 604 times, pointing to an expected variation in the dissemination of those studies.[8] Another indication of this reception is the data we can find on books published in recent years. Data on books are more complex to precisely establish, as most books are sold in bookshops, and data on distribution and the like are not always available. However, some books are available online as pdf-files, making it possible to monitor the extent of their circulation. Take, for example, Latifa Mohamad Salem's, 2009 book, which deals with Egypt's history during the First World War. Salem's book has been downloaded 5953 times since then (Salem, 2009, 2016).[9] These statistics, if varying and irregular, signify a significant reception among an Arabic reading audience.

Consequently, by bringing the First World War to the center of attention and treating it as a decisive event meriting further examination, Arab historians are recovering a past that until recently had been ascribed to minor importance. Hence, Arab historians are taking part in—and contributing to—the reconceptualization and reexamination of the Great War that has been unfolding since at least the centenary of the war. As maintained by Abdel Latif al-Hafar in his 2016 article on the Moroccan economy during the First World War: "the current phase requires [...] a reexamination of contemporary history based on substantivity, critical reading and analysis, to reach a deeper and better understanding [of the past]." This change in the way we consider the past is, according to al-Hafar, crucial today, as the heat of events has cooled, rendering it possible to yield new insights about the war. What al-Hafar and other Arab historians are calling for is an adjustment of the focus of World War I studies which takes social and economic aspects into consideration alongside the political and military dimensions. In this way, so the argument, we can reach an understanding of how the mass populations were affected by the war (al-Hafar, 2016: 35; see also Abdel Masih, 2016: 66). Such objectives as proposed by the Arab historians to a great extent echo what the above-discussed scholars of global history are advocating.

Another trait characterizing this budding field of research is the heterogeneity of its contributors in terms of national and generational backgrounds. Even more important are their educational levels and occupational backgrounds. Whereas some studies are produced by experienced historians, some of them professors in history who have had long schooling in research and publishing academic studies, others are penned by early-career historians or even students who lack the same level of training and proficiency. This renders this body of research highly heterogenous in terms of quality and impact. A case in point is Yossef Ragab, a graduate with a master of arts degree in modern and contemporary history from the College of Arts and Humanities at Tishreen University in Latakia, Syria. In 2020, the young Ragab published a paper dealling with the First World War and its repercussions on Egypt. Examining how Egypt became a puzzle piece in the struggle between Great Britain and the Ottoman Empire, Ragab seeks to present a narrative on how the Egyptian population and its national aspirations were affected by the war (Ragab, 2020: 231–232; see also Shamsi, 2019[10]). Mohamed Afifi, to take a different example, published a paper in 2016 addressing the image of Europe among Egypt's educated intelligentsia during the

First World War (Afifi, 2016). Afifi, unlike the young Ragab, is a history professor at Cairo University and the head of its history department. Thus, whereas younger historians are contributing to this growing body of historical research as the case of Ragab and Shamsi clearly illustrates, they are joining the company of established and recognized historians such as Afifi and Teniou (2016). This reinforces the notion that a growing segment of Arab historians, up-and-coming and established alike, have joined the global proliferation of World War I studies since the centenary of the War.

Geographically, I found a similar diversity in the authors' backgrounds. Moroccan, Egyptian, Syrian, Algerian, Iraqi, and Tunisian historians, just to mention a few, have contributed to this area of research. However, an examination of published material shows that some countries are substantially more represented than others. This preponderance of some nationalities vis-à-vis others correlates with those nations' histories and their degree of involvement in the First World War, as well as with differing opportunities for teaching, publishing, and research. North African historians figure prominently, and might even be the largest geographic group among Arab historians, even more so than scholars from countries with an established and seasoned historiographic tradition, such as Egypt. Certainly, this preponderance stems from the fact that North African societies were profoundly impacted by the war by dint of forced conscription to the French army and the migration of workers from the colonies to metropolitan France to work in mines, factories, and ports, inter alia.[11] Morocco, Algeria, and Tunisia, all three of which were French colonies at the time of the War, were thus drawn into it in various ways, and this has shaped the consciousness of the war and its legacy in those countries. This explains the prevalence of studies emerging from North Africa when compared to all other Arabic-speaking countries.

Furthermore, in most cases explored for the purpose of this chapter, historians opted for a study of the history of their own country and in the second place the subregion in which their country lies. Consequently, whereas we can make mention of "Arab historians" studying the First World War, it is obvious that within this general classification, several subcategories subsist and shape this body of research.

4.3.1 *Historiography in Arabic: Topics, Questions, and Themes*

In the works of North African historians, the forced conscription of young Maghrebi men to the frontlines appears to be one of the most scrutinized issues. This is conceived as an occurrence leading not only to entanglements across borders and the emergence of new ideas and social dynamics but also to death and suffering. As a case in point, the Algerian historian Halima Moulai published a study in 2019 dealing with forced conscription during the war. In her article, Moulai zooms in on Tlemcen in northwestern Algeria, examining how the arrival of this political decree in Tlemcen from metropolitan France sparked off different reactions and led to new dynamics and conscious responses by the local population. Forced recruitment, especially in the death-bringing context of the Great War, stirred things up in modest Tlemcen and gave rise to popular protests, expressions of discontent, and the abscondence of young men from the town to avoid conscription into the French army. At the same time, a vehement Islamic discourse rejecting conscription appeared, depicting it as Islamically illegal to join the French army and permitting the locals to seek refuge outside Algeria to avoid conscription. Overall focusing on mandatory conscription and the enrollment of young colonial men into the French war effort, historians, such as Moulai and Teniou (2016), seek to clarify how the Great War affected the local dynamics in a country such as Algeria.[12]

By so doing, those historians are in the process of bringing this "long obscured facet" of the war into the broader field of research. Such studies might help rectify the narrowness in terms of both race and class that has characterized many studies so far. Algerian men participated in and contributed to the war, just as British and French soldiers did, and this fact is being elucidated now. As eloquently stated by David Olusoga:

> What has been lost sight of is not the true geographic scope of the war but its fundamental demographics. More words have been written over the past century about a few dozen middle-class officers [...] than about the 4 million non white, non European soldiers who fought for Britain, France and their allies, let alone the millions of civilians who laboured at war work or who suffered hardships and loss when the war swept through their communities. (Olusoga, 2019: 40)

How the Great War and its reverberations affected and ultimately transformed the former Arabic-speaking provinces of the Ottoman Empire has been another major object of study among Arab historians (Abdel Masih, 2016; al-Qassab, 2016; Al-Rubei, 2016; Haddad, 2018; Hasan, 2018; Shamsi, 2019). Mainly authored by historians from the Fertile Crescent, i.e. Syria, Lebanon, Palestine and Iraq, these studies tend to combine a political history perspective with social history approaches to explore and explain how the war reshaped the geopolitical landscape of the region and affected its social and economic conditions. A concrete example is the Great Famine of 1915–1918, which, with its fatal outcome, struck greater Syria and claimed the lives of hundreds of thousands. Several interesting studies pertaining to this traumatic episode have been published, discussing its reasons, socioeconomic consequences, and implications in the region (Abdel Masih, 2016; Sheib, 2011).

The political agreements and secret correspondences that proliferated during the First World War have been another major subject area. How these arrangements shaped the geopolitical scene and altered the political landscape of the Middle East has occupied a number of excellent scholars and authors from the region. Conceiving the war as a watershed event that reshaped their societies and put their nations on an untrodden path, different scholars from different backgrounds focused on the immediate and longstanding political, social, and economic consequences of the war on the region.[13]

In this section, I have tried to map this growing body of research in Arabic on a general level. Outlining its main traits, the characteristics of its contributors, and the subjects it treats, I intended to signify that Arab historians are embarking on the same road as historians from other parts of the world. I will now discuss two specific contributions by Arab historians. Doing so, I intend to flesh out my argument by providing insights into how these case studies treated the First World War and its implications. It is the uncelebrated soldier, the ordinary woman and man, and the colonial regions and the experiences of the war within these regions that are the focus of those two Arab historians, as will become visible from the following discussion.

4.4 The First World War through the Lens of Arab Historiography: Two Case Studies

Historians from several Arab countries gathered at a conference in Beirut in 2015, commemorating and debating the centenary of the First World War. Studying various aspects pertaining to the war's causes, implications, and outcomes, they contributed to a two-volume anthology with 39 chapters. The publication of *Miʾat ʿĀm ʿalā al-Ḥarb al-ʿĀlamiya al-Ūla: Muqārabāt ʿArabiya* (World War I: A Century Later—Arab Approaches) (Kawtharani, 2016a, 2016b) was part of the above-sketched trend that saw similar projects of commemoration taking place around the world (Ulrichsen, 2014: 3). The contributors to this voluminous publication in Arabic took their own national histories as a steppingstone toward understanding the global ramifications of the First World War. I will discuss Noureddine Teniou's and Bashir al-Yazidi's studies dealing specifically with the impact of the War on Algeria and Tunisia.[14]

4.4.1 *Noureddine Teniou and the Algerian Contribution to the First World War*

Born in 1955, the first year of the Algerian War of Independence (1954–1962), Noureddine Teniou spent his formative years in the context of anti-colonial struggle and early postcolonial state formation. Teniou graduated with a bachelor's degree from law school before changing direction to pursue a master's degree in modern and contemporary history. This he achieved when he graduated in 1998 at the height of Algeria's ravaging civil war, also known as the "Dark Decade" (1991–2002). In 2010, he was awarded a PhD degree in modern and contemporary history, thus completing his education as a historian of modern Algerian history.

In his career, we observe the journey of a man shaped by the social history of Algeria and by the desire not only to grasp this history but also to shape the way in which it is comprehended, written, and taught. This desire and inquisitiveness led him, inter alia, to become chairman of a panel tasked with the formation of a department for Algerian History in 2013 and to head several study programs on, among others, "the French presence in Algeria before the occupation" and "modern reform movements in the Maghreb." Today, Noureddine Teniou serves as a professor at Emir Abd El Kader University in Constantine, Algeria, where he teaches Algerian history.[15] A diligent and industrious historian with a specific focus on the modern history of Algeria, reform movements in Algeria and North Africa, historiography, memory studies, and nation-building, Teniou has penned a number of important studies in Arabic. Among these are: "*Al-Dhākira wal-Shahāda fī Kitābat Tārīkh al-Thawra al-Jazā'iriya (1954–1962): al-Thawra al-Taḥrīriyya fī al-Tārīkh al-Rāhin*" (Memory and Testimony in Writing the History of the Algerian Revolution 1954–1962: The Liberation Struggle in History of the Present Moment) (2015a), "*Al-Thawra al-Jazā'iriya fī al-Umam al-Muttaḥida*" (The Algerian Revolution in the United Nations) (2015c), and the monograph "*Ishkāliyyat al-Dawla fī Tārīkh al-Ḥaraka al-Waṭaniyya al-Jazā'iriyya*" (State Problematic in the Algerian National Movement History) (2015b).[16] It is important to note that Teniou's publications are largely written in Arabic, indicating that he has made a deliberate choice to address an Arab readership rather than writing in French. This is not always the case with North African authors, among whom francophone literature is commonplace.[17] In the following, I will focus on how Teniou treated the Great War. Why, according to Teniou, is the First World War a key chapter in modern Algerian and North African history, and what hypotheses does he advance?

Noureddine Teniou puts his main argument in a nutshell when he contends that, "if the Algerian participation in the war was opaque and without a title or a definition at first [...] it did enable them [the Algerians], however, to extract positive results in terms of a consciousness of the necessity to liquidate colonialism." It was at the end of the war and because of its implications on Algerian society that a national consciousness emerged, necessitating the liquidation of colonialism in Algeria. The dragging of Algerians into the war and the serious consequences the war had on people and society turned out to be formative in the history of modern Algeria, so his contention goes (Teniou, 2016: 311).

With a particular focus on the mandatory conscription of thousands of young Algerian men into the French army, he analyzes how this conscription affected local society on different levels. From Teniou's perspective, the war, more than anything else, molded Algerian national awareness and gave rise to a political consciousness that became influential following the War (Teniou, 2016: 314). Teniou claims that when the Algerians were dying in their thousands for France "[t]hey did not realize at the time that it [the war] concerned them as much as it concerned France" (Teniou, 2016: 311). But by fighting and falling in this conflict, the Algerians were strongly affected by this war: "When war broke out and when it pulled in the colonies, it came to influence these countries in direct and lasting ways" (Teniou, 2016: 314–315, 325).

Sacrificing themselves for the French empire and participating in the "sacred obligation," the Algerians strongly lamented the unequal treatment with which they were met by the French authorities (Teniou, 2016: 311–313[18]). It was in this process of participation in a global conflict that the national awareness of the Algerian masses developed and was refined. Based on primary sources such as letters from the battlefront and official documents by Young Algerians, Noureddine Teniou argues that the rise of "political awareness of Algerians was concomitant with the conclusion of the Great War, when the Algerian intelligentsia became deeply involved in political work" (Teniou, 2016: 325[19]). The birth of the national Algerian movement took place in the postwar era, also as a result of the growing awareness that conscription had given rise to and by dint of the postwar principles of self-determination. Teniou's study should be seen as a contribution to the growing trend of World War studies that redirect our attention to the unheard masses.

I will now continue with an exposition of the ideas and arguments offered by Bashir al-Yazidi in his chapter in the 2016 anthology on the First World War (Kawtharani, 2016b).

4.4.2 *Bashir al-Yazidi: Tunisian Public Opinion in the Light of the First World War*

Bashir al-Yazidi resembles Noureddine Teniou in discipline, interests, and academic productivity. A professor of contemporary history and a researcher at the advanced institute for research in contemporary Tunisian history at the University of Manouba, al-Yazidi has published extensively on the modern history of Tunisia. Focusing on Tunisia's social and economic history during the colonial era and in its direct aftermath, al-Yazidi has had a lasting effect on the educational and academic field in Tunisia. His written work includes publications on the production and dissemination of historical knowledge among students and the teaching of history at Tunisian secondary schools (Kawtharani, 2016b: 13).[20]

In his article from 2016, Bashir al-Yazidi seeks to understand how the First World War and the dragging of Tunisia into it affected the Tunisian public opinion of the time. Published alongside Teniou's abovementioned study, this article is based on letters sent home by Tunisian conscripts and on military and diplomatic sources from Tunisian and French archives.

By being forced to fight in a war that did not concern them and against people who shared their religious convictions, the Tunisians developed a strong national awareness against the colonial system. It was in view of this participation, according to al-Yazidi, that the Tunisian public opinion took its nationalist and anti-colonial form. Rather than being a period of nationalist impasse due to the lack of political opportunities, the war years offered an incentive for further nationalist awareness (al-Yazidi, 2016: 250–251).

In addition, successful and convincing German and Ottoman propaganda had reached Tunisia, depicting in cruel terms the participation in the war on the French side as a religious sin. This propaganda designated support "of the infidels [entente powers]" as a "sin that brings the anger of God against the participants. Those who die while fighting alongside the enemies of religion will end up in hell (al-Yazidi, 2016: 236)." This led according to al-Yazidi's sources to an antipathy toward the French army and a willingness to desert its ranks to join the Ottomans or at least to avoid fighting Ottoman coreligionists (al-Yazidi, 2016: 235–240).

Many Tunisian soldiers wrote home describing the state of confusion and distress they found themselves in. Dispatched to hotspots on the French front, Tunisian soldiers from the Tirailleurs regiment lamented what they perceived as being subjected to "a slaughter" and bemoaned being made "cannon fodder" by the French army. Al-Yazidi contends that French army commanders intentionally used Tunisian Tirailleurs soldiers as shock troops during the most bloody and dangerous battles. Being put on the front lines and in the advanced trenches, the Tunisian soldiers faced certain death. These tactics adopted by the French army led to the death of 15,000 out of 73,000 Tunisian soldiers participating in the war (see, for example, al-Yazidi, 2016: 242–243).

Against this background, a growing sense of discontent grew among Tunisian soldiers at the fronts. This discontent was mainly rooted in dissatisfaction with conditions in the army and with the high numbers of casualties among the North African troops. Al-Yazidi argues that this discontent was echoed in the public opinion among most Tunisians, who were strongly opposed to French warfare against the Ottoman Empire. The War was interpreted by Tunisian troops as a war waged by "infidels" against the Islamic caliphate and thus "against Islam" (al-Yazidi, 2016: 244–245, 248). In other words, as opposed to the above-discussed Algerian case, where the Algerian elite had endorsed recruitment to the French army in exchange for a better standing of the Algerians, according to al-Yazidi, Tunisians were opposed to conscription to the French army on religious grounds. What made things even worse was the feeling that the French army was utilizing Tunisian conscripts as "cannon fodder."

It was in this atmosphere that the Tunisian national movement developed during the war years. Al-Yazidi argues, therefore, that we should understand anti-French sentiments and the abovementioned antipathy toward conscription as an embodiment of the nationalist movement and ideas. While organized and active nationalist agitation was unattainable during the war due to wartime restrictions, this period enhanced the nationalist awareness among Tunisians and developed their desire to achieve independence (al-Yazidi, 2016: 250–251).

4.5 Conclusions

"[T]o dismiss the Middle Eastern theatre as peripheral to the conflict as a whole would do a gross disservice to the near-total impact of the war on its societies" (Ulrichsen, 2014: 2–3). Kristian Coates Ulrichsen's book sheds light on the First World War's destructive ramifications on the region. Yet, despite these monumental implications, which made the war a disaster for peoples of the dying Ottoman Empire, we still do not have systematic studies about the ways in which Arab historians have dealt with this "catastrophe." In recent decades, a growing number of historians have turned their attention to the First World War, its causes, and its implications in what had hitherto been considered as "peripheral" regions. Inspired by the global history paradigm, those historians studied different aspects of the Great War and its consequences (Teniou, 2016: 309–310). As this chapter showed, Arab historians have contributed to this burgeoning field of research, and we should integrate their accounts when writing global history.

While being tremendously destructive and bloody, the war was also important in generating new ideas and articulating new concepts. According to al-Yazidi, the First World War gave rise to "political, geographic, and social" change in the national movement in Tunisia, leading to its maturation and expansion. This transformation was embodied in the rejection of colonization and endowed previously overlooked segments of society with a more vocal voice (al-Yazidi, 2016: 251). Studying a similar case, but in the Algerian context, Noureddine Teniou argued that the Algerian intelligentsia had uttered support for conscription at the beginning of the war. Seeing in conscription an opportunity for better conditions within the French colonial system, those Algerians strongly recommended this idea, thus pushing for assimilation within the French colonial system. This endorsement of conscription, however, generated a split in Algerian society between the pro-assimilation intelligentsia and the anti-conscription masses, the latter fearing that conscription would pull them away from their families. Yet, when eventually the horrors of war became evident for both the elite and the Algerian masses, a strong opposition against conscription became widespread in Algeria. It was during the war, so the contention of Teniou, that an anti-colonial consensus of sorts developed among Algerians, with anti-war sentiment being at its core (Teniou, 2016: 310–311, 316).

This chapter shows the close entanglement of Arab and European history writing. Historians writing in Arabic take part in similar debates and thematic changes as their European colleagues. In this sense, they are an intrinsic part of historiography as a global discipline. Even more important, they develop their historical narratives employing globally relevant categories and concepts of social theory such as nation, nationalism, resistance, and notions of collective and individual identities. However, the narratives they tell are different from mainstream literature on the First World War. They add new perspectives to this literature and contribute in this way to decentering the hegemonic role of European history in scholarly work on the Great War. If these works in Arabic were more broadly accessible through translation, they would also provide new sources for the conceptional work of social theorists who previously almost entirely relied on empirical data from Europe.

Notes

1. I will apply the terms Great War, The First World War, and World War I interchangeably when referring to this global event.
2. For a more detailed discussion of Eurocentrism in historical frameworks, see: Gran (1996).
3. See also: Barr (2011), Fawaz (2014), Liebau et al. (2010), McMeekin (2016), Rogan (2015), Fawaz (2014), Fantauzzo (2019), Ulrichsen (2014).
4. Prior to the war, Algeria, Egypt, Tunisia, Morocco, and Libya had fallen prey to Western colonization.

5. For the purpose of this paper, I understand the Arab world as stretching from the Atlantic Ocean in the West to the Arabian Sea in the East.
6. Samson (2010), Markovits (2010), Das (2011), Koller (2011), Jones (2011), Fawaz (2014), Rogan (2015), Hanna (2010), Hanson (2007), Omissi (1999), Prunty (2021), Ragab (2020).
7. https://bit.ly/3WSpbFU (accessed January 6, 2023).
8. https://bit.ly/3W0npkI (accessed January 10, 2023).
9. https://bit.ly/3X2ucMl (accessed January 11, 2023).
10. A postgraduate student at the time of this paper's publication.
11. See, for instance: Al-Hafar (2016), Teniou (2016), Bulfardi and al-Bar (2018), Bijawi (2018), al-Yazidi (2016), Walid (2019), Butafi (2022), Halayli (2019), for a Syrian study see, for example, Shamsi (2019), for an Iraqi, see Almehmedawy (2019), for an Egyptian, see Salem (2016).
12. Moulai (2019: 63–64): for similar studies, see: Teniou (2016), Fayid (2018), Bulfardi and al-Bar (2018), Bijawi (2018), al-Yazidi (2016), Walid (2019), Butafi (2022), Halayli (2019), Taouanza and Sbihi (2019), al-Hadik (2016), Halayli (2021).
13. For studies on the Levant, see: Sabbagh (2016), al-Karmi (2016), Mahafza (2016), al-Jamil (2016), on Egypt: Ali Ghazi (2016), Eid (2016), Ragab (2020), for studies on the Gulf: Almehmedawy (2019), al-Zahrani (2020); on Sudan: Abu Shuk (2016); for Libya: Maklouf (2020).
14. As they study two different settings, I do not expect the two authors to present uniform analyses.
15. For a resumé of Noureddine Teniou's professional life, see: https://bit.ly/3MseCVD (accessed October 13, 2022). For a list of Teniou's writings, see https://bit.ly/3D3EdBr (accessed October 13, 2022).
16. These studies are written in Arabic. Translations of titles are taken directly from the original texts.
17. This fact is also evident in the bibliography of Teniou's studies, where most of the literature is francophone, even when written by Maghrebi historians. See, for example, Abdallah (1915), Abdelkader (1959), Faci (1936), Kaddache (1980).
18. See also: https://bit.ly/3Tqysmx (accessed October 5, 2022).
19. See also: https://bit.ly/3Tqysmx (accessed October 5, 2022).
20. See https://bit.ly/3S1O1zX (accessed October 6, 2022).

References

Abdallah, E. H. (Lieutenant). (1915). *L'Islam dans l'armée française: (Guerre de 1914–1915)*. s.n.

Abdel Masih, S. (2016). Al-Majāʿa al-Kubrā wal-Iqtiṣād al-Ṭarfī, min Dirāsāt al-Ḥāla ilā Bināʾ al-Mafhūm [The Great Famine and the Peripheral Economy, from Case Study to Concept-Building]. In W. Kawtharani (Ed.), *Miʾat ʿAm ʿala al-Harb al-ʿAlamiya al-Ula Muqarabat ʿArabiya (al-Mujallad al- Thani): Mujtamaʿat al-Buldan al-ʿArabiya, al-Ahwal wal-Tahawwulat* [World War I: A Century Later—Arab Approaches (Vol. II): Arab Societies: Conditions and Transformations] (pp. 63–115). Arab Center for Research and Policy Studies.

Abdelkader, R. (1959). *L'affaire des officiers algériens*. Seuil.

Abu Shuk, A. I. (2016). Al-Ḥarb al-ʿĀlamiyya al-Ūlā wa-Tadāʿiyātihā fī al-Sūdān: Muqāraba Taḥlīliya [The First World War and its Implications for the Sudan: An Analytical Approach]. In R. Khashana (Ed.), *Al-Ṭarīq ilā Sykes-Picot: Al-Ḥarb al-ʿĀlamiyya al-Ūlā bi-ʿUyūn ʿArabiyya* [The Path to Sykes-Picot: The First World War through Arab Eyes] (pp. 149–190). Al Jazeera Centre for Studies.

Afifi, M. (2016). Ṣūrat Ūrūbā ʿind al-Muthaqqafīn al-Lībirāliyīn al-Maṣriyīn fī Al-Ḥarb al-ʿĀlamiyya al-Ūlā [The Image of Europe among the Educated Egyptian Intelligentsia during the First World War]. In W. Kawtharani (Ed.), *Miʾat ʿAm ʿala al-Harb al-ʿAlamiyya al-Ula Muqarabat Arabiya (al-Mujallad al- Thani): Mujtamaʿat al-Buldan al-ʿArabiya, al-Ahwal wal-Tahawwulat* [World War I: A Century Later—Arab Approaches (Vol. II): Arab Societies: Conditions and Transformations] (pp. 387–400). Arab Center for Research and Policy Studies.

Al-Hadik, Q. (2016). al-Diʿāya al-Almāniyya fī al-Maghrib Khilāl al-Ḥarb al-ʿĀlamiyya al-ʾŪla wa-Raddāt al-Fiʿl al-Maḥalliyya [German Propaganda in Morocco during the First World War and Local Reactions]. In W. Kawtharani (Ed.), *Miʾat ʿAm ʿala al-Harb al-ʿAlamiyya al-Ula Muqarabat Arabiyya (al-Mujallad al- Thani): Mujtamaʿat al-Buldan al-Arabiyya, al-Ahwal wal-Tahawwulat* [World War I: A Century Later—Arab Approaches (Vol. II): Arab Societies: Conditions and Transformations] (pp. 141–174). Arab Center for Research and Policy Studies.

Al-Hafar, A. L. (2016). Al-Iqtiṣād al-Maghribī khilāl al-Ḥarb al-ʿĀlamiyya al-Ūlā, Dirāsa fī al-Irshīf al-Faransī [The Moroccan Economy during the First World War, a Study in the French Archive]. In W. Kawtharani (Ed.), *Miʾat ʿAm ʿala al-Harb al-ʿAlamiyya al-Ula Muqarabat ʿArabiyya (al-Mujallad al- Thani): Mujtamaʿat al-Buldan al-ʿArabiyya, al-Ahwal wal-Tahawwulat* [World War I: A Century Later—Arab Approaches (Vol. II): Arab Societies: Conditions and Transformations] (pp. 33–62). Arab Center for Research and Policy Studies.

Ali Ghazi, A. A. (2016). Maṣr wal-Ḥarb al-ʿĀlamiyya al-ʿŪlā bayn 1914–1918 [Egypt and the First World War from 1914 to1918]. In R. Khashana (Ed.), *Al-Ṭarīq ilā Sykes-Picot: Al-Ḥarb al-ʿĀlamiyya al-Ūlā bi-ʿUyūn ʿArabiyya* [The Path to Sykes-Picot: The First World War through Arab Eyes] (pp. 117–148). Al Jazeera Centre for Studies.

Al-Jamil, S. (2016). Bilād al-Shām khilāl al-Ḥarb al-ʿĀlamiyya al-Ūlā [The Levant during the First World War]. In R. Khashana (Ed.), *Al-Ṭarīq ilā Sykes-Picot: Al-Ḥarb al-ʿĀlamiyya al-Ūlā bi-ʿUyūn ʿArabiyya* [The Path to Sykes-Picot: The First World War through Arab Eyes] (pp. 89–116). Al Jazeera Centre for Studies.

Al-Karmi, G. (2016). Min Muʿāhadat San Remo ilā al-Intidāb [From the San Remo Conference to the Mandate]. In S. Akram (Ed.), *Al-Ḥarb al-ʿĀlamiyya al-Ūlā wa-Athruhā fī Filisṭīn: Irth Miʾat ʿĀm* [The First World War and its Impact on Palestine: A Hundred Years of Legacy] (pp. 99–106). Al Jazeera Centre for Studies.

Almehmedawy, G. M. (2019). Iʿādat Rasim al-Ḥudūd fī Manṭiqat al-Khalīj al-ʿArabī baʿd al-Ḥarb al-ʿĀlamiyya al-ʾŪla (Al-Aḥwāz Namūzajan) [Redrawing Borders in the Arabian Gulf Region after the First World War: Al-Ahwaz as a Model]. *Dirasat: Human and Social Sciences, 46*(2), 297–305.

Al-Qassab, A. W. (2016). Al-Ḥamla al-Brīṭāniyya ʿalā al-ʿIrāq (1914–1918): al-Dawāfiʿ wal-Tadāʿiyāt al-Ijtimāʿiyya wal-Iqtiṣādiyya wal-Siyāsiyya [The British Campaign on Iraq (1914–1918): Objects and the Social, Economic, and Political Consequences]. In W. Kawtharani (Ed.), *Miʾat ʿAm ʿala al-Harb al-ʿAlamiyya al-Ula Muqarabat ʿArabiyya (al-Mujallad al- Thani): Mujtamaʿat al-Buldan al-ʿArabiyya, al-Ahwal wal-Tahawwulat* [World War I: A Century Later—Arab Approaches (Vol. II): Arab Societies: Conditions and Transformations] (pp. 651–664). Arab Center for Research and Policy Studies.

Al-Rubei, I. N. (2016). Miʾat ʿĀm min Shurūkh al-Wijdān al-Jamʿī: Al-ʿIrāq wa-Mīʾawiyat al-Ḥarb al-ʿĀlamiyya al-Ūla [A Hundred Years with Collective Cracks of Conscience: Iraq and the Centenary of the First World War]. In W. Kawtharani (Ed.), *Miʾat ʿĀm ʿalā al-Ḥarb al-ʿĀlamiyya al-Ūla Muqārabāt ʿArabiyya* (al-Mujallad al-Awwal): *Al-Asbāb wal-Siyāqāt wal-Tadāʿiyyāt* [World War I: A Century Later Arab Approaches (Vol. I): Arab Causes, Contexts and Implications] (n.p.). Arab Center for Research and Policy Studies (n.p.).

Al-Yazidi, B. (2016). al-Raʾī al-ʿAmm al-Tūnisī wal-Ḥarb al-ʿĀlamiyya al-Ūlā: Al-Junūd Namūdhajan [Tunisian Public Opinion and the First World War: The Soldiers as a Case]. In W. Kawtharani (Ed.), *Miʾat ʿAm ʿala al-Harb al-ʿAlamiyya al-Ula Muqarabat ʿArabiyya (al-Mujallad al- Thani): Mujtamaʿat al-Buldan al-ʿArabiyya, al-Ahwal wal-Tahawwulat* [World War I: A Century Later—Arab Approaches (Vol. II): Arab Societies: Conditions and Transformations] (pp. 229–251). Arab Center for Research and Policy Studies.

Al-Zahrani, M. S. A. (2020). Mawqif al-Umarāʾ wal-Mashāyikh fī al-Jazīra al-ʿArabiyya Min al-Ḥarb al-ʿĀlamiyya al-Ūlā [The Attitude of Rulers and the Elderly of the Arabian Peninsula toward the First World War]. *Majallat Buḥūth Kuliyyat Al-Ādāb, 31*(122), 3–30.

Barr, J. (2011). *A Line in the Sand: Britain, France and the Struggle That shaped the Middle East*. Simon and Schuster.

Bayly, C. A. (2004). *The Birth of the Modern World 1780–1914: Global Connections and Comparisons*. Blackwell Publishing.

Bayly. C. A. (2018). *Remaking the Modern World 1900–2015*: *Global Connections and Comparisons*. Wiley-Blackwell.

Bijawi, M. S. (2018). *Ishāmāt al-Ahālī al-Jazāʾiriyīn fī al-Ḥarb al-ʿĀlamiya al-ʾŪlā 1914–1918* [The Algerian Population's Contributions during the First World War (1914–1918)]. Al-Maktab al-ʿArabī lil-Maʿārif.

Bulfardi, J., & al-Bar, S. (2018). Al-Mujannadūn al-Jazāʾiriyūn Ḍimn al-Jaysh al-Faransī Athnāʾ al-Ḥarb al-ʿĀlamiyya al-Ūlā (1914-1918) [Algerian Recruits in the French Army during the First World War (1914–1918)]. *ElMaaref Review for Research and Historical Studies, Quarterly International Refereed, 4*(3), 240–270.

Butafi, A. S. (2022). Al-Ṣaḥāfa al-Faransiyya wa-Mushārakat al-Maghāriba fī al-Ḥarb al-ʿĀlamiyya al-Ūlā (1914–1918): Bayn al-Taʿtīm wal-Taḍlīl wal-Taḥkīr [The French Press and the Participation of Moroccans in the First World War (1914–1918): Between Opacity, Deception, and Denigration]. *Historical Kan Periodical, 15*(55), 151–161.

Conrad, S. (2016). *What Is Global History?* Princeton University Press.

Das, S. (2011). Indians at Home, Mesopotamia and France, 1914–1918: Towards an Intimate History. In S. Das (Ed.), *Race, Empire and First World War Writing* (pp. 70–89). Cambridge University Press.

Das, S., Maguire, A., & Steinbach, D. (2022). Colonial Encounters in a Time of Global Conflict: An Introduction. In S. Das, A. Maguire, & D. Steinbach (Eds.), *Colonial Encounters in a Time of Global Conflict, 1914–1918* (pp. 1–34). Routledge.

Eid, A. M. A. (2016). Athar al-Ḥarb al-ʿĀlamiyya al-Ūlā fī Mujtamaʿ Shibh Jazīrat Sīnāʾī [The Impact of the First World War on the Sinai Peninsula]. In W. Kawtharani (Ed.), *Miʾat ʿAm ʿala al-Harb al-ʿAlamiyya al-Ula Muqarabat ʿArabiyya (al-Mujallad al-Thani): Mujtamaʿat al-Buldan al-ʿArabiyya, al-Ahwal wal-Tahawwulat* [World War I: A Century Later—Arab Approaches (Vol. II): Arab Societies: Conditions and Transformations] (pp. 401–424). Arab Center for Research and Policy Studies.

Faci, S. (1936). *L'Algérie sous l'égide de la France contre la féodalité algérienne*. Impr. régionale.

Fantauzzo, J. (2019). *The Other Wars: The Experience and Memory of the First World War in the Middle East and Macedonia*. Cambridge University Press.

Fawaz, L. T. (2014). *Land of Aching Hearts: The Middle East in the Great War*. Harvard University Press.

Fayid, B. (2018). Al-Inᶜikāsāt al-Siyāsiyya li-Hijrat al-ᶜUmmāl al-Jazāᵓirīn naḥwa Faransā khilāl al-Ḥarb al-ᶜĀlamiyya al-Ūlā [The Political Repercussions of Algerian Workers' Migration to France during the First World War]. *Al-Majalla al-Tārīkhiyya al-Jazāᵓiriyya, 2*(2), 189–206.

Fromkin, D. (2009). *A Peace to End all Peace: The Fall of the Ottoman Empire and the Creation of the Modern Middle East*. Henry Holt and Company.

Goldschmidt, A., Jr., & Al-Marashi, I. (2019). *A Concise History of the Middle East* (12th ed.). Routledge.

Gran, P. (1996). *Beyond Eurocentrism: A New View of Modern World History*. Syracuse University Press.

Haddad, M. (2018). Falasṭīn wal-Masᵓala al-Sharqiyya/al-Gharbiyya (Palestine and the Eastern/Western Question). In S. Akram (Ed.), *Al-Ḥarb al-ᶜĀlamiyya al-Ūlā wa-Athruhā fī Falasṭīn: Irth Miᵓat ᶜĀm* [The First World War and Its Impact on Palestine: A Hundred Years of Legacy] (pp. 37–55). Al Jazeera Centre for Studies.

Halayli, H. (2019). Al-Jazāᵓiriyūn al-Farūn min al-Jaysh al-Faransī wa-Ittiṣālātihim bi-Almāniyā wal-Dawla al-ᶜUthmāniyya khilāl al-Ḥarb al-ᶜĀlamiyya al-Ūlā wa-Inṭibāᶜāt al-Mulāzim Bukābawiyya (1915–1917) [The Algerian Fugitives from the French Army and Their Contacts with Germany and the Ottoman Empire during the First World War and the Impressions of Lieutenant Boukabouya]. *Al-Ḥiwār Al-Mutawasaṭī, 10*(1), 67–80.

Halayli, H. (2021). Al-Jazāᵓiriyūn al-Mujannadūn fī al-Jaysh al-Faransī Khilāl al-Ḥarb al-ᶜĀlamiyya al-Ūlā (1914–1918): Aḍwāᵓ Jadīda fī Kitābāt al-Mulāzim Awal Rābiḥ Būkābawiya [The Algerians enrolled in the French Army during World War I (1914–1918): New Light on the Writings of Rabah Boukabouya]. *Majallat al-Dirāsāt al-Tārīkhyiyya al-ᶜaskariyya, 3*(1), 159–178.

Hanna, A. (2010). The First World War According to the Memories of "Commoners" in the Bilād al-Shām. In H. Liebau, K. Bromber, K. Lange, D. Hamzah, & R. Ahuja (Eds.), *The World in World Wars: Experiences, Perceptions and Perspectives from Africa and Asia* (pp. 299–312). BRILL.

Hanson, N. (2007). *The Unknown Soldier. The Story of the Missing of the Great War*. Corgi.

Hart, P. (2015). *Voices from the Front: An Oral History of the Great War*. Profile Books.

Hasan, J. H. (2018). Al-Ḥaraka al-Ṣahyūniyya wa-ᶜAlāqātuhā bi-Aṭrāf al-Nizāᶜ (Almānyā wa-l-Imbrāṭūriyya al-ᶜUthmāniyya wa-l-Ḥulafāᵓ) [The Zionist Movement and its Relations with the Elements of the Conflict (Germany, the Ottoman Empire, and the Allies)]. In S. Akram (Ed.), *Al-Ḥarb al-ᶜĀlamiyya al-Ūlā wa-Atharuhā fī Falasṭīn: Irth Miʾat ʿĀm* [The First World War and its Impact on Palestine; A Hundred Years of Legacy] (pp. 87–96). Al-Jazeera Centre for Studies.

Hureidi, S. A. (2009). *Urūbā min al-Thawra al-Faransiyya ḥattā al-Ḥarb al-ʿĀlamiyya al-Ūlā: 1815–1939* [Europe from the French Revolution until the First World War 1815–1939]. Kafr al-Duwwār: Maktabat Bustān al-Maʿrifa.

Jones, H. (2011). Imperial Captivities: Colonial Prisoners of War in Germany and the Ottoman Empire, 1914–1918. In S. Das (Ed.), *Race, Empire and First World War Writing* (pp. 175–193). Cambridge University Press.

Kaddache, M. (1980). *Historie du Nationalisme Algérien: Question Nationale et Politique Algérienne 1919–1951* (Vol. II, 2nd ed.). Société Nationale d'Èdition et de Diffusion.

Kawtharani, W. (Ed.). (2016a). *Miʾat ʿĀm ʿala al-Ḥarb al-ʿĀlamiyya al-Ūlā Muqārabaāt ʿArabiyya (al-Mujallad al-Awwal): Al-Asbāb wa-l-Siyāqāt wa-l-Tadāʿiyyāt* [World War I: A Century Later—Arab Approaches (Vol. I): Causes, Contexts and Implications]. Arab Center for Research and Policy Studies.

Kawtharani, W. (Ed.). (2016b). *Miʾat ʿĀm ʿala al-Ḥarb al-ʿĀlamiyya al-Ūlā Muqārabāt ʿArabiyya (al-Mujallad al-Thānī): Mujtamaʿāt al-Buldān al-ʿArabiyya, al-Aḥwāl wa-l-Taḥawwulāt* [World War I: A Century Later—Arab Approaches (Vol. II): Arab Societies: Conditions and Transformations]. Arab Center for Research and Policy Studies.

Koller, C. (2011). Representing Otherness: African, Indian and European Soldiers' Letters and Memoirs. In S. Das (Ed.), *Race, Empire and First World War Writing* (pp. 127–142). Cambridge University Press.

Koller, C. (2014). Colonial Military Participation in Europe (Africa). In U. Daniel, et al. (Eds.), *International Encyclopedia of the First World War*. Freie Universität Berlin. https://bitly.ws/326Ry. Accessed 12 November 2023.

Liebau, H., Bromber, K., Lange, K., Hamzah, D., & Ahuja, R. (Eds.). (2010). *The World in World Wars*. Brill.

Mahafza, A. (2016). Al-Athār al-Siyāsiyya wa-l-Iqtiṣādiyya wa-l-Ijtimāʿiyya wa-l-Thaqāfiyya li-l-Ḥarb al-ʿAlamiyya al-Ūlaā fī Filisṭīn wa-l-Urdun [The First World War's Political, Economic, Social, and Cultural Implications in Palestine and Jordan]. In W. Kawtharani (Ed.), *Miʾat ʿAm ʿala al-Harb al-ʿAlamiyya al-Ula Muqarabat ʿArabiyya (al-Mujallad al-Thani): Mujtamaʿat al-Buldan al-...Arabiyya, al-Ahwal wa-l-Tahawullat* [World War I: A Century Later—Arab Approaches (Vol. II): Arab Societies: Conditions and Transformations] (pp. 485–518). Arab Center for Research and Policy Studies.

Maklouf, A. A. M. (2020). Inʿikāsāt al-Ḥarb al-ʿĀlamiyya al-Ūlā ʿalā al-Ḥaraka al-Waṭaniyya al-Lībiyya bil-Manṭiqa al-Sharqiyya [The Repercussions of the First World War on the Libyan National Movement in the Eastern Region]. *Majallat al-Buḥūth al-Tārīkhiyya, 4*(1), 165–181.

Markovits, C. (2010). Indian Soldiers' Experiences in France during World War I: Seeing Europe from the Rear of the Front. In H. Liebau, K. Bromber, K. Lange, D. Hamzah, & R. Ahuja (Eds.), *The World in World Wars: Experiences, Perceptions and Perspectives from Africa and Asia* (pp. 29–54). BRILL.

Moulai, H. (2019). Mawāqif al-Sukkān wa-l-Nuwwāb al-Tilmisāniyyīn min al-Tajnīd al-Ijbārī athnāʾ al-Ḥarb al-ʿĀlamiyya al-Ūlā (1914–1918) [The attitudes of the Residents and Deputies of Tlemcen to Forced Recruitment during the First World War (1914–1918)]. *Historical Kan Periodical, 12*(43), 63–70.

McMeekin, S. (2011). *The Berlin-Baghdad Express: The Ottoman Empire and Germany's Bid for World Power 1898–1918*. Penguin Books.

McMeekin, S. (2016). *The Ottoman Endgame: War, Revolution and the Making of the Modern Middle East, 1908–1923*. Penguin Books.

Murphy, M. (2022). The British Military Occupation of Jerusalem, 1917–1920: Soldiers as Tourists and Pilgrims. In S. Das, A. Maguire, & D. Steinbach (Eds.), *Colonial Encounters in a Time of Global Conflict, 1914–1918* (pp. 79–97). Routledge.

Olusoga, D. (2019). *The World's War: Forgotten Soldiers of Empire*. Head of Zeus.

Omissi, D. E. (Ed.). (1999). *Indian Voices of the Great War: Soldiers' Letters, 1914–18*. Palgrave Macmillan.

Prunty, R. (2021). The Impact of French Algeria's Participation during the First and Second World Wars on the Algerian Nationalist Movement. *West Virginia University Historical Review, 2*(1), 19–33.

Ragab, Y. (2020). The First World War and its Repercussions on Egypt Between 1914–1918. *Tishreen University Journal—Arts and Humanities Sciences Series, 42*(4), 229–241.

Rogan, E. (2015). *The Fall of the Ottomans: The Great War in the Middle East*. Basic Books.

Sabbagh, K. (2016). Wuʿūd li-Falasṭīn min Murāsalāt al-Hussein-MacMahon ilā Waʿd Balfour wa-mā baʿdahu (Promises to Palestine, from the al-Hussein–MacMahon Correspondence to the Balfour Declaration and Beyond). In S. Akram (Ed.), *Al-Ḥarb al-ʿĀlamiyya al-Ūlā wa-Atharuhā fī Filisṭīn: Irth Miʾat ʿĀm* [The First World War and its Impact on Palestine: A Hundred Years of Legacy] (pp. 69–86). Al-Jazeera Centre for Studies.

Salem, L. M. (2009). *Maṣr fī al-Ḥarb al-ʿĀlamiyya al-Ūlā* [Egypt during the First World War]. Dar al-Shurūq.

Salem, L. M. (2016). *Maṣr fī al-Ḥarb al-ʿĀlamiyya al-Ūlā* [Egypt during the First World War]. Maṭbaʿat Dār al-Kutub wa-l-Wathāʾiq al-Qawmiyya bi-l-Qāhira.

Samson, A. (2010). The Impact of the East Africa Campaign, 1914–1918, on South Africa and Beyond. In H. Liebau, K. Bromber, K. Lange,

D. Hamzah, & R. Ahuja (Eds.), *The World in World Wars: Experiences, Perceptions and Perspectives from Africa and Asia* (pp. 483–498). BRILL.

Shamsi, A. F. (2019). Shuhadāʾ Ḥalab Khilāl al-Ḥarb al-ʿĀlamiyya al-Ūlā, 1914–1918 [Aleppo's Martyrs during the First World War, 1914–1918]. *Kan Journals, 12*(44), 187–218.

Sheib, A. (2011). Tadāʿiyāt al-Ḥarb al-ʿĀlamiyya al-Ūlā fī Jabal ʿĀmil [The Implications of the First World War on Jabal Amil]. In A. al-Qasis (Ed.), *Lubnān fī al-Ḥarb al-ʿĀlamiyya al-Ūlā* [Lebanon during the First World War] (Vol. II, pp. 435–496). Dāʾirat al-Manshūrāt fī al-Jāmiʿa al-Lubnāniyya.

Taouanza, M., & Sbihi, A. (2019). Tafāʿul Jarīdat al-Fārūq al-Jazāʾiriyya maʿ Aḥdāth al-Ḥarb al-ʿĀlamiyya al-Ūlā (1914–1915) [The Reaction of the Algerian newspaper Al-Farouk to the events of the First World War (1914–1915)]. *Al-Ḥiwār al-Mutawwasiṭī, 10*(3), 183–198.

Teniou, N. (2016). al-Jazāʾiriyūn fī al-Ḥarb al-ʿĀlamiyya al-Ūlā [The Algerians in the First World War]. W. Kawtharani (Ed.), *Miʾat ʿAm ʿala al-Harb al-ʿAlamiyya al-Ula Muqarabat ʿArabiyya (al-Mujallad al- Thani): Mujtamaʿat al-Buldan al-ʿArabiyya, al-Ahwal wa-l-Tahawwulat* [World War I: A Century Later—Arab Approaches (Vol. II): Arab Societies: Conditions and Transformations] (pp. 307–328). Arab Center for Research and Policy Studies.

Teniou, N. (2015a). Al-Dhākira wa-l-Shahāda fī Kitābat Tārīkh al-Thawra al-Jazāʾiriyya (1954–1962): Al-Thawra al-Taḥrīriyya fī al-Tārīkh al-Rāhin [Memory and Testimony in Writing the History of the Algerian Revolution 1954–1962: The Liberation Struggle in the History of the Present Moment]. *Oustour, 2*, 23–37.

Teniou, N. (2015b). *Ishkāliyyat al-Dawla fī Tārīkh al-Ḥaraka al-Waṭaniya al-Jazāʾiriyya* [State Problematic in the Algerian National Movement History]. Arab Center for Research and Policy Studies.

Teniou, N. (2015c). Al-Thawra al-Jazāʾiriyya fī al-Umam al-Muttaḥida [The Algerian Revolution in the United Nations]. *Oustour, 12*, 122–151.

Ulrichsen, K. C. (2014). *The First World War in the Middle East*. Hurst and Company.

Vince, N. (2020). *The Algerian War, the Algerian Revolution*. Palgrave.

Walid, B. (2019). Al-Tajnīd al-Ijbārī wa-Mushārakat al-Jazāʾirīn fī al-Ḥarb al-ʿĀlamiyya al-Ūlā [Mandatory Conscription and the Participation of Algerians in the First World War]. *Majallat al-Dirāsāt al-Tārīkhiyya al-ʿaskariyya, 1*(1), 79–86.

Werner, M., & Zimmermann, B. (2006). Beyond Comparison: Histoire Croisée and the Challenge of Reflexivity. *History and Theory, 45*(1), 30–50.

Zweig, S. (2011). *The World of Yesterday: Memoirs of a European*. Pushkin Press.

CHAPTER 5

The Islamization of Knowledge: Critique and Alternative

Sari Hanafi

5.1 Introduction

Far from the ossified reading of much of the literature on extreme secular social sciences and the simplified reading of the social sciences propounded by researchers of the *Shariʿa* sciences, in this chapter, I aim to confirm that integration can be achieved among the *Shariʿa* sciences and the social sciences, as well as other sciences, and attempt to bridge the gap between these sciences. This is an incredibly important subject if we

---

This chapter is an updated and revised version of Chapter 3. "The Islamization of Knowledge: Appraisal and Alternative," from the author's forthcoming publication with Routledge, Taylor & Francis, *Studying Islam in the Arab World: The Rupture Between Religion and the Social Sciences.*

S. Hanafi (✉)
Department of Sociology, Anthropology and Media Studies, American University Beirut, Beirut, Lebanon
e-mail: sh41@aub.edu.lb

D. Jung and F. Zemmin (eds.), *Postcolonialism and Social Theory in Arabic*, The Modern Muslim World,
https://doi.org/10.1007/978-3-031-63649-3_5

hope to return legitimacy to the social sciences in the religiously and politically authoritarian Arab world, thus enabling it to do its pioneering part in solving current economic, political, and social problems and creating new conceptions and visions. This could open the horizon for many deep *ijtihādāt* (innovations) that would enrich Islamic thought and knowledge in different fields.

In recent decades, there has been much discussion on "Islamically grounding" the social sciences, which some researchers have described as being traditionally "Western" in nature. This debate was particularly prominent in Middle Eastern countries in the early nineties and played out in books, articles, and doctoral theses. Nonetheless, while this project received a positive response from a small group of researchers, it attracted a largely negative response from many in the social science community.

As a sociologist, I have no qualms about using the terms "Islamic," "Arab," "Lebanese," or "Algerian" to describe where social science concepts and theories have been inspired by Islamic heritage and these societies. However, after undertaking a content analysis of 97 articles,[1] 32 books, and nine theses that have adopted this orientation, as well as conducting interviews with some of the proponents of the Islamization of Knowledge (IoK) or Islamic grounding (*taʾṣīl*) of knowledge, I believe that adding a geographical or religious adjective to the social sciences creates real problems.

This chapter describes the literature of the IoK, presents a synthesis of this literature, analyzes some of its problems, and ponders whether this project is theoretically insightful or instead serves as a form of identity politics. On the basis of my analysis, this chapter suggests a new approach that I refer to as "separation, connection, and pluralistic praxis," which acts as an alternative to IoK and similar projects. However, I will first show that the social sciences include several elements and dimensions that are not found in the Islamized social sciences. Furthermore, these Islamized sciences constitute a closed system in the face of "Western" social sciences, only searching for an Islamic social philosophy and thereby ignoring other important elements and dimensions.

5.2 The Five Dimensions of the Social Sciences

The social sciences, which for the purpose of this study particularly include anthropology, political sciences, psychology, and sociology, are made up of five dimensions: (1) a social philosophy and ontological concepts; (2) methodological tools; (3) "objective" analysis of social structures; (4) analysis of individual and group perceptions; and (5) public policy recommendations in a manner that takes into consideration the material possibilities and interests that make one social group dominate over others, individual and social consciousness, and the contradictions and paradoxes related to measuring benefits and harms. These recommendations, therefore, do not depend on ultimate good and evil, or ultimate *halal* and *haram*, but are instead equations that are as complex as the complexity of social phenomena and their changes.

When discussing the social sciences, IoK scholars tend to focus on the first and fifth elements, the two most normative elements compared to the others. They will most likely argue that there is a unified Islamic vision, in the manner of the slogan "Islam is the solution," which imbues it with an essence of being the antithesis of what they refer to as the Western (materialistic) vision. At the same time, we also cannot say that there is an "Islamic social science." Perhaps there is an Islamic social philosophy that discusses the first dimension of social science but is meaningless with regard to the other dimensions. Therefore, the social sciences are construed by IoK scholars as forming a closed system.

5.3 The Genesis of the Islamization of Knowledge Project

Social scientists, mostly non-Arab, were the driving force in early thinking about the Islamic perspective on the social sciences and included such scholars as the Pakistani Akbar Ahmed (1986), Iranians ʿAli Shariʿ ati (1979), and Shaykh Morteza Motahhari (1979) and the British Muslim scholar Merryl Wynn Davies (1988). Except for Motahhari, all were educated in the West and developed their ideas in this context, echoing the emergence of postcolonial discourse particularly in American universities. For example, Akbar Ahmed called for an Islamic anthropology, describing it as a specialization that would be concerned with studies of Islamic groups by researchers committed to the universal values of Islam (humanism, knowledge, and tolerance), a specialization that would connect studies, particularly on tribes and small villages, to Islam's grand historical ideological frameworks. The concern with Islam here is not as a theological concept but as a social science. Therefore, for Ahmad, the definition does not exclude non-Muslims (Ahmed, 1986: 56). There were likewise Arab attempts at Islamizing knowledge, the most important of which was possibly by Shaykh Muhammad Baqir al-Sadr, especially in his thematic exegesis of the Quran (al-Sadr, 1989).

The establishment of The Association of Muslim Social Scientists by the Muslim Students Association in the United States and Canada in 1972 was an important event in understanding the connection between the social sciences and Islamic values. This association convened many conferences and meetings that culminated in the establishment of the International Institute of Islamic Thought (IIIT) in Herndon, Virginia, in 1981.[2] This project was led by the late Palestinian philosopher Ismaᶜil al-Faruqi in order to "recast knowledge in the mold of Islam in relation to the Islamic vision" and thus "to redefine and re-order the data, to rethink the reasoning and relate the data, to reevaluate the conclusions, to re-project the goals and to do so in such a way as to make the disciplines enrich the vision and serve the cause of Islam" (IIIT, 1984: 46). He outlined the aims of his work plan as (1) mastering the modern sciences; (2) mastering Islamic heritage; (3) establishing the proper relationship between Islamic concepts and every field of the modern sciences; (4) establishing a creative connection between Islamic heritage and modern knowledge; and (5) launching Islamic thought on a path that will lead to the realization of God's laws on earth.

A group of contemporary Islamic intellectuals/researchers—most of them university professors in the social and human sciences—adopted ideas inspired by this project. These intellectuals belonged to four groups. The first group was centered in the IIIT itself (among them, for example, Emad al-Din Khalil, Taha Jabir al-Alwani, and al-Haj Hamed Abu al-Qasem). The second group was connected to the International Islamic University of Malaysia, which called for the Islamization of human knowledge (e.g. only in the humanities and the social sciences), under the leadership of Syed Muhammad Naquib al-Attas. The third group was connected to Saudi universities, especially al-Imam Muhammad Ibn Saud Islamic University, which was established in 1950. The fourth group was centered on the IIIT branch in Egypt (including, for instance, Muhammad ᶜImara and ᶜAbd al-Wahhab al-Masiri). From these beginnings, their intellectual efforts, which mostly took the form of non-research studies, spread widely in the Arab world.

IIIT's paradigm developed over many academic meetings convened to discuss the Islamization project in a general sense or related topics organized by the institute, among other bodies that shaped the project (see Table 5.1).

Table 5.1 Conferences and events related to the topic of the Islamization of knowledge

Conference/Event	*Organizer/Place*	*Convening year*
Establishment of the Association of Muslim Social Sciences	Muslim Students Association in the United States and Canada	1972
The International Conference for Islamic Economics	King Abdulaziz University	1974
Islam and Psychology Symposium	College of Education at King Abdulaziz University in Riyadh	1978
First International Conference on Islamic Education	Makka (at the invitation of King Abdulaziz University in Jeddah)	1977
First International Symposium on Islamic Thought[3]	Lugano, Switzerland	1977
Establishment of the International Institute of Islamic Thought	United States of America	1981
Islamization of Knowledge Symposium	Islamabad, Pakistan	1982
Establishment of the World Islamic Association of Mental Health (WIAMH)	Lahore, Pakistan	1983
The Forum of Islamic Thought on Islam and the Social Sciences	Sétif, Algeria	1986
Symposium on the Islamic Grounding of the Social Sciences	Research Center at Imam Muhammad bin Saud Islamic University (Riyadh)	1987
The Islamic Orientation toward the Sciences	al-Azhar University of Egypt in coordination with the League of Islamic Universities	1993
Social Sciences from an Islamic Perspective	Center of Epistemological Studies (Cairo)	2007
The Global Economic Crisis from an Islamic Perspective	IIIT and the International Islamic Sciences University-Amman	2010
The Methodology of Knowledge Integration	IIIT and the College of Shariah at the University of Jordan	2012

The IoK project branched out in several directions, generating positive and negative responses. Some outrightly rejected the social sciences, which they viewed as being founded on theories that could not be applied to any study or problem facing Islamic society. This response was championed by Ahmed Ibrahim Khudr, who demonstrated his opposition to the IoK project with articles like "Do our Countries need Social Scientists?" (Khadr, 2012). This approach is particularly prominent among some imams in Lebanon.

Another approach sought to focus on Islamic grounding (*taʾṣīl*) instead of IoK, taking a more theological bent (concerned with worries about the compatibility of social sciences with the current *fiqhi* rulings) rather than a knowledge-based one (epistemological concerns related to a scientific discipline), though this approach caused much confusion (ʿAbd al-Halim, 2014). The term *taʾṣīl* was formulated in several universities, especially Imam Muhammad Ibn Saʿud University, in which representatives from the Association of Muslim Social Scientists and IIIT helped formulate the plan for its social sciences colleges at the university's request. There were specific suggestions for the Islamic grounding of knowledge. For example, Bilqasim al-Ghali (1999) suggested the following steps: placing social issues in an Islamic framework, clarifying issues through reference to classical works, authoring Islamic works that have a social dimension, utilizing the works of Ibn Khaldun (1332–1406), and integrating the Islamic science with the social sciences.

Others, such as Fuʾad Abu Hatab, took up the term "Islamic orientation" (*tawjīh*) of knowledge. The concept of destination (*wijha*) for him is synonymous with a paradigm, or Islamic interpretation, of knowledge (al-Atiri, 2013).

There are other strands that are not necessarily influenced by IIIT but which aimed to connect the social sciences to Arabs' or Muslims' cultural particularities. Sometimes taking an eclectic approach, they called for the establishment of a bridge between European modernity's binaries and Arab or Islamic identity, or between the classical tradition and modernity, authenticity and contemporaneity, revelation and reason, or material and symbolic spiritualism.

In this section, I will discuss some of the many attempts at Islamization and Islamic grounding of knowledge. These efforts are extensive in some fields—according to the Dar al-Manthumah Database (research undertaken in 2020), there are 213 research papers and books on the Islamic grounding of psychology alone. I will discuss three types of these efforts at Islamization and Islamic grounding of knowledge.

5.4 Knowledge Produced Within IoK

In this section, I will outline some examples of IoK or Islamic grounding and will organize them under three headings: (1) social philosophy emphasis, (2) serious attempts, and (3) shallow attempts.

5.4.1 *Social Philosophy Emphasis*

There has been much theorizing on the need for an Islamic sociology, Islamic psychology, or Islamic political science. Upon examining many of the attempts to establish these approaches, one can find that in reality, they do not transcend being an Islamic social, psychological, or political philosophy. Debates revolved around the importance of the group over the individual and the necessity of replacing "instrumental rationality" with a normative rationalization that takes ethics into consideration, or around the importance of using concepts proposed by Muslim intellectuals such as Ibn Khaldun's *ᶜasabiyya* or Malik Bennabi's "colonizability." In general, many proponents of the need for these approaches have stressed the necessity of benefiting from classical Islamic literature or intellectuals in the social sciences (Alatas, 2013; Haque, 2004). There has also been an emphasis on the necessity of reforming the research methodology of the social sciences in addition to including revelation as a source of knowledge that completes and complements the senses and reason, which extreme positivist and empirical theories have respectively evaded and exclusively relied on (Rajab, 1996).

Despite the importance of Islamic social philosophy, IoK scholars ignored the importance of understanding the *Shariᶜa* through the geography and history of Muslim societies and hid behind ideals inspired by Qurᵓanic concepts, which they viewed as if they had a fixed meaning and application throughout the ages. Thus, the issue is not *what* will be of worth for such Islamic social philosophy but *how* this will guide a research agenda.

5.4.2 *Serious Attempts at Islamic Grounding*

There are new attempts, though rare, to study all the elements of the social sciences and ground them nationally (*tawṭīn*). I prefer to use the concept of an interactive ecology of knowledge, as it points not only to an Islamic cultural or value framework but also other factors, such as local and national culture. This is closer to the spirit of science as being (softly) universalist than describing it as Islamic. I consider a process of grounding to be serious if it possesses the following four dimensions:

- Admission that large sections of the social sciences (and especially their objective side) have developed due to the global accumulation of knowledge. Therefore, we should no doubt benefit from research produced globally, whether in the West or elsewhere.

- Because the social sciences are imprinted by local culture, including Islamic culture, the role of this culture should be taken into consideration when attempting to understand the social actors of any social phenomenon.
- The whole life cycle of research (i.e. including knowledge transfer and public or policy-oriented research activities) should be taken into account. Knowledge cannot be completed (when there is a local relevance) without interaction with the community concerned. Thus, the societal debate resulting from its reception by the community and how policy options can be received by society are inherent parts of the research.
- It is necessary for the social sciences to communicate with moral philosophy and Shariᶜa sciences (*fiqh* and *uṣūl al-Dīn*) in order for empirical findings to be integrated with normative analysis, and for there to be a *fiqh al-wāqiᶜ* (jurisprudence of reality) based on *maqāṣid*, which are two necessary paradigms for all Islamic reformist schools in our contemporary reality. As a result, social scientists need to understand the lexicon used by religious scholars and laypeople, while religious scholars should use the social sciences to think ethically before establishing jurisprudential rules (Hanafi, 2024).

I will now turn to discussing two examples of these serious attempts coming from economics and psychology. The first example is in the field of Islamic economics. There are two interesting synthetic and bibliometric works that studied the knowledge produced on Islamic economics. The first is offered by the study of Ahmad Balwafi and Abdelrazzaq Bilabas (2010), which was built on a content analysis of 33 research papers published on the global financial and economic crisis of 2008 from an Islamic economic perspective. The two researchers came up with alarming results on the content of most of these research papers, the majority of which they described as essays that merely make comments, embellish capitalism, and have poor methodological bricolage. They also noted an absence of strategic dimensions and methodological planning to the point that they concluded that Islamic economics is unprepared to present alternatives to neoliberalism. The second is more bibliometric, specifically on knowledge production in Jordan (219 master's and PhD theses, 118 articles, and 178 books) from 1974 to 2010. This study concludes that 60%

of the materials focus on Islamic finance, meaning that other aspects of economics are missing. This study also highlights the chaos in the field and some problems related to the quality of research (al-Awran & Hattab, 2016: 24). But in terms of content, this knowledge production mostly adopts a neoliberal paradigm influenced by the situation in the Arab Gulf and does not concern itself much with social justice or equitable distribution of wealth. However, in fairness, we must point to two serious and critical attempts whose source is more East Asian than Arab, notably that of Mohammad Najatuallah Siddiqi, who was chosen as the president of the International Association of Islamic Economics in 2001, and that of Masudul Alam Choudhury, both of whom studied economics before embarking on *Sharīʿa* studies. Here I will mainly focus on Choudhury's contributions.

There is serious critical debate on Islamic economics and attempts to mainstream it. One of the most influential figures in this regard is Professor Masudul Alam Choudhury, whose books are used as key readings at the International Islamic University of Malaysia (IIUM). Bridging the Islamic and Western fields in Islamic economics and finance, Choudhury's scholarship has been recognized in both Western and Muslim academic circles, and as such, plays an influential role in defining this Islamic discipline locally and internationally. After graduating from the University of Toronto, he occupied the Professorial Chair of Islamic Finance at the Institute of Islamic Banking and Finance at IIUM. As a way of providing validation of his work to peers in the scientific community, he asked a prominent figure in economics from California State University, John C. O'Brien, to write the foreword for his book, *The Principles of Islamic Political Economy: A Methodological Enquiry* (Choudhury, 1992). In addition, unlike many IoK scholars, not only did he emphasizes *tawḥīd* as an epistemology, highlighting that there is only one epistemology for all sciences guided by the notion of unicity of the universe created by God and thus following monotheistic law that stems from the Quran and *Sunna*, but he also provided three other resources. The first, which is called foundational epistemology, entails universal epistemes. The second is not an episteme per se, but discourse channeled through a shuratic process (i.e. consultation, which he considers as compulsory, making it closer to the notion of democracy). The third and final is the "formation of knowledge," which is a discursively interactive, integrative, and evolutionary process (IIE-learning process). Choudhury's methodology relies on epistemology while also remaining a process-oriented model, the combination of which is used to ensure innovation.

These sources establish the five aims (*maqāṣid*) of the shariᶜa (religion, life, intellect, offspring, property), organic unity of knowledge and the world system in its diversity, goodness, choice of the good things of life, and justice as balance. These five principles are used to guide four areas within economics: (i) *muḍāraba/mushāraka* (profit-sharing/equity participation) as interactively participatory joint venture instruments; (ii) avoidance of wastefulness (*isrāf*) in consumption, production, and resource utilization, and in interest-bearing transactions (*ribā*); (iii) the institution of wealth tax (*zakāt*) to ensure justice and goodness are carried out through the act of wealth distribution; and (iv) the diversification and continuity of evolutionary learning possibilities. These instruments ensure a complementary relationship between the broader world system and *maqāṣid al-shariᶜa*, allowing its sustainability and continuity through circular causation, in turn feeding the sources of knowledge and supporting general well-being.

It is clear that Choudhury's methodology was developed with the aim of creating harmony between Islamic political economics, the broader social sciences, and contemporary economics. This approach is very different from how the IoK was initially conceived, as simply *Tawḥīdi* epistemology, where Western social sciences are altered to work in line with Islamic principles. This epistemology provides some epistemes that will complement or enter into tension with the universal foundational epistemology, and the other sources of knowledge will come to resolve tensions and contradictions. This is why, for Choudhury, it is not only applicable to the Muslim world but to humanity generally. In his article "Islamic Political Economy: An Epistemological Approach" (2014), which uses the example of Canada's indigenous people, he demonstrates how his conception of Islamic political economy can be utilized to deal with the labor market problems this population faces.

In line with this, Choudhury's *Heterodox Islamic Economics: The Emergence of an Ethico-Economic Theory* (Choudhury & Bhatti, 2016) was an attempt to show that Islamic economics is an inherent part of heterodox and ethico-economics. By mainstreaming Islamic methodology in this interpretive way by combining it with international and reflexive epistemologies, he allows for the possibility that democracy and innovation can handle tensions that could emerge from the competing stances.

Beyond epistemology, details are important, and the more one examines issues of microeconomics, the more complications that require empirical work arise. In this regard, Choudhury's book (1992) does a thorough job of laying out the details of the principles of Islamic economics, as has the work of many IIUM faculty members. Looking at the titles within the publications by these researchers, the topics go beyond epistemological debates and Islamic banking, covering various areas of socioeconomic life, including Islamic microfinance, the Shariʿa screening of stocks that promote responsible consumption and production and support climate action, *zakāt*, *sadaqāt* (charity), *qarḍ ḥasan* (free loans), *waqf* (endowment), micro-*takāful* (mutual insurance), and poverty, hunger, well-being, and the sustainability of communities in "underperforming" Islamic economics.

Therefore, Islamic economics has begun to represent an important research and knowledge approach. Today we truly find researchers in many Arab universities, and more particularly in Malaysia, who are distinguished by their serious work.

The second example of a serious attempt at Islamic grounding is the pioneering work of Huda Muhammad Hasan Hilal, *The Theory of Aptitude: An Analytical and Comparative Study of Fiqh and Psychology* (2011). Hilal graduated from IIUM and specialized in *fiqh* and *uṣūl*, but her work shows a mastery of psychology. The importance of this book stems from it raising many thorny issues for research and discussion, such as women's aptitude as judges, rulers, and witnesses under Islamic law, distinguishing between physiological maturity and rational wisdom, and the subject of mental or rational disorders invalidating one's aptitude either temporarily or permanently. This approach represents a change from blunt and categorical discrimination between men and women to one based on maturity, as men—like women—may enjoy aptitude (i.e. no gender discrimination) or may lose it. She refutes the opinion of some scholars that a woman's disqualification from some roles has any relationship to her menses, postpartum condition, or other biological changes. She insists on the need for a sound contemporary theory of eligibility incorporating findings from *fiqh* and psychology and contemporary sciences in order to find solutions to old and modern problems and differences.

5.4.3 *Shallow Attempts*

While there have only been a few serious attempts at IoK and the grounding knowledge in Islam, theoretically shallow works are unfortunately far more plentiful, as they are mostly built on reflections that do not implement methodological tools to obtain positivist/empirical elements (structural or perceptual data about individuals and groups) which can understand reality. Some dress the social sciences in religious garb with Qurʾanic verses and Prophetic statements as decoration, while others impart the adjective "Islamic" to ethics that more closely resemble humanistic, Christian, or Jewish ethics, for example, in some of the literature related to the topic of the environment.

It is understandable for intellectuals to be inspired by the dominant Islamic culture in order to encourage Muslims to respect nature, but there is discussion on particularities that are not really particularly "Islamic." For instance, ʿAuda al-Jayyousi (2013) reminds us that the principles of Islamic thought are represented in notions of justice, *iḥsān* (in its many significations: quality, doing something well, and continual beautification), treating one's family well, and preventing corruption. He aimed to root this universally by studying sustainable development from an Islamic perspective. But to see these principles as contrary to Western principles is empirically incorrect, as these are general and abstract universal principles. As for saying that they are the negative effects of a Western paradigm that aims "toward happiness through excessive consumption and luxurious distractions from necessities," (al-Jayyousi, 2013, 47 [translation S.H.]) this is none other than a capitalist paradigm that can be found in both the West and the East, especially in the Gulf countries. Much of the literature around ecology and Islam (see, for example, al-Khoshn, 2011) is nothing but literature on general ethics that lacks a basic level of scientific research to identify a specific problem and present solutions that transcend wishful thinking. Despite the importance of *Shariʿa*-grounding to maintain an environmental balance (e.g. Saidi, 2013), it is insufficient to reduce the topic of the environment to this element alone.

Another example of these incomplete attempts is Jasser ʿAuda's study (2012) entitled "Employing *Maqāṣid al-Shariʿa* to Guide Policies of the Knowledge Economy." This study begins by presenting an understanding of the concept of the knowledge economy promoted by the World Bank and then presents a critique of the indicators of a knowledge economy. Yet the study's criticism was very general, with no reflection on specific indicators. ʿAuda did not benefit from the substantial literature that has highlighted the problem of the knowledge economy indicators, such as percentage of mobile phone use. As Tremblay (2011) reminds us, Arab countries have rarely developed typical knowledge economy industries, such as production or assembly of electronic components, biotechnology, or pharmaceutical industries. ʿAli Kadri (2014) even talks of policies of deindustrialization that have laid waste to the production of knowledge. As such, the indices used for postindustrial societies do not fit the reality of many Arab countries. All of this was absent in Jasser ʿAuda's discussion.

5.5 IoK: Six Problems

I will focus here on six problems that emerged from the dominant concepts of IoK projects and their lack of serious application. Some of these problems are related to the epistemological content of the discourse, while others are related to the working conditions of its knowledge production.

5.5.1 Reductionism

Some of those involved in IoK projects respond to Eurocentrism by using Islamo-centrism (Alatas, 1987): Islamic knowledge should be used to interpret phenomena in Muslim societies and Western science in the West. There is a reduction of the West's value framework to its Judeo-Christian inspiration. Evidently, this reductionism is being used to justify the necessity for an Islamic social science, with some highlighting the case of the Western financial crisis in 2007 (which began in the United States as a subprime mortgage crisis) as proof of the need for an alternative presented by Islamic economics. This religio-cultural reductionism conceals what is problematic in the West, namely capitalism and neoliberalism, which were the essential culprits of the financial crisis. Evidently, this reductionism only operates in one direction, meaning that the same people will not make the same assumption in reverse, i.e. "Our problem in the Muslim world is the presence of a religious culture." This is a form of straw-man fallacy that attributes the cause of Muslim countries' backwardness solely to an imperialist conspiracy and neocolonial influence. This kind of reductionist discourse is shared by many Islamists and the (illiberal) left alike in many Arab countries.

Syed Farid Alatas rightly called for the development of alternative discourses without these binaries. This is an essential demand in the process of popularizing the social sciences and protecting internationally recognized standards of scientific research. Introducing theories and concepts rooted in local practices and cultures must be counted as contributing to the universal social sciences—that is, they are not an alternative to them. Ibn Khaldun's theory of the dynamics of tribal-state formation could be applied to a myriad of other historical cases outside of his geographical area and periods of interest. Alatas, for instance, integrates the Marxist theory of forms of production with Ibn Khaldun's theory of state formation and applies them to the case of the political economy of the Safavid empire (Alatas, 1987). According to Alatas, the hypothesis that concepts and theories only apply to Asian phenomena holds the idea that Asians are so greatly different from non-Asians that both sides require separate special worlds of theories for us to be able to understand them. He views this as an extreme reaction to the problem of Orientalism. This represents one of the aspects of the problem of focusing on nativism, as it makes the local perspective the one judging things to the point that it denies Western bodies of knowledge, not on the basis of the extent of their benefit, power of proof, and accuracy, but on the basis of their national or cultural roots.

This reductionism takes on different forms, such as comparative reductionism that privileges one factor for the sake of comparative analysis like reading Islamic behavior as only the result of the Qurʾan without any influence from geography, history, or society. Therefore, some believe in the unity of truth, and that they, naturally, are the only ones who possess it.

5.5.2 *Emphasis on Normative Approaches and Empirical Laziness*

There is an emphasis on normative approaches, which makes it easy for many proponents of IoK or Islamic grounding to focus only on presenting ethical prescriptions. For example, talking about what the Muslim family or Muslim youth should be like without dealing with descriptive/positivist issues, that is, empirical research, which can present some sort of understanding of the nature of the family in the twenty-first century in a particular country. It is empirical research that clarifies how spiritual or religious rites influence individual or group behavior in society, the family, or the market.

While I acknowledge the importance of the Islamic worldview or life-worlds and certain ontological premises (e.g. the family as an overarching social structure for the protection of individual), the normative becomes meaningless by itself without the toil of empirical research.

5.5.3 The Changing and the Unchanging

There are those who view Islamic thought and *fiqh* as unchanging in their normativity and ethical values, and that the "positivistic" sciences must be subjugated to them. If we believe in *maqāṣid al-sharīᶜa* methodology, this means that those literal textual laws—except for the universals and foundations—can change with the changing nature of reality. Therefore, it is not only scientific knowledge that can change with the changing nature of reality.

Generally, there has been a claim that *fiqh al-wāqiᶜ* and *fiqh al-tawaqquᶜ* (jurisprudence of forecasting) and modernizing and updating old rules must refer to the social sciences, but we have noticed an absence of methodological tools, structural information, and perceptions capable of understanding reality in order to present solutions built on an understanding of the Qurʾan, *Sunnah*, and *Shariᶜa*. For jurisprudents to understand their reality they must generate the key questions: What? Why? Where? When? And how? Reality does not mean only the present, but also the past. Despite reality being globalized and transcending the local community (whether made up of a family, tribe, or neighborhood), is the changing nature of reality what is needed before *fiqh al-wāqiᶜ* can be grounded? In this case, who changes it? The ruler? The individual? The religious institution?

These subjects were at the heart of the *maqāṣidi fiqh* which was neglected by the dominant jurisprudential trend. Alyan Buzyan (2014) calls on researchers in the field of *maqāṣid* "to move away from comparative studies between *Shariah* and law whose intent is to demonstrate the difference and stress the height of the *Shariah* and its higher aims in obtaining human interests toward a stage of making them closer in a fruitful *maqasidi* approach" (76).

5.5.4 The Fiqh of Shariᶜa vs. The Fiqh of Applying the Shariᶜa

ᶜAbdullah al-Maliki (an opinion-maker currently imprisoned in Saudi Arabia who obtained a doctorate in the *Shariᶜa* sciences) championed an important intellectual development in *The Ummah's Sovereignty before the Shariah's Application* (al-Maliki, 2011). According to al-Maliki, there is a need for there to be sovereignty of the *ummah* (Muslim community) through its popular recognition, namely the democratic acceptance of a ruler. This will move the principle of the *Shari*ᶜ*a's* obligatory status from the individual level to the group level by establishing laws and constitutions before applying the *Shari*ᶜ*a*. Al-Maliki gives a witty reply to those who say that sovereignty in Islam only belongs to the *Shari*ᶜ*a* and not the individual or the people:

This saying has a problem in its understanding of the nature of the *Shari*ᶜ*a*, as it does not look at the *Shari*ᶜ*a* as an expression of a system of values, principles, and laws. Rather, it views as if it were close to a living being eating food, walking in the markets, sitting on its sofa, and enforcing its views and will on people. This is how some conceptualize it! I do not only say that this is a caricature, but rather some people really make you feel that this is how the *Shariah* is in its conceptualization. As such, they always contrast the *Ummah's* sovereignty and the *Shariah's* sovereignty, and present the *Shariah's* sovereignty as above the *ummah's*, as if the *Shariah's* values were living beings possessing a will and power (al-Maliki, 2011, 121).

From here, the political and social sciences have an important role to play in studying this sovereignty, power, and democracy, which are preliminary elements to applying the *Shari*ᶜ*a*. Enabling these sciences becomes a condition for those interested in spreading the *Shari*ᶜ*a*. It is apt for Islamic movements to raise the slogan "The Ummah's sovereignty is the solution" instead of "Islam is the solution" (al-Maliki, 2011, 7–9).

5.5.5 Epistemology vs Working Conditions of Researchers

I see the weakness of the social sciences (whether they claim to be from an Islamic perspective or not) as resulting from the social, political, and economic conditions that researchers in the Global South face and which shape their intellectual formation, more than it being an epistemological problem resulting from the internationalization of the social sciences (that is, incompatibility with Western concepts born in the limited contexts of European nation-states). Arab societies, for example, have been afflicted with fierce dictatorships which prevented any possibility of critical thought, in the sciences as well as in theology.

There is an excessive reductionism in many of these projects built for harmonization or Islamization, all of which tend to be purely epistemological methodologies. There is an exaggeration of the importance of values at the expense of interests and motivations. Khaled al-Hroub (2008) criticizes the current Arab and Islamic discourse on the issue of cultural particularity, as it becomes distant from the reality of these societies and their historical experience. He also views these obsessive delusions as transforming cultural particularism into a form of apologism for Arab societies' failures and hurting their chances of developing and catching up to scientific countries. It is necessary to criticize the Eurocentrism of the social sciences, but not to forget other local powers that push for self-censorship, as ʿAbdelkebir Khatibi (1983) did with his double criticism.

From here I prefer approaches that take into account both epistemology and the social condition of knowledge production as a means of understanding the crisis of the social sciences, such as the approach of Rushdi Rashid (2008), who used the concept of "localizing knowledge," describing it as a way of establishing science in contemporary Arab societies. According to Rashid, the localization of knowledge is built on two essential foundations: the necessity of focusing on the correct knowledge of the relationship between classical Arab-Islamic knowledge and modern knowledge, and the necessity of revising the pioneering role of the former in bringing the latter into being. In addition, we must recognize the necessity of both economic and political power in the process of harmonization in order to achieve the necessary infrastructure for knowledge production. One of the main messages of my *Knowledge Production in the Arab World: The Impossible Promise* (Hanafi & Arvanitis, 2015) was a clear call to improve the working conditions of knowledge production by enabling a national science system and the necessary political, economic, and social conditions for its realization.

5.5.6 *Internationalization of Knowledge*

The governance and predominance of science in political debates (about such things as climate change, genetically modified organisms [GMOs], international property rights, and negotiations on drugs, biodiversity, and the like) have changed. Scientific questions have become global. Scientists of the natural and social realms have become accustomed to thinking about issues at the global level. Of the two scientific fields, this phenomenon possibly occurs more among the natural sciences. Objects are global; communities of specialists are global; training specialists has become a question of feeding an international distribution of competences, making every new PhD candidate a future emigrant. Caroline Wagner (2008), among many other authors, has defended the idea that international scientific networks are essentially made up of individuals who seek collaboration with peers with mutual interests and complementary skills around the world. In this globalized world, international collaboration functions as a global self-organizing system through collective action at the level of researchers themselves (Leydesdorff & Wagner, 2008).

Overall, all sciences contain universalist dimensions as well as dimensions related to the culture of a population group and its needs. What is needed is a form of dialectical exchange between the particular/contextual and the universal which can each benefit from their different experiences and accumulation of knowledge. This is what is lacking in IoK, as its scholars do not sufficiently acknowledge the effect of globalization and how it is difficult to resolve any problems without intervening not only in cultural particularities but also in how people are impacted by global factors (including global culture).

5.6 The Alternative: "Separation, Connection, and Pluralistic Praxis"

No knowledge exists today that has meaning without mutual enrichment and cross-pollination between scientific disciplines and domains of knowledge. The social sciences have come to observe local, national, and global forms of religiosity, their impact on political, economic, and social spheres, and how they are impacted in turn. Theology studies religion and religious rites from the perspective of their religious meaning, and in connection with their values to achieve salvation for people. Yet theology, at least in many Western universities, is interested in practical theology, i.e. how people perceive religion and how religion can help in human development through individual integrity and social cohesion and by maximizing religious congruence. Thus, there is no subject that can be considered as a purely religious subject (Adnali, 2016).

Returning to the *Shariʿa* sciences, what is needed is to teach them with two approaches: an approach of knowledge built on faith and an approach built on the academic methodology of liberal arts, remembering that one will complement the other. This was adopted in the Master of

Arts program in the Islamic Sciences (part of the School of Humanities and Social Sciences) et al.-Akhawayn University in Morocco, with the aim of educating students in the human and social sciences necessary for research in religious studies. The Master of Arts in Islamic Studies has two tracks: a track for students who have an academic background outside of Islamic studies, and a "Religious Studies" track for students who have a solid background in Islamic studies (Monette & Roy, 2016).

How can we understand and work toward the integration of knowledge or pedagogies between the natural and human and social sciences and the *Sharīᶜa* sciences? I will use an approach that I call the Separation, Connection, and Pluralistic Praxis Approach (SeCoPP), which takes its premises from Egyptian philosopher Samir Abuzaid's (2009) bi-dimensional approach of separation and connection, and develops it further, adding a third dimension (pluralistic praxis). In order to understand this concept, I will unpack these three dimensions.

First, by separation, any problem can be divided into issues related to different fields: for instance, social distancing related to a pandemic should be the subject of medicine (how important it is to isolate the virus), the social sciences (the psychological, social, and economic ramifications of social distancing), and religion (what is the opinion of Islamic texts on holding the Friday prayer during a pandemic?). There is an acknowledgment that each knowledge field has its own methodology and that some of the field's aspects are objective and others subjective. One cannot reduce all sciences to one episteme. Even knowledge can share the same ontology but not the same epistemology.

Second, connection is the art of providing a synthesis of the results from all fields about a problem in a way that ensures consistency. For Abuzaid, "consistency" is related to a "worldview." For if every human has a view of the world, the essential characteristic which distinguishes this view is that it is consistent with itself and with the real world. This, in his view, was the secret of classical Arab-Islamic civilization's success (Abuzaid, 2013). However, here I tend to disagree with Abuzaid and others like him who strip pluralism from a worldview in a particular space–time context, especially if we consider the Islamic worldview as fixed and unitary. Therefore, in my opinion, worldviews must be seen as *lifeworlds*, a phenomenological concept dear to Muhammad Bamyeh (2019), and *rules of discussion and dialogue*. The concept of lifeworlds refers to the range of acts and practices through which old ideas continue to generate voluntarily accepted meaning, rather than enforced rules by an institution or state. The Islamic lifeworld is thus related to historical Muslims' experience rather than the systems that result from economic and political techniques of standardization, which seek to obstruct individual agency. Thus the concept of lifeworlds enables the possibility of having a specific ontology (e.g. Islamic ontology) for a given issue (for instance, the centrality of the family as a social structure in our society; what are the master conceptions of family in Islamic thought and corpus) but not a specific epistemology, unless related to a specific science (e.g. how sociology determines the validity of sociological reasoning, or how *hadith* science determines the authenticity of *hadith* through a method that investigates the chain of transmission of a given *hadith*). Using the Michael Walzer's (2019) metaphor of "thick" and "thin" moral terms, ontology is thin, as it has several premises and cannot be thick enough to encompass details on how to moralize human behavior.

Concerning the *rules of discussion and dialogue,* I would like to use here the seminal methodology that the Lebanese philosopher Mouchir Basil ʿAoun (2023) proposes to help us in the phase of connection to deal with different levels (circles) of "truth" (the outcome of phase one, i.e. separation) and what can be a matter of discussion or not in order to carry out moral reasonings. The first circle is about scientific truth. One can distinguish between the not-for-discussion outcome of the descriptive and conceptual epistemological imperatives of the sciences and what comes from the paradigm that should be the subject of discussion. The second circle concerns moral principles as universal truths that become stable as anthropological truths (something stable through history and geography) framed by the values of dignity, freedom, equality, justice, brotherhood, and other ideals. However, this circle should be understood as a theoretical one and guidelines that are not-for-discussion, but how these guidelines are applied to each society is a matter of discussion. For example, gender equality (which is part of the universal declaration of human rights) will be implemented in a society that has a specific culture and a division of labor between men and women, making this implementation vary from society to society. The third circle concerns the moral reasonings that apply the principles of the second circle (i.e. how gender equality will be implemented) and which also deal with aesthetics (one society may appreciate a certain kind of music while others may not). This can be fully discussed. The fourth and last circle concerns the truth of beliefs (or comprehensive doctrines, in the language of John Rawls), including religious beliefs. These beliefs, in the form of theology, are difficult to discuss, such as why one should believe in the prophet Mohamad and not Jesus, but of course, one can discuss whether warriors' behavior in historical wars waged in the name of the religion is just or not. As society has different communities with different beliefs, one can only *respect* the beliefs of others as long as they do not contradict the second circle. ʿAoun, in the line of Paul Ricoeur, rightly thinks that beyond the outcome of the two descriptive and conceptual epistemological imperatives of science, the other truths are a sort of existential truth which is, in essence, rhetorical, metaphorical, and interpretive and should be taken as it is in order to facilitate innovation (*ijtihād*) and the possibility of discussion and dialogue. For example, religions did not ban slavery—is this because it was so common at the time of the revelation? Or is slavery something ethical that should be maintained? Holy scripts should be interpreted in order to privilege the former explanation.

One of the means by which some philosophers and theologians have tried to solve the contradiction between science and religion has been to separate them on the basis that each has its own unique language. In the theory of linguistic analysis, interpretations are given to each—one for the language of religion and one for the language of science—with a complete contrast between them where one does not refer to the other, and with each having its own special role. In this regard, Wittgenstein uses the phrase "language games," as he and his followers believe that both science and religion have their own specific language games. In light of this, both religion and science have special roles that differ from the role played by the other. As such, neither of them can be judged by the standards and criteria of the other. The language of science is a basis that benefits uncertainty and estimation and is distinguished in its pragmatic functional nature (Sajdi, 2008).

Third, by pluralistic praxis, I mean that after connecting the outcomes of different fields in order to deal with an issue, we need to consider different actions for different audiences taking into account the plurality of people in terms of culture, social classes, religions, ethnicity, etc.

Let me illustrate the SeCoPP approach through the example of the issue of women's share of inheritance. For the *faqīh*, there is a Qurʾanic verse on the distribution of inheritance. For others, there is a sort of contradiction between both the noble virtues of Islam (and other religions) and liberalism, such as equality and justice. In Tunisia, there was an important debate on this topic. However, those who supported maintaining the dominant interpretation of the Qur᾿anic text and their peers who supported gender equality in distributing inheritance ended up using pieces of evidence that had the same epistemological repertoires for their moral justifications (using textual, legal, and sociological arguments).[4] After both sides had used their different methodologies, they sought connection by using different justificatory repertoires of arguments and disseminating them in the public sphere, which is the third phase, that is, pluralistic praxis.

Pluralistic praxis is that action which reflects the debate of ethical dilemma and research on reasonable accommodation (and not only rational, as it is also influenced by feelings) between virtue and a choice that takes into account consequences. By pluralistic, I intend to emphasize that we always have different publics: at the very least citizens and believers. This is because arguments and justifications, which are presented to the citizen who comes from a different social, cultural, and religious background, will most likely differ from the one the preacher presents to believers. In the latter case, it suffices to cite a holy text and its exegesis. Afterward, action comes in, which is this peaceful debate in the public sphere which leads to a coming together of views through both sides accepting that no matter how much civil legislation may be preferable to a particular means of distributing inheritance, the other side may choose the other means. If there are democratic means to resolve the choice of the majority (most likely in the form of civil legislation), the preacher can always call believers to their religious choice and ratify it in the form of *fiqh*.

Ultimately, the separation step is an analytical step. This means that the same actor can use different disciplines in order to come up with a position before the connection. I am thinking particularly of those who are interested in *maqāṣid al-sharīʿa*. To resolve a problem related to different disciplines, they need to do this by outsourcing the research to those who are experts in each discipline.

5.7 Conclusion

The process of integrating and grounding knowledge does not mean adopting a completely local theoretical context vs. "Western materialist" theories. Rather, it means benefiting from global and local traditions at the same time and sifting through them to form a theoretical framework valid for studying the topic under consideration.

The late Isma^c^il al-Faruqi, who conceived IoK, put together a work plan for his project in 1981, calling on everyone to adopt his approach. A third of a century later, we have found that this project did not produce much substantial research and knowledge. Perhaps, its secondary effect has been to scientize Islamic culture rather than Islamize the sciences. Yet I see some important reflexivity within IIIT, the institutional bearer of the al-Faruqi project, as it has abandoned this slogan, instead adopting "integrating knowledge" or "Islamic perspectives on knowledge." What I tried to show here is that there are epistemological problems that grew out of some concepts of IoK, with one of its results being that it was more a collective self-view (identity politics project) than a view of knowledge. There are good seeds, but in soil that is still poor and in need of care and tilling before it can bear fruit.

Finally, I argued that good social knowledge is a science that has the potential to enact change and perhaps even be subversive, which means raising critical questions on economic and political interests and some pathologies of strong ideologies that affect all levels of society. It is this knowledge which clarifies how ideologies are built and how symbolic systems are utilized.

Notes

1. I rely here on some of the specialized journals in this field, the most important of which is the "Islamization of Knowledge" journal published by IIIT (in Arabic), as well as JSTOR, the Arabic E-marefa, and al-Manhal Databases.
2. The institute has several branches and offices in Muslim and Arab capitals, and its work is supervised by a board of trustees, whose members include a president rotated cyclically.
3. This resulted in a call to establish the "International Institute of Islamic Thought" to lead the efforts of the "Islamization of knowledge."
4. For more on this topic, see Hanafi and Tomeh (2019).

References

ᶜAbd al-Halim, M. (2014). *al-Taʾṣīl al-Islāmī li-ᶜIlm al-Ijtimāᶜ, Muqāraba fī Islāmiyyat al-Maᶜrifa* [The Islamic Grounding of Sociology, An Approach to the Islamisation of Knowledge]. University of Setif 2.

Abu Zayd, S. (2009). *Al-ᶜIlm wa-l-Naẓra al-ᶜArabiyya ilā al-ᶜĀlam: al-Tajriba al-ᶜArabiyya wa-l-Taʾsīs al-ᶜIlmī li-l-Nahḍa* [Science and the Arabic World-view: The Arabic Experience and the Scientific Founding of the Arabic Renaissance]. Markaz Dirasat al-Wahda al-ᶜArabiyya.

Abu Zayd, S. (2013). Tārīkh Falsafat al-ᶜIlm min Manẓūr Islāmī bi-Waṣfihi Asāsan li-Taḥqīq al-Takāmul al-Maᶜrifī [The History of the Philosophy of Science from an Islamic Perspective as a Basis for Achieving Cognitive Integration.] In R. J. ᶜUkasha (Ed.), *al-Takāmul al-Maᶜrifī: Atharuhu fī al-Taᶜlīm al-Jāmiᶜī wa-ḍarūratuhu*, 109–154. Maᶜhad al-ᶜAlami li-l-Fikr al-Islami.

Adnali, A. H. (2016). Al-Dirāsāt al-Islāmiyya: Naẓra Muᶜāṣira min Turkiyya [Islamic Studies: A Contemporary View from Turkey.] In N. Tabbara (Ed.), *Al-Dirāsāt al-Islāmiyya amām Taḥaddī al-Tanwīᶜ al-Thaqāfī fī al-ᶜĀlam al-Muᶜāṣir*, 78–107. al-Farabi/Maᶜhad al-Muwatana wa-Idarat al-Tanawwuᶜ.

Ahmed, A. (1986). *Toward Islamic anthropology: Definition, dogma and directions*. New Era.

Alatas, S. F. (1987). Reflections on the Idea of Islamic Social Science. *Comparative Civilisations Review*, 17.

Alatas, S. F. (2013). *Ibn Khaldun*. OUP India.

al-ᶜAtiri, ᶜA. S. (2013). Naẓarāt fī al-Aslama wa-l-Taʾṣīl [Insights into Islamization and Grounding]. *Majallat al-Muslim al-Muāṣir, 149*, 65–93.

al-ᶜAwran, A. F., & Ḥaṭṭāb, K. T. (2016). *Dalīl al-Bāḥithīn fī al-Iqtiṣād al-Islāmī wa-l-Maṣārif al-Islāmiyya fī al-Urdun (1974–2010)* [Researchers' Guide to the Islamic Economy and Islamic Banks in Jordan (1974–2010)]. al-Maᶜhad al-ᶜAlami li-l-Fikr al-Islami.

al-Ghali, B. (1999). Muḥāwalāt fī Taʾṣīl ᶜIlm al-Ijtimāᶜ [Attempts at Grounding Sociology]. *Majallat Shuʾūn Ijtimāᶜiyya, 63*, 9–41.

al-Hroub, K. (2008). From Privacy to Historic Disability? Qantara website for dialogue with the Islamic world. https://ar.qantara.de/content/llm-lrby-lwlm-wjdl-lhwy-mn-lkhswsy-l-lq-ltrykhy

al-Jayyusi, ᶜAwda. (2013). "Al-Bīʾa wa-l-Taḥawwul Naḥwa al-Istidāma: Naẓra Islāmiyya" [Environment and the Transition Towards Sustainability: An Islamic View]. *Majallat Islāmiyyat al-Maᶜrifa, 72*, 43–59.

al-Khushn, H. (2011). *Al-Islām wa-l-Bīʾa... Naḥwa Fiqh Bīʾī* [Islam and the Environment... Steps Towards an Environmental Jurisprudence]. Dar al-Malak.

al-Maliki, A. (2011). Siyādat al-Umma Qabla Taṭbīq al-Sharīᶜa [The Sovereignty of the Umma Before the Implementation of Shariᶜa]. http://www.almqaal.com/?p=922

al-Sadr, M. B. (1989). *Al-Tafsīr al-Mawḍūʿī wa-l-Falsafa al-Ijtimāʿiyya* [Objective Interpretation and Social Philosophy]. Al-Dar al-ʿAlamiyya li-l-Tibaʿa.

ʿAwn, M. B. (2023, April 10). Hal yajūz an Tataḥawwal al-Ḥaqīqa ilā Mawḍūʿ Ḥiwārī? [Is it Permissible to Turn the Truth into a Topic of Discussion?] *al-Sharq al-Awsaṭ*. https://aawsat.com/home/article/4262981

Bamyeh, M. A. (2019). *Lifeworlds of Islam: The pragmatics of a religion*. Oxford University Press.

Balwafi, A., & Bilabas, A. (2010). Researchers in Islamic Economics' *Treatment of the Global Financial Crisis: An Analytical Study*. https://bit.ly/415OfLB

Buzyan, ʿA. (2014). Tawẓīf Maqāṣid al-Sharīʿa fī Aslamat al-Maʿrifa al-Qānūniyya [The Employment of Maqasid al-Sharia in the Islamization of Legal Knowledge] *Majallat Islāmiyyat al-Maʿrifa, 78*, 40–76.

Choudhury, M. A. (1992). *Principles of Islamic Political Economy: A Methodological Enquiry*. St. Martin's Press.

Choudhury, M. A. (2014). Islamic Political Economy: An Epistemological Approach. *Social Epistemology Review and Reply Collective, 3*(11), 53–107.

Choudhury, M. A., & Bhatti, I. (2016). *Heterodox Islamic Economics: The Emergence of an Ethico-Economic Theory* (1st ed.). Routledge.

Davies, M. W. (1988). *Knowing One Another: Shaping Islamic Anthropology*. Mansell.

Hanafi, S. (2024). *Studying Islam in the Arab World: The Rupture Between Religion and the Social Sciences* (1st ed.). Routledge.

Hanafi, S., & Arvanitis, R. (2015). *Knowledge Production in the Arab World: The Impossible Promise* (1st ed.). Routledge.

Hanafi, S., & Tomeh, A. (2019). Gender Equality in the Inheritance Debate in Tunisia and the Formation of the Non-Authoritarian Reasoning. *Journal of Islamic Ethics, 3*(1), 207–232.

Haque, A. (2004). Psychology From Islamic Perspective: Contributions of Early Muslim Scholars and Challenges to Contemporary Muslim Psychologists. *Journal of Religion and Health, 43*(4), 357–377.

Hilal, H. M. H. (2011). *Naẓariyyat al-Ahliyya: Dirāsa Taḥlīliyya Muqārana Bayna al-Fiqh wa-ʿIlm al-Nafs* [The Theory of Eligibility: A Comparative Analytical Study between Jurisprudence and Psychology]. al-Maʿhad al-ʿAlami li-l-Fikr al-Islami.

IIIT. (1984). *Islamization of Knowledge: General Principles and Work Plan*. IIIT.

Kadri, A. (2014). *Arab Development Denied: Dynamics of Accumulation by Wars of Encroachment*. Anthem Press.

Khadr, A. I. (2012). Hal Tuḥtāj Bilādunā ilā ʿUlamāʾ Ijtimāʿ? [Does Our Country Need Sociologists?]. http://www.alukah.net/culture/0/44114/

Khatibi, ʿA. (1983). *Maghreb Pluriel*. Denoël.

Leydesdorff, L., & Wagner, C. (2008). International Collaboration in Science and the Formation of a Core Group. *Journal of Informatics, 2*(4), 317–325.

Monette, C., & Roy, E. (2016). "Master in Islamic Studies at Al Akhawayn University," In N. Tabbara (Ed.), *Islamic Studies Facing the Challenge of Cultural Diversity in the Contemporary World*, 17–30. al-Farabi/Institute for Citizenship and Diversity Management.

Motahhari, M. (1979). *Al-Mujtamaᶜ wa-l-Tārīkh [Society and History]*. Wizarat al-Irshad al-Islamiyya.

Rajab, I. ᶜA. al-R. (1996). Al-Taʾṣīl al-Islāmī li-l-ᶜUlūm al-Ijtimāᶜiyya: Maᶜālim ᶜalā al-Tarīq [The Islamic Grounding of the Social Sciences: Milestones on the Road]. *Majallat Islāmiyyat al-Maᶜrifa*, 3.

Rashid, R. (2008). Al-Waṭan al-ᶜArabī wa-Tawṭīn al-ᶜIlm [The Arab World and the Localization of Science]. *Al-Mustaqbal al-ᶜArabī*, 354.

Saidi, Y. (2013). The Legitimate Grounding for Maintaining Environmental Balance. *Islamic Studies*, *16*.

Sajidi, A. al-F. (2008). Ishkāliyyāt al-Taᶜāruḍ bayna al-ᶜIlm wa-l-Dīn: Qirāʾa Naqdiyya fī al-Ḥulūl al-Muqtaraḥa [The Problem of the Conflict between Science and Religion: A Critical Reading of the Proposed Solutions] In *Ishkāliyyāt al-taᶜāruḍ wa āliyyāt al-tawḥīd: al-ᶜilm wa-l-dīn min al-ṣirāᶜ ilā al-aslama*. Markaz al-Hadara li-tanmiyat al-fikr al-Islami.

Shariᶜati, ᶜA. (1979). *On the Sociology of Islam*. Mizan Press.

Tremblay, A. (2011). *Les Classements Internationaux Sont-Ils La Clef d'accès à l'économie de La Connaissance? Analyse Des Universités Du Liban et Dubaï*. In Université Saint-Joseph de Beyrouth.

Wagner, C. (2008). *The New Invisible College: Science for Development*. Brookings Institute Press.

Walzer, M. (2019). *Thick and Thin: Moral Argument at Home and Abroad*. University of Notre Dame Press.

PART II

Social Theory Beyond Academic Disciplines

CHAPTER 6

Liquid Modernity in Arabic

Haggag Ali

6.1 Introduction

This chapter opts for a comparative approach to explore diverse Arab engagements with the metaphor of "liquid modernity." This term was introduced by Polish-born British sociologist Zygmunt Bauman (1925–2017) and Egyptian intellectual Abdelwahab Elmessiri (1938–2008). The question of who first introduced this metaphor is highly controversial. On the one hand, Elmessiri repeatedly acknowledged Bauman's deep influence on his way of thinking and writing on Nazim, Zionism, and secularism (Elmessiri, 1999, 2001, 2002b, 2005). On the other hand, Bauman did not explicitly use the metaphor of "liquid modernity" until 2000, and it was foregrounded later in his book titles thanks to the suggestion of the editor at Polity Press (Wagner, 2020: 352–354). As for Elmessiri, he extensively used the liquidity metaphor in his 1999 encyclopedia on *Jews, Judaism and Zionism.*

What is certain, however, is that in a posthumous publication, Elmessiri referred to the problematic question of conceptual influence among

H. Ali (✉)
Academy of Arts, Giza, Egypt
e-mail: Haggag.ali@gmail.com

D. Jung and F. Zemmin (eds.), *Postcolonialism and Social Theory in Arabic*, The Modern Muslim World,
https://doi.org/10.1007/978-3-031-63649-3_6

academics through four cases in his intellectual journey and described Bauman's case as the most astonishing in his life. At one point, Elmessiri admitted that Bauman was among the most important sociologists, lamenting Western marginalization of Bauman's radical critical vision. Elmessiri also acknowledged that he had engaged with Bauman's writings, which broadened his intellectual horizon (Elmessiri, 2009a: 181–182), while at another point he elaborated on the deep significance Bauman's *Modernity and the Holocaust* (1989) had for him. Yet he claimed precedence over Bauman in his use of the liquidity concept in an earlier book on Zionist ideology (1981). Moreover, Elmessiri mentioned that he had already been approaching Western civilization as a progression from solidity to liquidity, and that he was very surprised when Bauman published a book entitled *Liquid Life* (2005). Then again, Elmessiri himself speaks of, "an association of ideas" between two intellectuals adopting similar stances to modernity (Elmessiri, 2009a: 252).

Indeed, it is more fruitful to move away from this controversy over precedence and focus on the common appreciation of metaphor in formulating social theory. Despite the deaths of both Bauman and Elmessiri, their metaphor is still alive, and I argue that the ongoing Arab engagement with this metaphor via Bauman and Elmessiri, as well as via my Arabic translations of Bauman's major works, is not a case of mere replication or easy reproduction but instead a critical engagement with social philosophy that explores ever-changing realities.

This chapter consists of three main sections. First, I will underline the relevance of metaphors in social theory in relation to Bauman's and Elmessiri's social philosophy. Second, I will explore the critiques directed at Bauman's and Elmessiri's uses of the metaphor of liquidity. In the final section, I will show how this metaphor is used in approaching contemporary transformations in three pertinent discourses: political Islam, Salafism, and Maqāṣid al- Sharīʿa.

6.2 The Relevance of Metaphors in Bauman's and Elmessiri's Social Theory

Social theory itself can be regarded as a metaphor that is not expected to be tested by facts (Brown, 1976: 178). Social theory is constituted by metaphors, and many analytical concepts—including system, society, social movements, and social trends—are originally metaphors, but their repeated use over time makes them so familiar that they lose their original metaphorical force and become, *à la* Paul Ricoeur, "dead metaphors." The function of metaphor is neither to reflect exact realities nor to indulge in romantic fantasies. Rather, metaphors are expected to provide new ways of understanding that can be elaborated into competing models or ideal types (Brown, 1976: 185–186). Master metaphors are often used in social theory, and they gradually give rise to debates, critiques, polemics, and attempts to modify them. With their connotative and suggestive power, metaphors never equate the subject and the predicate, stressing instead that the subject and predicate are identical and not identical at the same time (Swedberg, 2020: 244). And it is within this discursive ambivalence that social theories are developed in relation to very complex realities.

6.2.1 Root Metaphors in Social Theory

Root metaphors in social theory often compare society to a machine, a living organism, a system, a structure, a network, or even a theater. Each metaphor is meant to identify some phenomenon and make it more visible. For example, in the nineteenth century, biologists used the notion of "society" to better understand the nature of a living organism, and then, according to Richard Swedberg (2020: 252), some sociologists borrowed the notion of a living organism from the biologists to better understand the nature of human society. Metaphors, however, might be partial and biased. For example, structural-functionalists compared important social actions to biological organs, assuming that they are by nature long-lasting and inherently non-conflictual. Also, Herbert Spencer's pseudo-scientific metaphor "the survival of the fittest" played a key role in the infamous eugenics movement, and it was used to justify the brutal type of nineteenth-century capitalism that prevailed in both Europe and the USA. Spencer's formulation was also adopted by Darwin and was instrumental in promoting social Darwinism (Swedberg, 2020: 248–252).

As for twentieth-century social theorists, they used technology metaphors to underline the profound impact of technological developments in the industrial age, particularly the loss of human agency due to dominant structures, among which were Max Weber's "iron cage of capitalism," Theodor Adorno's and Max Horkheimer's "culture industry," and Charles Wright Mills' "cheerful robots" (Ossewaarde, 2019: 11).

In Bauman's social theory, the scientific and the academic are infused with the metaphoric and imaginative, and this is why his social insights, from an empiricist point of view, are critiqued for "conflating social science with literature" (Jacobsen, 2017: 16). Bauman, however, never claimed that metaphors reflect reality itself or constitute a coherent grand theory (Jacobsen, 2006: 313). Rather, Bauman's metaphors are by nature eclectic strategies that may rescue sociology itself from any residual functionalism (Pollock, 2007: 112).

Almost the same view regarding the nature and function of metaphor is embraced by Elmessiri, and this opens an interactive global horizon for social theory. Bauman theorizes the ambitions and consequences of modernity as a dynamic sequence of paradigms that starts with "solid modernity" and culminates in "liquid modernity." Elmessiri used almost the same master metaphors, but he developed them into a more complex explanatory paradigm under interchangeable designations and metaphors: "liquid non-rational materialism," (*al-māddiyya al-lā-ʿaqlāniyya al-sāʾila*), "comprehensive immanentism," (*al-kumūniyya al-shāmila*), and "comprehensive secularism" (*al-ʿalmāniyya al-shāmila*).

6.2.2 Bauman's "Solid Modernity" and Elmessiri's "Solid Rational Materialism"

"Solid modernity" is a master metaphor used by Bauman to theorize the grand narratives of capitalism and socialism under the modern nation-state. In his critique of the ideology of the notion of progress under the exclusivist practices of the modern state, Elmessiri refers to Bauman's sub-metaphors of the "gardening state," the "therapeutic/surgical state," and the "space-managing state" (Bauman, 1992: 179).

These metaphors, according to Elmessiri, map very well the nature of secularization, which subjects human beings to such secular absolutes as "the interest of the state" and "the will of the *Volk*" (Elmessiri, 2002b: 83, 142). Like Bauman, Elmessiri holds that the emphasis on the notions of *Blut, Boden und Volk* is a good example of immanent materialist monism (*al-wāḥidiyya al-māddiyya al- ḥulūliyya*), which is reminiscent of the pantheistic immanent trinity of God–Nature–Man. Elmessiri was deeply impressed by Bauman's *Modernity and the Holocaust* (1989), particularly Bauman's reference to Hannah Arendt's definition of the Jews as a non-national element in a world of existing or growing nations. Within the nation-state ideology, members of nations without a state are perceived and treated as strangers, vagabonds, pariahs, sub-men, and middlemen.

In Elmessiri's terminology, they are "functional groups" to be utilized, excluded, transferred, or even exterminated (Elmessiri, 2002b: 83, 142).

The metaphor of "functional group" (*al-jamāʿa al-waẓīfiyya*) in the stage of liquid modernity goes beyond the context of the so-called "Jewish problem/question" in Europe. It covers a wide range of strangers who are either imported from outside society or recruited from within its ranks and who are generally defined in terms of a definite function rather than their complex humanity. Functional groups are not a unique product of modernity, since they have existed throughout history, but it is modernity that makes their experience a universal human condition, reducing them to their function (Elmessiri, 2002c: 41–51).

The phenomenon of functional groups, according to Elmessiri, is not confined to the West, and it expresses a global human condition that needs also to be explored in Arab countries. For example, foreigners who work in the oil-rich Gulf countries are referred to as "contract employees" within the guarantorship system (*Kafāla*), which underlines the privilege of nationals and their superiority to foreigners. Contract employees usually live in their own ghetto, whether it consists of barracks for laborers or air-conditioned flats for professionals (Elmessiri, 2005: 588–590). In the 1980s, Elmessiri resided for a number of years in Saudi Arabia, working as a professor of comparative literature, and he noted the social and psychological barriers that separated foreign workers and nationals. Once these "contract holders" have carried out their functions, they are replaced by nationals. They are asked to leave the host country once the contract term ends, or at very short notice, or without any notice at all (Elmessiri, 2005: 588–590). It is interesting to note that when Egyptian scholar Hany Abdel Fattah discusses the dark aspects of *Kafāla* in Mohamed El-Bisatie's fictional novel *Drumbeat*, he does not draw on Elmessiri's analysis of functional groups but on Bauman's *Liquid Modernity* (Abdel Fattah, 2019: 29).

6.2.3 Bauman's "Liquid Modernity" and Elmessiri's "Liquid Non-rational Materialism"

"Liquid modernity" is a master metaphor used by Bauman to theorize the current stage of global sociocultural transformations. It underlines a time of endemic uncertainty, freedom of maneuver, openness to choices, and the privatization of life struggles (Bauman, 2001: 126–127). Progress is no longer a metaphor of "sweet dreams and expectations," "radical optimism," and "promise of universally shared and lasting happiness," but a terrible nightmare and a sinister real "game of musical chairs" in which a second's inattention results in irreversible defeat and exclusion (Bauman, 2005: 68). In every social game, human beings become players with few deep relations and many superficial ones (Bauman, 2001: 61–69). They avoid creating lasting social structures and indulge in "free-floating eroticism" (Bauman, 1998: 21). All people are plotted on a continuum stretched between the poles of the "perfect tourist" and the "vagabond beyond remedy" (Bauman, 1997: 93). Vagabonds include refugees, asylum-seekers, the poor, the socially excluded, and the underclass. Fundamentalism becomes an attractive option for those people who are impoverished and deprived of human dignity in the world of instantaneous consumption and instantaneous gratification. It promises an attractive shelter, endowing both life and death with meaning and purpose as opposed to the inequalities and injustices in the global space (Bauman, 2004: 86).

Using very similar terminology, Elmessiri describes the current stage of secular modernity as "liquid non-rational materialism" (*al-māddiyya al-lā-ʿaqlāniyya al-sāʾila*). The underlying philosophy of liquefaction declares the death of humankind in favor of such nonhuman categories as the market and power or in favor of such one-dimensional categories as the body, sex, and pleasure (Elmessiri, 2003: 15). The process of liquefaction is explained by other sub-metaphors, including "first class air travel." The airplane is compared to a womb that the traveler enters and in which he then sits down on a chair to be treated like a spoiled child by the flight attendants. This state of happiness can also be traced in almost all commercials for luxury products and commodities that sexy celebrities promote. Elmessiri even argues that the deep structure of any commercial is to show a problem emerging and then claim the best solution to it. There is always a happy ending, a total control, and a return to a world without problems (Elmessiri, 2005: 382).

Arabs and Muslims are no exception to the dominance of consumerism and the entertainment industry. They are bombarded with ads and video clips that give primacy to the body and sex (Elmessiri, 2009a: 172). This "liquid non-rational materialism" is related to the philosophy of postmodernity, and it is explained in terms of the dominance of an "embryonic tendency" (*nazʿa janīniyya*). The latter is very close to Bauman's "return to the womb" metaphor in *Retrotopia* (2017), and it suggests a withdrawal from complex reality, a dissolution of the self, and a reduction of the whole universe into one single materialist principle, without genuine possibilities of free choice and the transcendence of nature or matter. This tendency reveals itself in the semantic field of womb, body, mother's breast, territory, and sexual organs (Elmessiri, 2002a: 47).

It is in this sense that the world "resembles a tremendous artificial womb that mashes the self in a delicious and pleasurable manner" (Elmessiri, 2002a: 57). Time vanishes, boundaries collapse, the family is dissolved, and people are pushed to live in "the great cosmic womb without boundaries or constraints," reducing humans to pure bodies dissolved in the natural whole (Elmessiri, 2002a: 60).

Elmessiri uses these metaphors to address the optimistic claims of postmodernity, the end of history, and the New World Order, advocated not only by Francis Fukuyama in the West but also by Shimon Peres in the Middle East. The advocation of postmodern pluralism, in Elmessiri's view, is not a genuine invitation to openness and tolerance, but the celebration of an era of comprehensive liquefaction and the dissolution of all dualities: subject/object, truth/falsity, good/evil, justice/injustice, and friend/enemy. Within the notion of the "New World Order," economic factors are given primacy over cultural ones, and thus the issues of the Middle East are turned into purely economic issues. Prosperity is expected to be achieved by the best utilization of Saudi oil, Turkish water, the Egyptian market, and Israeli know-how (Elmessiri, 2002b: 222). The Arab world is thus reduced to "the region," and this term refers to a geographical area without history, memory, identity, or autonomous interests. The very notion of the Middle East Market emerges from this materialist philosophy as an attempt to impose the image of *homo economicus* in place of the image of the Arab Muslim (Elmessiri, 2002b: 226). The first enemy of the New World Order, according to Elmessiri, is not Arab nationalism but everyone who stands against global consumerism (Elmessiri, 2002b: 228) This new liquid stage entails a transformation from the Western imperial strategy of oppression to the consumerist strategy of seduction. It entails the domestication of both Arab intellectuals and political elites so that they put aside identity issues and advocate a more realist and pragmatic stance (Elmessiri, 2002b: 89).

6.3 Critiquing Bauman's and Elmessiri's Uses of Metaphor

Bauman's metaphor of "liquid modernity" and Elmessiri's metaphor of "liquid non-rational materialism" capture significant structural transformations from the industrial era of factories into the era of service economy and digitalization. However, they face three major critiques.

6.3.1 Hiding the Solid Systems of Colonization and Brutalization

In my doctoral dissertation on Bauman and Elmessiri, which was later developed and published in 2013, I criticized major aspects of their social theories, especially their pessimist tendency in the tradition of Max Weber's iron cage of capitalism and Herbert Marcuse's one-dimensional man (Ali, 2008, 2013). Explicating my own involvement in the debate, I wish to focus here on three critical questions that I posed to Bauman in a private conversation. His kind response to my first question on metaphor as a method informed the above analysis. For the other two questions, he recommended that I read two of his books: *Globalization* (1998) and *Identity* (2004). Both critical points do, however, still apply.

My second question was about the gardener metaphor that prevails in most of Bauman's writings on solid European modernity, although it was not used in relation to the attempts of European imperialism to turn the rest of the world into useful substance/matter that can help Europe establish its modern garden or earthly paradise. My third and most fundamental point concerns the sub-metaphor of "hunters" Bauman used within the master metaphor of liquid modernity to underline opportunism, individualization, and deregulation rather than solid grand narratives of collective progress of humankind:

> You have used the hunter metaphor in connection with liquid modernity to place a great emphasis on the fragmentation of identity in what you refer to as the modern liquid era. Don't you think that this metaphor can be used in connection with solid modernity and the European attempts to perform hunting practices in the rest of the world to achieve its utopian dreams? (Ali, 2008, 2013: 153).

Bauman's anti-colonial and anti-imperialist stance is undoubtable, yet his writings deal with colonialism and imperialism *en passant*, as if their legacy of violence were something that belonged to the past and did not hide itself in hybrid forms, both solid and liquid. Bauman relates the colonial legacy of solid modernity to the conquest of territory and capitalist exploitation of labor, claiming that the present problem of capitalism "is shifting in its current planetary stage from exploitation to exclusion" (Bauman, 2004: 41). Only recently, professor of sociology Marinus Ossewaarde observed a similar point. According to Ossewaarde, Bauman's metaphor of "liquid modernity" hides the reliance of digital technologies on energies that are mostly produced in industrial ways. It is argued that such technology firms as Apple, Amazon, and Google use vast amounts of natural resources and electricity that are produced through industrial extractivism (Ossewaarde, 2019: 12). This phenomenon relies on solid, concrete machinery whose brutalization is disassociated from digital transformation. The problem is that such metaphors as "data is the new oil," "data is the new gold," and "data mining," present data as a natural resource, thus hiding the brutal violence that comes with extractivism. The presentation of data as a natural resource that is ready to be industrially exploited has made data and data analytics into the business of tech oligarchs like Google and Facebook, with misinformation, mischaracterization, and stereotyping typically being a profitable business (Ossewaarde, 2019: 13).

6.3.2 *Reducing Religion to a Form of Fundamentalism*

Bauman's social theory of liquid modernity is also critiqued by Nilufar Allayarova, a scholar of Muslim consumption practices who is originally from Uzbekistan and currently residing in New Zealand. According to her, Bauman's metaphor of liquid modernity wields a powerful explanatory power among theorists of consumerism, yet it ignores the continuing significance of social structure. In particular, Bauman's analysis of liquid modernity does not pay much attention to religion, seeing it only through the prism of fundamentalism and defining fundamentalists as "flawed consumers." It seems to Allayarova that Bauman is not aware that there is almost no tension between Muslim religiosity and the market as long as consumption choices and services are considered *ḥalāl* (Allayarova et al., 2023). As for the consumption of non-essential goods, the position of most Islamic scholars is ambivalent, since Islam neither condemns nor prohibits the consumption of luxuries. This means that Islamic materialism in the sense of moderate consumption is a matter of fact, although

Muslims are often reminded of the superiority of developing and maintaining an ascetic consciousness (*zuhd*). It is precisely for this reason that market relationships and consumption practices in a Muslim context entail both fluidity and solidity. They may enhance such forms of solidity as spiritual sincerity, faithful submission, and existential gratefulness, but other consumerist practices may lead to a drift toward disbalance and excessive materialism (Allayarova et al., 2023).

A similar critique against Bauman is raised in a Catholic context by sociologist of religion Kees de Groot, author of *Liquidation of the Church* (2018). According to de Groot, religion has to do with such everyday life activities as communicating with people, learning, teaching, and making love. However, Bauman, from his agnostic position, fails to appreciate the relevance of religion throughout history (Groot, 2008: 278). Bauman is equally negative about the possibilities of all forms of genuine communities Only two options are available to individuals in Bauman's social theory of liquid modernity: (1) fundamentalism as a liberating option from the agony of choice, and (2) aesthetic gatherings in theater plays, exhibitions, and concerts. These momentary gatherings are described metaphorically in Bauman's theory as "cloakroom communities" and "carnival communities." These metaphors underline the fact that these communities are not genuine communities, but symptoms and sometimes factors of the social disorder of liquid modernity. Bauman, however, is aware that the "community of individuals" is a concept that belongs to the semantic field of hope. It is a metaphor, a critical category, a dystopia with hope for solidarity, and a utopian ideal rather than an empirical reality (Groot, 2008: 278–281). But it is always a hope threatened by the rise of fundamentalism as an expression of the "return to the womb" proclivity (Bauman, 2017: 166–167).

As for Elmessiri's position on religion, he partially expresses similar views, inasmuch as he, too, stresses that the real enemy is neither Christianity nor Judaism, but liquid consumerism, Western hegemony, and colonization (Elmessiri, 2009b: 96). However, for Elmessiri, Islamic discourse is not homogeneous, and it has three different levels: populist, political, and cultural. Populist Islam is a haven for the masses that find their way of life threatened by global powers and attacked by TV commercials that sell them impossible dreams. To face the liquefaction process, the Muslim masses take refuge in Islamic rituals and the extended family. In this case, populist Islam manifests itself in either charity work or terrorism. As for political Islam, it represents Islamic movements that aspire to carry out their programs via legitimate political channels. Giving these Islamic movements the chance to express themselves is the best means to stop terrorism, which is always fueled by political, social, and economic reasons rather than purely religious motives (Elmessiri, 2009b: 53–54).

Regarding cultural Islam, which Elmessiri associates himself with, it gives attention to architecture, history, philosophy, law, and arts, reflecting on such global issues as the environment, consumption, and progress (Elmessiri, 2009b: 53–55). This Islamic cultural critique of global modernity is optimistic in spirit, unlike Western cultural critique, which is known for its pessimism and nihilism (Elmessiri, 2009b: 60). However, Elmessiri's claim about the uniqueness of Islamic critical discourse is itself based on Western self-scrutiny discourse, including Bauman's critical sociology (Ali, 2018: 568–576).

6.3.3 *Focusing on Negative Globalization*

For many years, I thought that I was the first Egyptian scholar to notice the significance of making a comparison between Bauman and Elmessiri. However, I recently realized that the late Egyptian sociologist Mona Abaza preceded me, raising two serious questions regarding the relevance of global entanglement of social theory: "How much is [sic] Bauman's observations appropriate for understanding the changes taking place in the Third World? Could unexpected uses of spaces in the Third World by the youth and women be a new field for social investigation?" (Abaza, 2006: 82). In her endeavor to answer these questions, Abaza attempted to go beyond Bauman's pessimism about globalization. She presented the positive sides of globalization, even within the consumerist paradigm in so-called Third World countries. Egypt as a Third World country, according to Abaza, witnesses a process of "hybridity in consumerism whereby a McDonald's, a shopping mall or a consumer brand is recycled according to local tastes" (Abaza, 2006: 48). Unlike shopping malls in Europe and the USA, shopping malls in Egypt fulfill different functions, since Egypt has a shortage of public gardens. In other words, shopping malls provide spaces not only for shopping, but also for the youth and families to socialize and mix in groups (Abaza, 2006: 83–84).

In her critique of Elmessiri's metaphor of "liquid non-rational materialism," Abaza claims that Elmessiri is an example of an intellectual trend that advocates a way of Islamizing lifestyles by altering dress, food, and furniture. She saw this as a familiar reaction from traditionalists to "Westernization" within the broader Arab debate over *turath* (heritage/ tradition). Abaza also saw this call for Islamization of lifestyles as an aspect of the "folklorization" of culture, the "recycling" of authenticity, and the rediscovery of "local beauty," all of which are celebrated and adapted for the tourist industry to promote "distinction" and refined taste, thus raising the market for "local" tastes and elevating popular items to the status of high culture, or marketing them as mass culture (Abaza, 2006: 213–216).

6.4 Arabic Receptions of Bauman: Liquid Political Islam, Liquid Salafism, and Liquid Maqāṣid Discourse

6.4.1 *Translations and Receptions of Bauman in the Political Context*

Mohammed Bamyeh (this volume) speaks of the uncompromising spirit of the popular uprisings in the Arab region in 2011. This optimistic discourse of the revolution is introduced by Bamyeh as an implicit refutation of the dominance of liquid consumerism and apoliticism among the young Arab masses. The so-called dominance of consumerism was suddenly interrupted by Arab revolutions, protests, and demonstrations. Young people were not apolitical as one might have believed. Rather they embraced revolution as the solution, proving that they were revolutionary forces rather than egocentric consumers.

According to professor of Arabic and Islamic studies Luz Gómez, the Arab uprisings encouraged street politics and opened negotiations among secularists and Islamists in their struggle against authoritarianism. The openness of Islamists to the notions of the civil state and good governance ushered in a post-Islamist turn or a new form of "liquid Islamism" that necessitates "the end of the liberating Islamic utopia" and the liquefaction of "the solid nature of past ideological undertakings" (Gómez, 2018: 61). In other words, Islamism was expected to "dilute itself in a liquid modernity [and the ongoing processes of globalization] as it had in the Enlightenment, Liberalism or Socialism" (Gómez, 2018: 61).

But there were many obstacles, and the Arab uprisings did not liberate the masses from authoritarianism and exploitation. Rather, counterrevolutions dominated the scene. It was during that period of political turmoil and uncertainty (2014–2018) that I devoted myself to translating Bauman's theory of liquid modernity into Arabic. This endeavor led to the Arabic translation of ten books with introductions by Bauman himself and by Egyptian scholar Heba Raouf Ezzat: *Liquid Modernity*, *Liquid Life*, *Liquid Love*, *Liquid Fear*, *Liquid Times*, *Liquid Surveillance* (with David Lyon), *Culture in a Liquid Modern World*, *Liquid Evil* (with Leonidas Donskis), *State of Crisis* (with Carlo Bordoni), and *Of God and Man* (with Stanislaw Obirek). The translations were published between 2016 and 2018 by the Arab Network for Publishing and Research. The publisher has a number of branches in the MENA region, and its branch in Cairo was very successful until it closed in 2022 to avoid a security crackdown and harassment. A third edition of some of the Arab translations of the liquidity series, including *Liquid Love*, was published in 2019, and the entire series was also reprinted in two large volumes (Bauman, 2019).

It might be argued that Bauman's writings and their Arabic translations have encouraged a number of writers and intellectuals to engage with his theory of liquid modernity. In an article on current Arab cultural production in the humanities and the social sciences, Lebanese intellectual and professor of Islamic Studies Ridwan al-Sayyid notes that the second decade of the third millennium is witnessing the production of stimulating Arabic translations. He, however, blames Arab publishers for choosing very bleak, melancholy, and pessimistic books that appeal to Arab readers, including *Liquid Modernity*: "there is an author named Bauman, and ten of his books have been translated into Arabic! It occurs to me that Bauman resembles Colin Wilson, whose populist writings were very well received in the 1960s!" (al-Sayyid, 2020). Al-Sayyid does not dismiss the seriousness of Arab cultural production in the field of translation, but he does seem very anxious about "populist writings" and "populist receptions." His fears are obviously related to his explicit secularist stance against any Islamic cultural alternative, and his sensitivity to any critique of the ideals of the Enlightenment and the modern state. These fears show in his earlier rejection of "populist" Arab receptions of the cultural critique of Western modernity introduced by Abdelwahab Elmessiri and Edward Said (al-Sayyid, 2008), as well as his rejection of the "populist writings" of Moroccan philosopher Abdurrahman Taha, whose work will be explored in the following section (al-Sayyid, 2018).

There are now countless Arabic reviews and essays and many books, theses, and dissertations on Bauman in a number of Arab countries.

Therefore, in this section, I will be selective, dismissing descriptive studies and focusing only on the uses of the metaphor of liquid modernity in three pertinent discourses: political Islam, Salafism, and Maqāṣid discourse.

6.4.2 *Liquid Political Islam*

The metaphor of "liquid modernity" is used to approach an understanding of the nature and role of political Islam. In 2020, Egyptian scholar Ashraf Mansur, for example, made a general reference to Bauman's *Liquid Modernity*, but did not state whether he had read Bauman in English or in Arabic. I suspect the latter, since his article appeared in 2020, after the publication of more than ten of Bauman's books in Arabic. Mansur argues that political Islam is a phenomenon that takes place within the context of modernity, and therefore, it is conditioned by the liquefaction of all that enters into its realm. This is true in some aspects, especially in terms of adaptation to the requirements of the modern liberal state and economic globalization. But the problem is that Mansur compares political Islam to the chameleon's ability to change its skin color in response to environmental conditions, its fast adaptability to the surroundings, and its ability to blend in or keep a low profile. This metaphor is not innocent, and its usage might be appropriated to demonize all political Islamists, since it underlines not only the extraordinary flexibility of political Islam, but also its strategic maneuvers "to infiltrate the political sphere to achieve gains inside the political apparatus of an existing state," as well as its "increasing penetration in the institutions of civil society, the entry of its representatives into many Arab Parliaments, the multiplication of its funding resources, and thus the aggravation of its terrorist danger" (Mansur, 2020).[1]

Unlike Elmessiri, who advocated the political participation of Islamists through legitimate channels and saw this openness as the best means to stop terrorism, corruption, and oppression, Mansur dismisses this possibility, stressing instead their deception and pragmatism. The discourses of political Islamists, as Mansur argues, include a "conservative tendency" and "strong fanaticism" that play on religious emotions, imagination, and collective consciousness (Mansur, 2020). It is interesting to note that Mansur's critical piece featured on an electronic website associated with an Emirati research center based in Egypt (Daal Research and Media), which belongs to the Emirati think tank Mominoun Without Borders.

This think tank was established in 2013, and it has been instrumental in demonizing the Arab Spring and political Islam. In a recent dialogue with Moroccan scholar Hasan Ahjij, published on the website of Mominoun Without Borders, Mansur claimed that violence is a basic component of the identity of political Islam (Ahjij, 2022).

6.4.3 *Liquid Salafism*

The impact of the Arabic translations of Bauman can be traced in the articles and papers written by young Egyptian scholar Muhammad Tawfiq and young Egyptian journalist Ahmad ʿAbd al-Halim. In his short essay on "Liquid Salafism," Tawfiq argued that the transformations that Salafism has witnessed since 2011 in Egypt bring it closer to Bauman's metaphor of liquidity (Tawfiq, 2018). In his discussion of the state in the Salafist imaginary, Tawfiq argued elsewhere that Salafism witnessed a state of fragmentation, uncertainty, and perplexity after the coup d'état of 2013 in Egypt. Young Egyptian Salafists kept moving from one order of Salafism to another: traditional Salafism, activist/ revolutionary Salafism, Madkhaliyya, Jihadist Salafism, and reformist Salafism (Tawfiq, 2020: 168). The very idea of classification became difficult, and a state of loss prevailed regarding the most convenient Salafist position toward the state, the constitution, and modern political practices. This state of perplexity culminated in the theorization of "post-Salafism" and a call to abandon or broaden the discourse of the saved sect or *"al-firqa al-najīya,"* (Tawfiq, 2020: 169).

A similar stance is taken by Ahmad ʿAbd al-Halimin his reflections on the political turmoil that followed the ousting of Egyptian president Mohammed Morsi. In his paper "Liquid Islamism," ʿAbd al-Halim did not cite Bauman, Elmessiri, or any Arabic translations, but Mohammad Tawfiq himself. His major point is that there was a "season of migration" of young Salafists to "virtual Salafism" (online/cyber Salafism), which distanced itself from political issues and instead discussed the issues of faith and atheism. These "young migrants" included diverse groups: (1) those who were hopeless regarding the Muslim Brothers, (2) the "repentant" from the pragmatic Salafism of the Nur Party and its chameleon-like politics, (3) the returnees from jihadism after the fall of ISIS, and (4) traditionalists and religiously committed young people who were observant of Islamic rituals. Virtual Salafism provided online outlets and platforms beyond formal state institutions and the concentration of religious preaching sessions in Cairo and Alexandria. This virtual space was seen as the only alternative, constrained neither by geographical borders nor by censorship. It was open to all the perplexed who were looking for good models in Islamic knowledge and action. This virtual Salafism included the following platforms and outlets: (1) *silsilat al-yaqīn* (Series of Certainty), a series of lectures delivered on the formal YouTube Channel of Jordanian pharmacologist and preacher Eyad Qunaibi, now with five million followers; (2) lectures delivered by Kuwaiti preacher Muhammad al-ʿAwadi; (3) research centers like the Takween Center for Studies and Research in Saudi Arabia; (4) online curricula in religious sciences and humanities; and (5) online platforms such as Zad Academy, Masaq Academy, Barnamij al-binaʾ al-manhaji, and Sinaʿat al-Muhawir. These platforms, according to Egyptian journalist Ahmad ʿAbd al-Halim, are without political imagination, and they represent a solitary educational migration away from ideology, albeit with a sense of alienation and uniqueness that might lead to separatism (ʿAbd al-Halim, 2021).[2]

6.4.4 *Liquid Maqāṣid*

Maqāṣid al-Sharīʿa may be defined as the ultimate objectives of Islamic law. Traditionally, there are five objectives that seek to guarantee the public good of Muslim community: (1) the protection of soul/life (*nafs*), (2) the protection of wealth/property (māl), (3) the protection of faith/religion (*dīn*), (4) the protection of mind/intellect (*ʿaql*), and (5) the protection of offspring/progeny (*nasl*). However, these five domains have been submitted to various interpretations in view of global changes and pressures. This interest is embraced by many Muslim research centers, institutes, and journals to underline the extension of public good to all humankind, including International Institute of Islamic Thought in Washington, Maqāṣid Centre for Research and Studies in Morrocco, Maqāṣid Institute in Tennessee in the USA, the journal *al-Muslim al-Muʿ āṣir*, and the Arabic Bibliographical Guide to Maqāṣid al-Sharīʿa. The number of publications on Maqāṣid shows an increasing trend from 2006 to 2021, with 126 papers in the Scopus database, most of which were written in English, and only one in Arabic (Pratami et al., 2022: 234). The Arabic paper, even if the data is hardly representative, is highly pertinent, as it engages with liquid modernity and speaks metaphorically of *al-fiqh al-sāʾil* (liquid Fiqh), as we will see shortly.

Sari Hanafi (this volume) underlines the significance of Maqāṣid discourse, but in his enthusiastic attempt to bridge the gap between the religious and the empirical production of knowledge, he does not hesitate to regard most of the contemporary publications in the field of Maqāṣid as "shallow attempts" and "nothing but literature on general ethics that lacks a basic level of scientific research to identify a specific problem and present solutions that transcend wishful thinking." Most of this literature, according to Hanafi, is incapable of "understanding reality in order to present solutions built on an understanding of the Qu'ran, Sunna, and Sharīʿa." Hanafi is right in suggesting that most of this literature is a mere recycling of over-generalized attacks on positivism, but Hanafi's perception of the production of knowledge in terms of problems and solutions is itself consistent with a positivist, instrumental, and functionalist approach to social theory, with a very limited appreciation of the role of ethics in the dynamics of human praxis. This point is better addressed by both Moroccan philosopher Abdurrahman Taha and Palestinian-American scholar of Islamic law Wael Hallaq.

Hallaq makes a very brief and general reference to Bauman's *Liquid Modernity*, arguing that the "progress" and "liquidity" of modernity itself, with its ever-changing secular and colonial legacy, pose key challenges to the application of classical Maqāṣid (Hallaq, 2011: 12). These challenges manifest themselves in the following facts: (1) the ever-changing realities in positive law as opposed to the limitedness of the semantic field of Maqāṣid; (2) the centrality of the modern nation-state as the major disciplinary agency, which puts the category of the "national citizen" in the place of religious loyalty (without being in conflict with an increasingly globalizing and consumerist world); (3) the marginalization of communal bounds in the mediation of conflicts and disputes; and (4) the tremendous changes in the social conditions of women and their ever-growing presence in the public sphere of capitalist morality (Hallaq, 2011: 14–15). The nation-state and Islamic law are even seen as incompatible categories, since the punitively oriented state subdued the citizen along with society at large, whereas Islamic law mediates conflicts to mend the ruptures of the social fabric. In other words, the Sharīʿa's prescribed harsh punishments, if ever applied, are intended to deter the forces of corruption that disrupt social harmony (Hallaq, 2011: 21). From a European and colonialist perception of the world, Islamic criminal law is seen as "unduly lenient," "hermeneutic," and "ijtihādic," thus leading to a pluralism that runs counter to the modern spirit of homogenization and transcends the limitations of technocracy. Unlike the modern lawyer-judge, the *fuqahā'*, the *mujtahidūn*, and muftis were known for their interest in interdisciplinary knowledge to produce the law. In other words, the epistemic, rather than the legislative, was their highest form of authority that spoke truth to power (Hallaq, 2011: 22–25).

In an attempt to support his argument, Hallaq draws on Abdurrahman Taha's philosophy. According to Hallaq, Taha mitigates the external, regulatory, institutional, political, instrumental, or functionalist force of Uṣūl al-Fiqh, placing emphasis instead on ethicization of Maqāṣid. In other words, Taha gives primacy to the spiritual, mystic, gnostic dimension or ethical substance in Maqāṣid. This return to the ethical in Maqāṣid is not an innocent move, since it represents an explicit critique and rejection of both European rationalist secularism and political Islamism. Hallaq puts it this way:

> If Europe's hegemonic liberalism and secularism came to blot and obliterate Islamic values between 1850 and 1950, and if political Islamism appeared as a misconceived reaction to the problems of colonialism and hegemony, then Taha's philosophical project is the synthesis that comes after but rejects both the thesis (colonialism) and anthesis (political Islamism). Ultimately, his is a temporarily modern project that attempts to resuscitate and harness Islamic ethical time for what we can easily describe as a postmodern critique, an ethical philosophy par excellence. (Hallaq, 2019: 25)

Taha's philosophy, according to Hallaq, gives primacy to praxis over intellectual-theoretical knowledge and interests. In other words, the various overlapping forms of Islamic episteme (including *Kalām*, *Uṣūl al-Fiqh*, and *Maqāṣid*) are ways of living in the world; and therefore, "the traditional text is much more amendable to humanism (*ta'nīs*) than politicization" (Hallaq, 2019: 54). Politicization is related more to instrumental reason, whereas Maqāṣid is closer to enhanced reason that "acquires its most perfect form in the Sufi arena," and "cultivates in the individual the special capacity to avoid certain character faults, such as lack of humility, love of appearances, unthinking conformism, indulging in (useless) abstractions, engaging in politics [*tasyīs*], and love for domination and mastery" (Hallaq, 2019: 168). Perhaps Hallaq is implicitly criticizing the politicized reconsiderations of Maqāṣid as introduced by Tariq Ramadan and Yusuf al-Qaradawi (March, 2011: 2–7).

Like Hallaq, Egyptian Azharite scholar Muhammad al-Marakeby cited *en passant* Bauman's *Liquid Modernity* in English. The aim was to underline the liquidity metaphor in relation to two transformations that liquefy Maqāṣid discourse: the reinterpretation of the meanings of the five objectives of Sharīʿa and the addition of new objectives (al-Marakeby, 2019: 19). Protection of faith, for example, once referred to fighting non-Muslims and the defense of Muslim land, as well as the killing of the apostate (*al-murtad*). This objective, according to al-Marakeby, is reinterpreted by Tunisian politician and intellectual leader of the Ennahda Party Rachid al-Ghannouchi as allowing non-Muslims to spread their religion in the same way Muslims are allowed to spread their religion among non-Muslims, in accordance with the Maqṣad of freedom. Another example mentioned by al-Marakeby is the reinterpretation of protection of mind made by the late Islamic scholar Yusuf al-Qaradawi, who saw it not only as the traditional refrainment from the consumption of inebriants, alcoholic beverages, and intoxicants, but also as a divine call to seek knowledge. Accordingly, Qaradawi argued that Muslim female students in some European countries are religiously allowed to uncover their heads if forced to take off their ḥijāb. The same approach, according to al-Marakeby, can be seen in the reinterpretation of the protection of property/wealth, not by cutting off the hands of thieves, but by introducing economic development and success as opposed to the materialist progress that dominates the global market (al-Marakeby, 2019: 19–20).

As for the expansion of Maqāṣid, al-Marakeby shows that they now go beyond the five classical objectives and have been expanded to include freedom, equality, dignity, welfare, health, love, diversity, solidarity, world peace, economic progress, scientific research, pluralism, and sovereignty of law. With this second transformation, qualitative and quantitative changes have thus been introduced to Maqāṣid according to modern values and in response to the challenges of modernity, reshaping religion and its role in the public sphere. Maqāṣid are no longer certain and fixed, but changeable according to spatial and time transformations. It is in this sense that al-Marakeby sees Maqāṣid as now moving from universalism to "relativism," "modern liquidity," and "liberalisation of Fiqh" (al-Marakeby, 2019: 20–21).

Maqāṣid studies are thus globally entangled with social theory and its traveling metaphors. It is a kind of authentication of the global discourse from within the local tradition itself in an attempt to confront the challenges and pressures of global liberalization. This liberalization of Fiqh might easily slip into a comprehensive state of liquidity leading to the adoption of ever-changing local rules that adapt themselves to rules of globalization and liberalization. In Bauman's writings, liberalization, as I explained elsewhere in a paper on identity under my Arabic pen name Hajjaj Abu Jabr, is always associated with three major metaphors in liquid times: players as pleasure seekers, tourists as the ultimate incarnation of consumerism, and vagabonds as the new poor, the flawed consumers, and the underclass (Abu Jabr, 2022).

6.5 Conclusion

The global entanglement of social theory is manifested in the embrace of similar stances and approaches to modernity, regardless of geographical and cultural differences. Bauman's intellectual journey was influenced by his life experiences in Poland, his two-year stay in Israel, and his lifelong exile in Britain, as much as Elmessiri's journey was influenced by his life in his native Egypt, his period of education in the USA, and his time working as a university professor in Saudi Arabia. Also, the intellectual formation, encounter, and convergence of the two scholars express a global entanglement due to their common Marxist background, with its emphasis on social justice and critique of capitalist exploitation.

The metaphor of liquid modernity has given rise to scholarly critiques, reviews, and translations, all of which underline a global entanglement of social theory. Late Egyptian sociologist Mona Abaza and I wrote monographs in English to underline this entanglement, critiquing Bauman and Elmessiri for focusing on negative globalization. In addition, Marinus Ossewaarde from the Netherlands and I critiqued Bauman's metaphor of liquid modernity for hiding the solid systems of brutalization and neocolonial violence. Nilufar Allayarova from Uzbekistan and Kees de Groot from the Netherlands critiqued Bauman's liquidity metaphor for ignoring the continuing significance of social structure and for focusing on religion in the form of fundamentalism.

Meanwhile, Egyptian scholar Ashraf Mansour made a general reference to Bauman's liquid modernity to polemically warn against the pragmatism and terrorism of political Islamism. As for Egyptian scholar Mohamad Tawfik and Egyptian journalist Ahmad ʿAbd al-Halim, they made use of the popularity achieved by the Arab translations of Bauman in their analysis of liquid Salafism and liquid Islamism, respectively. Palestinian-American scholar Wael Hallaq's brief reference to Bauman's *Liquid Modernity* underlined key challenges to the application of classical Maqāṣid. The global entanglement of social theory is enhanced by Hallaq's extensive exploration of the question of ethics in the philosophy of Moroccan intellectual Abdurrahman Taha. Again, with a very general citation of Bauman's *Liquid Modernity*, Azharite scholar al-Muhammad al-Marakeby explored the promise and risk of the liberalization of Maqāṣid away from the solid classical understanding of them over centuries.

These engagements fuel two major conclusions. First, social theory in contemporary times has a global horizon that pushes intellectuals to think globally and relate their traditions to global challenges. Second, the purpose of social theory is no longer to set a grand theory about society but to comment on an ever-changing reality on both the local and global levels. None of the above scholars has proposed a grand theory, but they have used the liquidity metaphor to express a point of view regarding a specific point in the discourse under study. In this regard, I am fully convinced of Bauman's suggestion that liquid modernity *avant la lettre* uncovers an abandonment of the legislative role of social theory (providing foundations, general principles, rules, laws, and overarching theories) in favor of a critical and interpretive role that gives primacy to the ethical core of both theory and praxis (Bauman, 1987).

Notes

1. Mansur, Ashraf (2020): Kayfa takayyafa al-Islām al-Sīyāsī maʿa siyūlat al-Ḥadātha [How did Political Islam adapt with the Liquidity of Modernity? [*Ḥafriyyāt*, October 29].
   https://hafryat.com/ar/blog (accessed on November 6, 2023).
2. ʿAbd al-Halim, Ahmad (2021): al-Islāmiyya al-Sāʾila [Liquid Islamism: Season of Migration to Contemporary Salafism], *Al-Safīr al-ʿarabī*, February 24. https://assafirarabi.com/ar/36196/2021/02/24 (accessed on November 6, 2023).

References

Abaza, M. (2006). *Changing Consumer Cultures of Modern Egypt: Cairo's Urban Reshaping*. Brill.

ʿAbd al-Halim, A. (2021, February 24). al-Islamiyya al-Sāʾila [Liquid Islamism: Season of Migration to Contemporary Salafism]. *Al-Safīr al-ʿarabī*. https://assafirarabi.com/ar/36196/2021/02/24 (accessed on November 6, 2023).

Abdel Fattah, H. (2019). Liquid Modernity at the Time of Interregnum: A Critical Reading of Moḥamed El-Bisāṭie's Drumbeat. *Philology, 36*(72), 27–52.

Abu Jabr, H. (2022). Hal min makān li-l-huwiyya fī ʿālam muʿawlam? [Is There a Place for Identity in a Globalized World?]. *Tabyyun for Philosophical Studies and Critical Theories, 42*, 153–173.

Ahjij, H. (2022, July 29). Ḥiwār maʿa al akādīmī Ashraf Mansur [A Dialogue with the Academic Ashraf Mansur]. *Mominoun Without Borders*. https://www.mominoun.com/articles (accessed on November 6, 2023).

Ali, H. (2008). *Cognitive Mapping of Modernity and Post-Modernity: A Comparative Approach to Zygmunt Bauman and Abdelwahab Elmessiri*. PhD dissertation, Cairo University.

Ali, H. (2013). *Mapping the Secular Mind: Modernity's Search for a Godless Utopia*. IIIT.

Ali, H. (2018). Abdelwahab Elmessiri's Islamic Humanism. *International Sociology Reviews, 33*(5), 568–576.

Allayarova, N., et al. (2023, March 20). Liquid Consumption and Islam: The Continual Drift Adjustment (CDA) Framework. *Journal of Islamic Marketing*, ahead of print.

al-Marakeby, M. (2019). al-Ḥadāṯha wa-taḥawwūlāt al-khiṭāb al- maqāṣidī: Naḥwa fiqh saʾil [Modernity and the Transformations of Maqāṣid Discourse: Towards a Liquid Fiqh?].

al-Sayyid, R. (2008, July 8). Abdelwahab Elmessiri wa-laʿnat al-gharb (Abdelwahab Elmessiri and the Curse of the West), *Voltairenet*. https://www.voltairenet.org/article157654.html (accessed on September 13, 2023).

al-Sayyid, R. (2018, November 29). Fiṣāmāt al-waqiʿ wa-l waʿī lada al-*muṯhaqafī*n al-ʿarab [Schizophrenia of Reality and Consciousness with Arab Intellectuals], *al-Sharq al-Awsat*. https://aawsat.com/home/article (accessed on November 6, 2023).

al-Sayyid, R. (2020, May 14). al-Nitāj al-ṯhaqāfī al-ʿarabī [Arab Cultural Production], *al-Sharq al-Awsat*. https://aawsat.com/home/article/2284461 (accessed on November 6, 2023).

Bauman, Z. (1987). *Legislators and Interpreters: On Modernity, Post-Modernity and the Intellectuals*. Polity Press.

Bauman, Z. (1989). *Modernity and the Holocaust*. Polity Press.

Bauman, Z. (1992). *Intimations of Postmodernity*. Routledge.

Bauman, Z. (1998). On Postmodern Uses of Sex. *Theory, Culture & Society, 15*(3–4), 19–33.
Bauman, Z. (1997). *Postmodernity and its Discontents.* New York University Press.
Bauman, Z. (2001). Identity in the Globalising World. *Social Anthropology, 9*(2), 126–127.
Bauman, Z. (2004). *Identity: Conversations with Benedetto Vecchi.* Polity Press.
Bauman, Z. (2005). *Liquid Life.* Polity.
Bauman, Z. (2017). *Retrotopia.* Polity.
Bauman, Z. (2019). Silsilat al-Siyula (Liquidity Series), eight books in two volumes (H. Abu Jabr, trans.). Arab Network for Publishing and Research.
Brown, R. (1976). Social Theory As a Metaphor. *Theory and Society, 3*(2), 169–197.
Elmessiri, A. (1999). *Al-Yahūd wa-l-Yahūdiyya wa-l-Suhyuniyya* [Jews, Judaism and Zionism], eight volumes. Dār al-Shurūq.
Elmessiri, A. (2001). *Al-Suhyuniyya, al-naziyya wa-nihāyat al-tārīkh* [Zionism, Nazism and the End of History] (3rd ed.). Dār al-Shurūq.
Elmessiri, A. (2002a). *Al-lugha wa-l-majāz: Bayna al-tawḥīd wa-waḥdat al-wujūd* [Language and Metaphor: Between Monotheism and Pantheism]. Dār al-Shurūq.
Elmessiri, A. (2002b). *Al-ʿAlmāniyya al-juzʾiyya wa-l-ʿalmāniyya al-shāmila.* Dār al-Shurūq.
Elmessiri, A. (2002c). *Al-Jamāʿat al-waẓīfiyya al-yahūdiyya* [Jewish Functional Groups]. Dār al-Shurūq.
Elmessiri, A. (2003). *al-Ḥadāṯha wa-mā baʿda al-Ḥadāṯha* [Modernity and Postmodernity]. Dār al-Fikr.
Elmessiri, A. (2005). *Riḥlatī al-fikriyya* [My Intellectual Journey]. Dār al-Shurūq.
Elmessiri, A. (2009a). *al-Thaqāfa wa-l-manhaj* [Culture and Method]. In S. Herafi (Ed.), *Ḥiwārāt.* Dār al-Fikr.
Elmessiri, A. (2009b). *al-Huwiyya wa-l-Ḥarakiyya al-Islāmiyya* [Identity and Islamic Mobility]. In S. Herafi (Ed.), *Ḥiwārāt.* Dār al-Fikr.
Gómez, L. (2018). Post-Islamism: Lessons from Arab Revolutions, In M. A. Rumman (Ed.), *Post-Islamism: A New Phase or Ideological Delusions?* (W. Joseph Ward, Trans., pp. 57–68). Friedrich Erbert-Stiftung.
de Groot, K. (2008). Three Types of Liquid Religion. *Implicit Religion, 11*(3), 277–296.
Hallaq, W. (2011). Maqasid and the Challenges of Modernity, *Al-Jāmiʿah: Journal of Islamic Studies, 49*(1), 1–31.
Hallaq, W. (2019). *Reforming Modernity: Ethics and the New Human in the Philosophy of Abdurrahman Taha.* Columbia University Press.

Jacobsen, M. (2017). Introduction. In M. Jacobsen (Ed.), *Beyond Bauman*. Routledge.
Jacobsen, M., & Marshman, S. (2006). Metaphorically Speaking: Metaphors as a Methodological and Moral Signifier of the Sociology of Zygmunt Bauman. *Polish Sociological Review, 3*(155), 307–324.
Mansur, A. (2020, October 29). Kayfa takayyafa al-Islām al-sīyāsī maʿa siyūlat al-ḥadātha [How Did Political Islam Adapt with the Liquidity of Modernity?] Ḥafriyyāt. https://hafryat.com/ar/blog (accessed on November 6, 2023).
March, A. (2011). Theocrats Living under Secular Law: An External Engagement with Islamic Legal Theory. *Journal of Political Philosophy, 19*(1), 28–51.
Ossewaarde, M. (2019). Digital Transformation and the Renewal of Social Theory: Unpacking the New Fraudulent Myths and Misplaced Metaphors. *Technological Forecasting and Social Change, 146*(c), 24–30.
Pollock, G. (2007). Liquid Modernity and Cultural Analysis: An Introduction to a Transdisciplinary Encounter. *Theory, Culture & Society, 24*(1), 111–116.
Pratami, C., et al. (2022). A Decade of Maqasid Shariah Research: A Bibliometric Analysis. *Management and Accounting Review, 21*(2), 211–238.
Swedberg, R. (2020). Using Metaphors in Sociology: Pitfalls and Potentials. *The American Sociologist, 51*(2), 240–257.
Tawfiq, M. (2018, August 29). *al-Salafiyya al-sāʾila* [Liquid Salafism], *Iḍāʾāt*. https://www.ida2at.com/transformations-of-salafism-in-egypt/ (accessed on September 13, 2023).
Tawfiq, M. (2020). al-Dawla fī al-mikhyāl al-salafī al-muʿāṣir [The State in Contemporary Salafist Political Imaginary]. In R. al-Mesibly (Ed.), *al-Salafiyya: taḥawwulātuhā wa-mustaqbaluhā* [Salafism: Its Transformations and Future] (pp. 145–170). Forum of Arab and International Relations.
Wagner, I. (2020). *Bauman: A Biography*. Polity Press.

CHAPTER 7

Crisis and Creativity: Tradition and Revolution in Arab Social Theory

Mohammed A. Bamyeh

7.1 Introduction

On the day following the Arab defeat in 1967, a professor of engineering at Damascus University[1] asked an imam about the reason for the defeat. The imam's response was that it was God's punishment for a nation that allowed its women to go out unveiled. Finding the explanation unpersuasive, the professor went to a communist friend and posed the same question. The communist friend replied that the defeat happened because our people still adhered to antiquated customs, such as fasting during Ramadan. Finding both answers, delivered by two opposing ideological camps, equally unfulfilling, he realized that he needed to find the answer himself. A self-consciously modernizing intellectual with no prior training in Islamic studies, he then devoted the rest of his life to *turath* (heritage) studies. Within two decades, he began to publish a number of bestselling

M. A. Bamyeh (✉)
University of Pittsburgh, Pittsburgh, PA, USA
e-mail: Mab205@pitt.edu

D. Jung and F. Zemmin (eds.), *Postcolonialism and Social Theory in Arabic*, The Modern Muslim World,
https://doi.org/10.1007/978-3-031-63649-3_7

books on Islamic reason, religion and civil liberties, the state, and the art of interpreting revelation.

The point here concerns not the validity of his or any other approach to heritage. Rather, it concerns the sociology of knowledge: What social crises drive intellectual activity, and what accounts for the social impact of this activity? This article explores how social theory emerges out of a feeling of "crisis," meaning an event that seems to require answers not convincingly provided by available knowledge. The introductory remarks below outline what I understand by "social theory"—a theme revisited in the conclusion. This is followed by showing how the most fruitful sites of social theory in contemporary Arab thought have resided in two specific genres—critical heritage studies and the historical novel. The use of these genres as venues for generating theoretical knowledge seems related to Arab intellectuals' perceptions that the crisis they were addressing emerged out of deep cultural and historical roots.

In studies of intellectuals, one proposition that is often encountered (e.g. Shils, 1972) is that intellectual activity can be understood as an outcome of some alienation, generally experienced as dissatisfaction with ready explanations. This dissatisfaction results in a quest for deeper causes for the appearance of things. The energy expended on the intellectual quest is then proportional to the profundity of the need to explain the otherwise unexplainable.

What should one expect from this type of intellectual effort? One would expect a "social theory" to emerge at the end. Which is another way of saying that one has finally arrived at an original explanation: an account that has not been available before, targeting the deep roots of the problem, and disregarding its immediate, technical causes. Yet, at the end this account may not actually explain the original problem. The deeper an intellectual digs, the more she may find herself enmeshed in a different problem that had not been recognized as such before.

Neither outcome is unusual in the quest for social theories, understood as the pursuit of explanations for a newly encountered reality for which available knowledge is inadequate. "Theory," after all, is a name we give to a method of organizing scattered information into a coherent pattern. The fact that we are talking about a theory that is "social" means that it is constrained by human reflexivity, by the time and space horizons of a humanity investigating itself. In other words, social theory cannot be simply construed as an act of singular authorship, although that is often the form by which it is delivered. Rather, social theory gains resonance when it is produced in an environment that is receptive to it, an environment that demands original "explanations." It is to be expected that in such an environment, social theory would be delivered in the form of a socially distributed effort to rearrange observations so that a broadly felt, large problem is shown to benefit from new perspectives that go beyond already available ways of seeing. In this sense, any single social theory is always liable to be contested by another social theory, not necessarily because it is "falsifiable" à la experimental natural sciences, but because the social world always contains alternative time and space horizons that generate alternative accounts. In other words, a basic property of social theory—unlike theories of the natural sciences—is that it is a communicative enterprise in a public sphere, rather than a "falsifiable" proposition.

7.2 Two Projects on the Way from Tradition to Revolution

It is often the case that the building of social theories begins from what some intellectuals regard to be social traditions, even when these intellectuals regard such traditions with skepticism or outright rejection. In this case, the theoretical effort tends to be geared toward exploring pathways to social change that is presumed to be shackled by traditional resistance to the new. It is often the case that the more resistant to social change social traditions are assumed to be, the more likely it is that the intellectuals will regard revolutions, rather than incremental progress, to be the preferred way forward.

In 2011 and again in 2019, most of the Arab region witnessed large popular uprisings. One of the questions that these events raised concerned whether the works of Arab intellectuals prior to the revolts reveal a radical critique that parallels the uncompromising spirit of the uprisings. The question here does not concern whether or how intellectuals influence social movements. Rather, it is whether intellectuals showcase a radical critique of the present that parallels the radical spirit that had apparently been building up in the populace of various Arab countries during the years preceding 2011.

We know that after 1967 many Arab intellectuals embarked on quests to determine the large, comprehensive, historical, and cultural roots of a crisis for which there appeared to be no parallel in contemporary history, and which appeared to defy ordinary comprehension (Kassab, 2009: 48–115). Several projects emerged and began to appear in the late 1960s written by intellectuals who shared a foundational critical attitude toward the Arab sociopolitical order, while also becoming highly visible in Arab public spheres. Generally, they made use of two genres: critical heritage studies and the historical novel. The critical heritage studies were undertaken by modern intellectuals who generally did not regard themselves as religious or conservative, including Muhammad 'Abid al-Jabiri (1935–2010), Hasan Hanafi (1935–2021), Tayyeb Tizini (1934–2019), George Tarabishi (1939–2016), the poet Adonis (b. 1930), Husayn Muruwwah (1910–1987), Abdallah Laroui (b. 1933), and Hadi Alwai (1932–1998), among others. They all had a totalistic orientation toward heritage, meaning that it could only be understood in its totality, rather than by focusing on a subset of its teachings or a specific historical period. They often understood "heritage" as a historical structure that had produced the modern Arab mind, which in turn produced a profound crisis that became most visible in 1967. Indeed, a cursory look at the contributions of Arab intellectuals between 1967 and 2011 shows them to be highly attuned to the concept of "crisis" (Bamyeh, 2015; Hammoudi, 2017), perhaps in a way that is not substantially different from intellectuals elsewhere in the Global South.

The other genre that witnessed a great efflorescence after 1967 was the historical novel, which also shared similar propositions to those of the critical heritage studies: totalistic in character, oriented to capturing essential elements of a national culture, rich in detail, and with portrayals more attuned to capturing a panorama of social psychology and sketching out logics of power than to helping narrative flow. In that sense they must be distinguished from earlier historical novels, such as Naguib Mahfouz's *Kifah Ṭiba* or Ahmad al-Shaykh's *Al-Nas fi Kafr ʿAskar*, which addressed themselves to a specific location or delimited historical period, and in ways that made claim to the significance of what was portrayed but not to its generalizability. By contrast, the clear objective of post-1967 historical novels, just as in the critical heritage studies, was to deliver a verdict on the present as a whole—not the present as simply a political system, but also as malignant social psychology and arrested development. The most notable works in this genre include the multivolume reconstructions of the sociopolitical histories of Saudi Arabia, Iraq, and Jordan by Abdulrahman Munif (1933–2004). Similar in spirit is the five-volume novelistic treatment of modern Libyan social history *al-Khusuf* by Ibrahim al-Koni

(b. 1948). Noteworthy in this genre as well is the three-volume novel on modern Egyptian sociopolitical history *Thulathiyyat al-Amali* by Khairy Shalabi (1938–2011). The same can be said of other works, such as the Palestinian social history as rendered in *Gate to the Sun* (*Bab al-Shams*) by Elias Khoury (b. 1948), which he had originally intended as a sociological collection of life narratives by refugee camp residents, or some of earlier works by Gamal Ghitani (b. 1945), notably *Zayni Barakat*.

One possible reason for the popularity of the historical novel as a genre of critique is the role of literature and the creative arts in general as venues for expressing critique or dissent, especially in illiberal situations. This is evident in the fact that parallel to this literary activity we also witness a few film projects that had an equally ambitious documentary relation to national history, most importantly being Mohamed Malas's (b. 1945) trilogy of modern Syria, which he began with *Night*, as well as various critical theater projects during the same period, especially in Egypt and Syria. It is possible that we are speaking here not of a specifically Arab phenomenon but of a general postcolonial cultural movement, since one can identify similar projects elsewhere in the Global South, such as Bibhutibhushan Bandopadhyay's novel *Aparajito* (the basis of Satyajit Rai's equally classic, three-part film *The Story of Apu*), or Semih Kaplanoğlu's *Yusuf* trilogy. In all such works, national stories are retold through experiences of socially marginal characters rather than great heroes, testifying perhaps to democratizing aspirations of a postcolonial intelligentsia.

This suggests a point to which I will return later: while 1967 was an enormous catalyst for Arab intellectuals, these intellectuals also lived in a general global climate typified by the global cultural revolutions of the 1960s and the more general anti-colonial environment in the Global South. In addition, while 1967 may have served as a catalyst for new directions of creativity, it was preceded by a significant *turath* movement, which had been more religious in character and whose notable figures just prior to the critical heritage school included Taher ben Ashour and Malek Bennabi. The distinct feature of the post-1967 critical *turath* school was its largely secular mode of posing the question of heritage and its relation to the present, while also being in communication with a global anti-colonial *Zeitgeist*.

The Arab cultural scene between 1967 and 2011 was therefore characterized by a twin reality: on the one hand, it was a substantially dark age (especially from 1973), an era characterized by an overwhelming popular desire for radical change, coupled with a frozen political reality designed to resist any change. On the other hand, that era housed a silent cultural revolution in which the entire history and cultural meaning of the region was being reworked, long before the uprisings of 2011. Dark ages (for example, Europe between 1815 and 1848 or the Arab region between 1973 and 2011) tend to be slowly undermined in the less policed cultural sphere rather than the more heavily fortified political structure. Understood this way, a dark age ends not with utopia, and not even with a better political system, but—from 2011 in this case or 1848 in Europe—with the spread of a feeling of capacity and dynamism in the culture. A new historical memory of revolution begins to take form, out of which a different kind of radical critique is formulated, and new networks establish themselves in civil society.

7.2.1 The Critical Heritage Studies

The critical heritage studies, which took shape during the dark age, generally adopted an anti-clerical attitude, even when they did not contest the principle of divine revelation. Rather, they contested the capacity of the traditional clergy to become truly modern, since they were regarded to be too scholastic and arcane in their reading of heritage. But this was already an old complaint, registered by Hasan al-Banna (1906–1949) and, after him, Sayyid Qutb (1906–1966), both of whom saw Islam as requiring liberation from the deathly grasp of the traditional clergy. The conclusions varied from showing the essential "liberalism" of Islam, as in the case of Muhammad Shahrur or Fatima Mernissi (1940–2015), to highlighting the historical situatedness of revelation, as in the case of Tarabishi, and from stressing one part of the heritage, namely, the progressive part, against more retrograde parts, as we see in the works of Muruwwah and Tizini, to arguing on behalf of the creative part of the heritage against its more conservative part, as in the projects of Hasan Hanafi and Adonis.

While the critical heritage studies arrived at no uniform conclusion, they did enter the public sphere as important new ways of thinking about heritage. And while they did expand the interpretive scope of Islamic studies, they generally did not directly address the crisis of 1967 out of which they were born. This may seem predictable, since in reality "Islam" had little to do with 1967. But "Islam," as a heritage, mindset, or cultural disposition rather than as a religion, was assumed to lie at the root of a crisis worthy of an appropriately profound foundation. However, while eliciting much debate in the Arab World, these works were generally ignored in the West, where no comparable sense of crisis needed to be confronted. This difference in time–space horizons points again to the essentially reflexive and bounded nature of what we call "social theory." I will come back to this point at the conclusion.

7.2.1.1 Identity, in Tradition and Beyond

One underlying assumption of the critical heritage studies concerned the question of collective identity. The issue of "our" identity was latent in terms like the "Arab mind (al-ʿaql al-ʿarabi)," as in Jabiri, and, in general, "identity" was then understood to refer to the internal character of the person, rather than to a simple proclamation of identity by the person. In other words, the question of "our" identity was inseparable from "our" structure of behavior and reasoning. Al-Jabiri, for example, had no problem peppering his writing with a general "we" as an addressee, even in the titles of some of his book—for example, the early *Nahnu wa-l-Turath* (Our Relation to Heritage). That approach to identity was justified by the claim that what "we" were was a question that required a serious and lengthy analysis of the internal structures of a whole cultural heritage. In other words, identity did not simply consist, as it would in a later stage, of a simple proclamation of who we were. Simple proclamation was itself a suspect practice from the point of view of the critical heritage studies, which were generally wary of slogans. Slogans were at that time understood as themselves symptoms of crisis. Rather, the attempted answer to the question of identity, from the point of view of the critical heritage approach, meant uncovering the content of a historical culture, out of which behaviors and styles of reasoning were presumed to emerge.

By 2011 and its aftermath, this older conception of identity appears to have become replaced by a very different understanding. An important example of this transformation came to the fore in the occupation of the Egyptian Ministry of Culture by some Egyptian intellectuals, shortly before the removal of Mohamed Morsi from the presidency in the summer of 2013. In her analysis of that episode, Dina Ramadan (2018) regarded it as a struggle over Egyptian "identity" vis-à-vis the Muslim Brotherhood notion of *huwiyyat al-umma*.

However, in the heat of the battle between Islamists and "liberals" back then, few noticed the degree of transformation in the meaning of "identity." Whereas in an earlier period and continuing through the critical heritage studies, identity was understood to refer to structures of thought and the *internal* intellectual composition of the person, in the aftermath of 2011, identity was seen more as an *external* proclamation: our "heritage" is less an object of extensive intellectual work and more a matter of verbal announcement of who we are, and (especially in the context of the deadly Egyptian struggles of 2013) who we are not. In other words, what is understood by "identity" became a matter of external appearance or a statement of allegiance.

Explaining this transformation requires an in-depth empirical research. It is possible that the earlier conception of identity was associated with one style of creativity, namely the totalistic, whereas the latter to another style that relies on appearances, intuition, exhibition, or other external validation. It may have emerged, or been encouraged, by the more confrontational aspects of contemporary culture, as in street art, songs, popular poetry, or popular cinematic portrayals, all of which rely on capturing immediate visual or other sensorial attention, even though they may not always be experienced as exterior to the self-understanding of the consuming subject.

7.2.1.2 Crisis and the Responsibility of the Intellectual

While the critical heritage studies served as creative responses to a profound crisis and showcased immense intellectual energy, they generally suffered from lack of sufficient sociological grounding. That is, they did not show why, how, or even if historical thought systems sedimented into the general contemporary Arab culture, or even into the culture of past centuries. The projects may therefore be considered elitist, in the sense that they simply assumed that ideas produced by historical intellectuals were formative of a culture, when in reality they may have been ignored, or contested by other contemporaneous authority—which the critical heritage studies actually do show.

In addition, the critical heritage approach sidestepped another primary question: Islam itself had in fact little to do with 1967. Yet, Islam seemed to offer the only framework for collective historical cultural analysis that would allow for an examination of an entire culture, from its deep historical roots down to the present moment. What this orientation disregarded were questions of sole responsibility of the present conditions for the crisis. As I see it, this stemmed from viewing 1967 as such a grand shock that something much deeper than a simple present could account for: the reason for the crisis must be as grand as the crisis itself appears to be.

While one sees similar anguish about heritage and modernization during the last decades of the Ottoman Empire, the answers then did not seem to require the nearly encyclopedic compendia we encounter in this case.

In this case, there are a number of notable features about this intellectual activity which seem common to the most public of those Arab intellectuals who have also sought to grapple with the soul-searching questions raised by 1967:

1. Critical heritage studies, produced in Arabic since the late 1960s, were sometimes carried out by autodidacts, who generally ignored approaches common in traditional Islamic studies. Here, the gravity of 1967 is indicated in the fact that the need to find satisfactory answers required many to depart from their professional training and invest an immense effort in seeking out the root causes of the crisis. As indicated in the plethora of authors each writing multivolume books, the effort seemed warranted by a sense that the crisis was historically structured.
2. It is the responsibility of the intellectual to find the answers. One cannot rely on traditional authorities, presumably because those authorities are themselves implicated in the cultural system that had produced the crisis. Failure of the established order is taken as a sign that one must conduct the inquiry directly, and that the intellectual part of managing the crisis has become an individual responsibility.
3. The crisis is assumed to be deep-rooted, that is to say, cultural and historical in nature. This does not negate the possibility that the immediate cause of the crisis may be bad leadership or even a simple accident. But leadership itself is produced by a history and a culture. And if it were an accident, something in our culture had made us incapable of properly planning for accidents. The crisis, in other words, is assumed to be necessary rather than accidental in character, an expression of deep structures rather than technical issues, a logic of history rather than an exception to its laws of movement. The search for deep answers, in other words, is an effort to banish accidental or personalistic explanations in favor of systematic ones.
4. The search for deep-rooted answers assumes a totalistic character. The intellectuals who responded to 1967 typically understood an entire heritage or a vast historical structure spanning centuries, to lie at its root. The inquiry, therefore, was as broad as the scale of the crisis itself was seen to be. The inquiry covered centuries

of scholarship and all areas of religious sciences, philosophy, and literature.

5. It was often understood that if culture is the reason for the crisis, then that culture had a name: it was Islam—not as a religion as much as a sociocultural system. This assumption, ironically, tended to be held especially by those intellectuals who had little connection to religion or even relation to religiosity prior to the inquiry process. In this case, "Islam" should not be understood as a religion, and certainly not a guide for everyday life or even pious life, but rather as a shorthand for cultural repertoires that form underlying cultural dispositions that also apply to non-believers sharing the same cultural cosmos.
6. The rediscovery of *turath* as a prime source of critical thought seems associated with another social fact. During the Arab dark age (1973–2011), we note the decline of all sources of social trust, with the exception of customary tradition. Tradition, in other words, remained as the only source of trust that is felt to be proximate and therefore empirically manageable, especially in comparison to more distant sources of authority (al-Werfalli, 2011: 84, 87, 141; Bamyeh, 2019). Under such conditions, tradition operated as a readily available source of open possibilities that could be creatively managed by the critical intellectual.
7. The critical heritage projects may in some sense be conceived as one strategy of resistance. What is resisted is not any specific regime. Rather, it is an overall condition of darkness permeating everything. The projects were motivated by a sense that, first, radical enlightenment (e.g. Kassab, 2019) is the first step to emancipation from darkness and, second, that such enlightenment is a personal responsibility that cannot be delegated to any other authority.

7.3 The New Historical Novel

While the critical heritage studies, along with the historical novel, adopted a totalistic outlook, they differed somewhat in the central axis that structured the inquiry. For some, such as Hasan Hanafi or Adonis, the question was the relationship of heritage to the problem of innovation. For others, such as Munif or Koni, it was the techniques of organizing social conflict.

For most, including Naguib Mahfouz from an earlier generation, it was the more generic and continuing problem of social change.

The historical novel shared with the critical heritage studies an orientation to the past, the past being understood as responsible for having given us this present. And like the critical heritage studies, the historical novel does not actually arrive from history directly in the present, since we rarely see the present represented: these works tend to stop at a moment in the past, but the narrative itself clearly concerns existing structures. Thus, in Ghitani's *Zayni Barakat*, the long novel remains focused entirely on a specific point in time—the takeover of Egypt by the Ottomans in 1517. Critics have typically understood the novel as a euphemistic commentary on the structure of power in Nasser's Egypt, although the portrayal is actually more generic. Zayni Barakat is an unprincipled, Machiavellian officer in the Mamluk state who, understanding the reality of the coming Ottoman conquest, manages to position himself so that he could be of service to the new masters of the country, rather than be executed as a high officer in an enemy camp. While the tale may be a reference to the unprincipled character of modern leaders, it may also be seen as a critique of excessive reliance on such leaders for the salvation of the nation. This is evident in how, in the same novel, there are more principled actors who either die in battle as heroes should or survive the change of regime by adhering to their same old moral mission in society, as in the case of Abu al-Su'ud, sheikh of the Sufi order.

The tale here delivers a twin lesson: the moral forces in our culture are historically continuous and continuously virtuous. The same cannot be expected of political functionaries, who must play by the equally continuous Machiavellian games of power. Abu al-Su'ud is portrayed as the one source of reliable and consistent morality in the entire system. He mentors young men pursuing just causes, and is so well-regarded that at the beginning of his career in the Mamluk state, Zayni makes a show of refraining from power, accepting the office only after the intercession of the Sufi Sheikh. Eventually, the two fall out as the sheikh becomes more aware of Zayni's double dealings and orders his arrest as the Ottoman army is marching on Egypt. The amoral nature of politics resumes after the invasion: Zayni comes out of his brief captivity, and is returned to office now to serve the victorious Ottoman state.

The theory of power that Ghitani introduces in this novel—his only theoretically developed work—comes out in Zayni's speech to an imaginary world conference of spies. There, Zayni defines the core of the mission of the spy to consist of establishing justice and—presumably as an aid to justice—"truth" (the more direct mission of spies). However, the spy cannot accomplish this core mission of justice without loyalty to the political system that shows surviving capability. The Darwinist theory of power spelled out here is straightforward: the power to which the spy must remain loyal is one that cannot show weakness, because in doing so it also reveals its incapacity to accomplish justice. Now, if the loyalty of the spy is to justice (and truth) but not to any particular state or power, it follows that all spies in the world share the same mission, and therefore must be seen as collaborators rather than competitors, with each serving a parochial and passing power. At the end, Ghitani offers no way out of this deadly impasse.[3]

The most open and radical rejection of the modern state is perhaps the most monumental historical novel of the period, Abdulrahman Munif's *Cities of Salt*, which portrays several decades of sociopolitical transformation that gave rise to the entity we now know as "Saudi Arabia" (and which Munif never acknowledges by the name). A new ruling elite emerges out of machinations carried out by a foreign oil company and around which an oppressive modern state slowly emerges, with surveillance apparatus, concentrated power, arbitrary exercise thereof, and much violence. That state is contrasted throughout to a popular culture that is characterized by pragmatic conservatism, accustomed to consultation, generous in spirit, but at the same time suspicious of concentrated rule and resistant to the influence of outsiders. In Munif's portrayal, the new elite is corrupt by virtue of becoming an elite of a new, modern kind, even though they may have come from a prior tradition of ephemeral rule that did not look like the modern state. The older tradition of ephemeral rule was more oriented to arbitrating disputes than to actually governing a society, and had none of the accouterments of modern power, such as prisons, police, army, an intelligence service, or even permanence.

In Munif's work, there are no central figures like Zayni Barakat, but a vast social panorama of characters that portray the complexity of a society undergoing total transformation from top to bottom. Various folk heroes, virtuous if fallible local characters, stand in for the local culture and occupy a good number of pages before they disappear and are replaced by new characters. The flow of characters across thousands of pages corresponds to the influx of migrants and participants in this new economy of oil, but also to a society typified by convivial variety though increasingly governed by a power monolith. Positing "the culture of the people" squarely against "the power of the state" is here similar to most contemporary Arabic historical novels, with the main difference being the amount of attention given to one side over the other.

It is society that gains prominence in *Cities of Salt*, especially in the first volumes, before the state—always portrayed as oppressive, conspiratorial, self-serving, or an incompetent pawn in foreign hands—begins to occupy the rest of the narrative into contemporaneity. Society is portrayed as if in a slow-motion film, with minute daily gestures and small, charitable acts, partial knowledge of nonlocal realities, and sustained by hospitality and mutual aid in spite of its austerity. As a new world, represented by the cooperating two powers of a foreign oil company and an emerging new state, descends upon this population, a general feeling of vulnerability ensues, a trope which is also encountered in much postcolonial literature from elsewhere in the Global South (Bamyeh, 2000: 104–111).

In this case, the slow pace of narration allows all kinds of new forces to be introduced in lavish detail. Once we have seen all the colorful characters comprising aspects of local society, we begin to see a dual process: the increasing size and alien nature of the new elite on the one hand, and the increasing fragmentations and dislocations of society on the other. Thus, in addition to a new style of governing and the mighty oil company that ends up knowing more about society than the emir himself knows, big merchants from the larger region begin to show up and claim a major share of local markets in various commodities. They drive out the locals, who are increasingly concentrated in wage labor in service of the new oil economy, and who possess fewer and fewer of their traditional rights and autonomy as this transformation takes its course.

In Munif's critical portrayal of this "modernization," the native becomes a spectator to rather than an agent of the process. Yet, the local responses are not uniform, reflecting a notion of "society" as an argumentative theater rather than a unified body following a single traditional form of resistance. This is evident in the variety of responses to the transformation, ranging from departure in disgust and conservative resistance to any change to wallowing in material bounties and—which seems to be the majority attitude—detested cooperation. All these responses suggest a sense of alienation and loss of social cohesion.

But the final nail in the coffin of the old society is in fact the least suspect, namely the "modern" doctor who comes in with his fancy equipment and, importantly, a strongly anti-traditional attitude. Munif sets him in opposition to a local healer, who treated people for free and lived off their charity, exemplifying an attitude that even the emir expresses when he hears of the coming of the modern doctor: "with someone around who profits from the illness of others, where would good health come from?" But the emir's argument does not last long, as the modern doctor proves his invaluable service in other areas, such as offering to build an internal intelligence agency so powerful as to allow the emir to "hear the steps of an ant in darkness." It is unclear to me whether Munif had read Michel Foucault, but the portrayal of the "helping hand" as the most insidious technique of modern power is clearly visible here, and the modern doctor eventually proves to be the most valuable source of advice for building a new system that completely destroys antecedent tradition. Indeed, in the novel, the traditional healer becomes the first prisoner of the new system. His end seems to signify the end of the gift economy, which anthropological studies have shown to decline gradually with the introduction of capitalism, with items like food and medicine being the last to convert to money rather than gift exchange (see, e.g., Gailey, 1987).

In other locations in the region that had witnessed great modernizing processes, such as Libya, we see even more disdain for the new postcolonial governing order. Across the entire five volumes of Ibrahim al-Koni's *al-Khusuf*[2] for example, the postcolonial governing order in Libya is barely present. King Idris makes a fleeting and unflattering appearance only once. The entire work, similar to Munif's, lingers on the trials and tribulations of a local community deep in the desert, which is self-governing for all practical purposes, and which is determined to resist the outside world—including Italian colonial intrusions but also the functionaries tied to the postcolonial system.

Here, too, we find elements of a social theory that are critical of the assumption that formal systems matter more than personality traits. This is most evident when the senior sheikh, Ahar—whose continuing presence, unlike Munif's characters, provides the novel with a sense of cohesion and continuity—criticizes his next in line, who looks forward to his role at the helm of that society: "he thinks that local seniority (*mashyakha*) makes the person, and forgets that it is Ahar who made the *mashyakha* what it is, not that it made him who he is." If we wish to develop this principle further, it would seem to be a critique of what Max Weber calls "legal-rational" authority, in which power is possessed by the office rather than the person who occupies it. But it does show a clear preference for a specific interpretation of "traditional" authority—namely that personal traits and standing are fundamental to it, and that it has no problem being a prosaic form of authority, since (unlike modern government) not too much depends on it. The society is otherwise self-organized and self-governing.

Al-Koni, who was invited to give the keynote address at the 5th conference of the Arab Council for the Social Sciences (ACSS), as someone whose literary works should be relevant to Arab social scientists, elaborated a vision that aligns well with the description above. Speaking of the Arab revolutions, he criticized the notion that revolutions were needed more than personal transformation, since revolutions would not take us far if we continued to be the people who we were at that moment. One sees here a deep suspicion of modern systems, all the more striking since they come from someone who did in fact work in such systems and as a diplomat no less. While not explicitly mentioning the neopatriarchy thesis of Hisham Sharabi, al-Koni registered a similar understanding of cultural transformation as a transformation of personal psychology or disposition. The priority of personality seems to emanate from al-Koni's understanding of tradition as a less-governed system than what we have become accustomed to. And what we have become accustomed to must be overthrown by a revolution, but one that begins from within the person. Without that, revolution is destruction: if Ghaddafi's takeover had destroyed the state, the 2011 revolution threatened to destroy the nation (al-Koni, 2021).

7.3.1 *The Spirit of Revolution*

Thus, while the critical heritage studies approached "our" culture as conveyed through historical intellectual systems, the historical novel approached the same issue as a popular system of mores that had little to do with the inescapably Machiavellian character of political power. And while the historical novel appears to be more sociologically grounded than the critical heritage studies, it seems to share with the latter a certain hope for a revolution. In either case, the revolution is more cultural than political: either the more enlightened, "materialist," progressive or liberal part of our historical "mind" expunges the more conservative, backward looking, conspiratorial part of it, or the convivial social psychology of the nation somehow triumphs over the pure venom that is our political systems.

In other words, while these two projects emerged out of a sense of profound crisis in 1967; while their conclusions may be varied and debatable; and while they may not have a direct relation to the uprisings of

2011 and 2019, they share with the uprisings the general spirit of revolution (Kassab, 2019: 149–156), of rejecting all that rules us. Those acts of creativity, therefore, may be regarded as part of a general climate, of which the wish for a revolution began to take broader roots, in the same culture that had been the object of study of these intellectual movements. Creativity, after all, is less about finding solutions than about expanding the realm of choices, even in one's own mind, within an environment that otherwise restricts choice. The critical heritage studies and the historical novel, therefore, were not so much "accurate" as they were intellectual manifestations of militant opposition to unaccountable elites, and this miltancy would inform the spirit of the later popular revolts.

7.4 Conclusion: What Is Social Theory?

Obviously, the critical heritage school and the panoramic historical novel were not the only genres that proved useful for contesting what intellectuals perceived to be the roots of Arab thought after 1967. What made these genres distinctive, however, was their capacity to house a critique in the form of a comprehensive verdict, and in so doing approximate the character of "social theory." Of course, the value of such a "theory" in this case lay not in its academic character, but in the fact that it was meant, and was also received, as a set of original rearrangements of cultural and historical materials for the benefit of a public sphere. The fact that Muruwwah, for example, was murdered for his work demonstrates the public significance with which his work was regarded.[4] Given that all the other figures addressed here also occupied prominent roles in Arab public spheres, the same conclusion also applies to them.

The other distinctive feature of the comprehensive critiques considered here consisted in their obsession with what we call "tradition." In principle this is not unique to Arab thought, and what we call "modernity" everywhere included countless engagements with "tradition," whether as an obstacle to a necessary renewal, as a possible aid to orderly social change, or as an unsuspected catalyst for a revolution. These various engagements with "tradition" are obvious in the critical heritage school. They are also obvious in a different way in the panoramic historical novel. Each genre housed different sorts of materials: classical texts in the heritage studies and social life in the historical novel. Together, the two genres delivered social theory in its most elaborate form: as a fusion of lives and texts, of realities and commentaries on realities. But such a "theory" was not unified in the manner we expect: it was not to be found in a single book or delivered by a single author. Rather, it is to be regarded as a *social* theory in a different sense than what we are accustomed to: not simply a single theory about a social reality, but a socially distributed effort, across different genres and by a significant number of scattered intellectuals, all addressing the same crisis. Here, the "social" in the theory illustrates its communicative nature: theory not as an act of singular authorship, but as inputs flowing from different authors and different genres pouring into the same question.

While the above point illustrates the communicative character of social theory in this case, its second feature is its relational character. All social theories construct relations between different fields of observations, and the more such relations they construct, the more comprehensive the scope of the theory appears to be. In the cases addressed here, the most sustained relation is one between past and present, a relation that is understood as a route to theory. The difference lies only with the question as to what to do with the past, that is to say, with "tradition," as we move either beyond it or into another facet of it.

Finally, there is the question of social theory as an open enterprise, or as an aid to inquiry rather than as a last word—something that modern social theories since Talcott Parsons have unsuccessfully attempted to reach. The openness of the theory in this case is rooted less in its essentially "liberal" spirit than in the multiplicity of locations and agendas addressing the same issue, which is also responsible for its communicative character. The works addressed here, taken as a whole and in spite of their comprehensive aims, lack a sense of finality. But in their totality they place "tradition" as a fundamental question for modern times, while at the same time showcasing the vastness of such tradition, rather than it being an outworn residue that can be dispensed with, or be used, as the present prepares for its revolutions.

This is of course not to say that the authors discussed here, while public intellectuals and in many ways also popular, were read by the millions of Arabs who rebelled in 2011 and 2019. The question of the sociology of knowledge here is not that of direct "influence" as much as it is an intellectual anticipation of popular radicalism. This anticipation was done in the manner and according to styles of investigation preferred by intellectuals who, each in their own way followed, however intentionally or not, a specific understanding of the role of tradition in fostering freedom, structures of thought, rationality, or the opposites of these terms. But as

I have argued elsewhere (Bamyeh, 2012), revolutions tend to bring their own theories with them as they explode, and also to foster, as we see especially in the aftermath of 2109, an "anarchist enlightenment": a style of inquiry that is broadly communicative; one whose relation to the past is informed less by deep archaeology of knowledge than by available historical memory; one that rejects not only reality but even more realism as a perspective; and one whose "theory" assumes the character of intuitive thought rather than complex scholastic structures. Of course, the authors of the approaches discussed here do not consider themselves anarchists. But they share with the popular revolutions a similar radicalism. Both social revolutions and the intellectuals who preceded them may be seen to express two styles of doing the same thing: rejecting established authorities in favor of a future that, while not always clearly defined, will be more under the control of the agent who now languishes under them.

Acknowledgements I would like to thank participants in the workshop "Writing Social Theory in Arabic" (Freie Universität Berlin, November 2022) for comments that helped improve this paper. In particular, Mounir Saidani, who encouraged me to think about intellectual precursors to 1967; Claudia Derichs, for highlighting the role of literature as one site of contestation under controlled conditions; Sune Haugbolle, for reminding me of the context of the global cultural crisis of the 1960s within which Arab intellectuals were working; Florian Zemmin and Dietrich Jung for a broad range of comments that helped bring the article into sharper focus.

Notes

1. The reference is to Muhammad Shahrur (1938–2019), known for his widely read books that seek to align the Islamic tradition with a broad spectrum of what today would be called humanistic and liberal values in politics and society. Shahrur related the story personally during a meeting with the author in Berlin.
2. See previous note.
3. The references to Machiavelli or Darwin are not meant to convey the sense that any of the authors discussed here consciously based their theses on such sources. As I argued elsewhere (Bamyeh, 2009), "Machiavellian" theses abound in Arabic *siyāsa* manuals ("mirrors of princes") as well as in similar South Asian treatises for centuries preceding Machiavelli. Add to this the fact that simplified uses of

Darwinian logics of survival seemed well suited to the analyses of new political regimes obsessed with the question of their own survival.

4. Husayn Muruwwah (b. 1908) was assassinated in his home in Beirut in 1987, presumably by members of the Amal militia.

References

al-Koni, I. (2021, December 2). Al-Taghyir: Ru'ya fi al-Mafhum [The Concept of Change: A Perspective]. In *5th ACSS Conference*. Casablanca.

al-Werfalli, M. (2011). *Political Alienation in Libya: Assessing Citizens' Political Attitude and Behaviour*. Ithaca Press.

Bamyeh, M. A. (2000). *The Ends of Globalization*. University of Minnesota Press.

Bamyeh, M. A. (2009). *Anarchy as Order: The History and Future of Civic Humanity*. Rowan & Littlefield.

Bamyeh, M. A. (2012). Anarchist Method, Liberal Intention, Authoritarian Lesson: The Arab Spring Between Three Enlightenments. *Constellations, 20*(2), 188–202.

Bamyeh, M. A. (2015). *Social Sciences in the Arab World: Forms of Presence*. ACSS.

Bamyeh, M. A. (2019). *Lifeworlds of Islam: The Pragmatics of a Religion*. Oxford University Press.

Foucault, M. (1975). *Surveiller et punir: Naissance de la prison*. Gallimard.

Gailey, C. W. (1987). *Kinship to Kingship: Gender Hierarchy and State Formation in the Tongan Islands*. University of Texas Press.

Hammoudi, A. (2017). *Al-ʿUlum al-Ijtimaʿiyya fi al-ʿAlam al-ʿArabi: Muqarabat al-Intajat al-Sadira bi-l-Lugha al-'Arabiyya (2000–2016)* [Social Sciences in the Arab World: An Approach to Arabic Language Outputs (2000–2016)]. ACSS.

Kassab, E. S. (2009). *Contemporary Arab Thought: Cultural Critique in Comparative Perspective*. Columbia University Press.

Kassab, E. S. (2019). *Enlightenment on the Eve of Revolution: The Egyptian and Syrian Debates*. Columbia University Press.

Ramadan, D. (2018, November 7). *Culture Is the Red Line: Scenes from a Sit-In and the Battle for Egyptian Identity*. EUME Berliner Seminar, Berlin.

Sharabi, H. (1993). *Neopatriarchy: A Theory of Distorted Change in Arab Society*. Oxford University Press.

Shils, E. (1972). *The Intellectuals and the Powers and Other Essays*. University of Chicago Press.

Weber, M. (1922). Die Typen der Herrschaft. In *Wirtschaft und Gesellschaft: Grundriss der verstehenden Soziologie*. Mohr Siebeck.

CHAPTER 8

The Road Out of Marxism: Entangled Thought in 1970s Lebanon

Sune Haugbolle

8.1 Introduction

The Lebanese Civil War was a monumental event in recent Arab history which left significant marks on social thought. As part of the catastrophic internecine wars of the post-1967 era, the civil war involved deep ideological splits inside Lebanon but also in the wider Arab realm. The first part of the civil war period coincided with what Fadi Bardawil (2020: 165–187) has called the "fork" in theoretical agendas that would gradually separate Arab modernists from Saidian critics. Whereas the former performed self-critique in the wake of the defeat of 1967, the latter focused their analyses of the Arab predicament on colonialism. Another theoretical schism that crystallized in the late 1970s was a shift in momentum from secular Marxism and Arab nationalism to culturalist and Islamist ideology. These transformations are important not just for

S. Haugbolle (✉)
Department for Social Sciences and Business, Roskilde University, Roskilde, Denmark
e-mail: suneha@ruc.dk

D. Jung and F. Zemmin (eds.), *Postcolonialism and Social Theory in Arabic*, The Modern Muslim World,
https://doi.org/10.1007/978-3-031-63649-3_8

Lebanon, but for Arab social theory as such. They place the decline of Arab Marxism in a different context than the more obvious one of the late 1980s and early 1990s when world Communism collapsed. This chapter aims to contribute to the reappraisal of the 1970s as a transitional period by studying how two prominent Arab Marxist intellectuals found two very different ways out of Marxism, and how the Lebanese Civil War influenced their respective theoretical development.

Marxism as a theoretical tradition is a good avenue for analyzing the theoretical "fork" of the late 1970s. Not so long ago thought of as a dead tradition, Arab Marxism has in recent years received new scholarly attention, coinciding with a revival of Marxist theory globally. The work of Yasin al-Hafiz (1930–1978), Waddah Charara (b. 1942), Jurj Tarabishi (1939–2016), Fawwaz Traboulsi (b. 1941), and Hassan Hamdan (1936–1987), along with several other Levantine thinkers who began writing in the 1960s and continued under influence of the war, has been rediscovered, translated into English, and subjected to academic reevaluation. The revival of Arab Left historiography as a scholarly field partly springs from the renewed relevance of revolutionary theory and praxis after the Arab uprisings and defeats of the past decade. This relevance runs parallel with a global tendency to link our current crises and uprisings to radical theory and rediscovery of its historical roots. In the Middle Eastern branch of this literature, the Lebanese Civil War is an inescapable and complex setting for memory work and reflection, firstly, because the war involved a clear revolutionary project with theoretical annotation—mainly in the form of Marxism—and secondly, because its revolutionaries of the 1970s suffered defeats not unsimilar, and certainly not unrelated, to those of the 2010s. Although the context was different, these two decades forty years apart both showcase attempts to transform and liberate Arab societies which were both largely defeated. Reflecting on this interest and in conversation with the relevant literature, my chapter asks how Arab Marxist thought and particularly social theory changed during the war, and why and how some of its thinkers began to find a way out of Marxism.

My two protagonists, Yasin al-Hafiz and Mounir Shafiq, represent two positions in the trajectory of Arab Marxism that both contrast with the mainstream position, which we could call Marxist persistence. By that I do not mean a blind continuation of Marxist dogmas despite changing local and global conditions, but rather a persistent belief in the ability of Marxist theory to innovate and adapt and thus remain relevant. This position is most prominently represented by Hassan Hamdan, who is known under the pseudonym Mahdi Amel. Hamdan was one of the Lebanese Marxists who rethought his positions because of the war without abandoning Marxism altogether. Hamdan used his reading of Marx and Gramsci to theorize the Lebanese condition with a special focus on the class origins of sectarianism. Although he was highly reflexive and took positions that often contradicted his Communist peers, Hamdan maintained the relevance of Marxist theory and remained a committed member of the Lebanese Communist Party until his assassination in 1987 (Amel, 2021).

Hamdan's persistence can be counterposed with two trajectories that created fissures in Arab Marxism from the inside. The first position is represented by Yasin al-Hafiz, a Marxist turned liberal, whose work points to the longstanding dialogue and overlaps between liberal and Marxist intellectual traditions in the region. I call his position Marxist liberalism because I see his work as characteristic for the incubation of liberal thought from inside Marxist tradition that began in the early 1970s and culminated in the early 1990s (Khatib, 2022: 101–104). The second position is represented here by Mounir Shafiq, a Marxist-Maoist turned Islamist (of sorts, as we shall see), whose transformation represents a deep engagement with cultural specificity and religious identity from the mid-1970s onwards. While Marxist Islamism may sound oxymoronic, it is a well-documented phenomenon in the intellectual history of the region that there are overlaps and mutual inspirations between these two families of thought (Garcia, 2019). Through a reading of Shafiq's work, I discuss the emergence and development of this position resulting from social transformations in the mid-1970s. For both al-Hafiz and Shafiq, I pay special attention to the continuous dialogue in their respective bodies of work with other intellectual traditions like Maoism, liberalism, and Islamism, and how entanglement with these traditions in combination with their social experience created roads out of Marxism.

8.2 Arab Social Thought and Entangled Globalization

Before turning to my thinkers, this section develops the idea that Arab social theory should be studied as entangled traditions. Entanglement refers to interconnections inside and outside the region, but also to notions of interdependency and mutual influence. Not all corners of contemporary Arab thought are equally influenced by Western, Asian,

Latin-American, or African currents, but it is hard to find an Arab thinker in the past fifty years who only makes references to Arab tradition—and whose personal life and experiences that inspired the work were not in some sense transnational. Entanglement as a way of evaluating social theory also allows us to go beyond a sharp separation of thinkers into distinct schools of thoughts and isms, and instead consider mutual influences, overlaps, and gray zones between, for example, liberalism and socialism (Haugbolle, 2016). To say that Arab social theory is entangled may seem like a fancy way of stating the obvious. What I am aiming at, however, is to think through *how* exactly it is entangled, and what entanglement means for the way we read and evaluate social theory produced in the region. My method combines social history with intellectual history. At a theoretical level, my aim is to test the idea that social thought is not just (individual) thinking about the social at a particular moment, but equally (collective) thought resulting from social experience over time. Such a conception of social theory—inspired by the Greek-French philosopher Cornelius Castoriadis' (1975) work on the imaginary institution of society–may help us understand the nature of Arab intellectual tradition and its boundaries and overlaps with "Western," "global South," and "global" social theory.

There are two reasons why I find it pertinent to test this idea in the context of Lebanon. First, the country exemplifies the globalization of Arab social thought by being extremely exposed to global intellectual trends. Secondly, the Lebanese Civil War as a particular event produced significant intellectual innovation and reflection. We could call these strong international influences, but that would not capture the dynamic nature of cultural flows. Instead, I have increasingly come to favor the word "entanglement." Entanglement is a relatively recent term in globalization theory, and is mainly found in cultural globalization theory. When it comes to conceptualizing cultural globalization, theorists tend to speak in metaphors to visualize the hidden flows (Tsing, 2000), the scapes (Appadurai, 1996), and horizons that stretch across and beneath the visible terrain, creating infrastructures for information, communities, customs, and transportation of ideas that make up the architecture of globalization. These metaphors are taken from the natural world, suggesting that the borders that separate—visibly and invisibly, legally and culturally, socially and politically—are *not* natural and given, but rather a product of human organization. Globalization, in its most celebratory liberal rendition, describes the process of overcoming these borders and reverting, as it were, to the natural state of things where objects and subjects flow in a planetary continuum, freed from the restrictions of the nation-state. Critical globalization theorists, in contrast, pay attention to the forces that restrict these flows or create disjuncture and frictions, inequality, and injustice, as part of the globalization process (Tsing, 2000).

Sociologists, historians, and anthropologists are increasingly aware that theorization of the social in the age of globalization must account for the process of cultural meeting, exchange, and blending. This is where the term "entanglement" has proven to be a popular concept. Entanglement and "entangled" traditions, histories, and identities now appear in book titles, conferences, and project descriptions. The word defines a subdiscipline of global history (entangled history), a critical reassessment of modernity (entangled modernities), and redefined conceptions of the man–nature relationship (ecological entanglements). Such studies overlap with and take inspiration from entanglement in the natural world (quantum entanglement and the entangled lifeforms of mycelium).

All these new literatures point to the fact that globalization processes entail increased circulation of goods, peoples, and ideas and therefore lead to transgressions of boundaries separating social units and cultural identities. The result is not just clash, conflict, and homogenization, but also heterogenization and the creation of new, hybrid subjectivities and cultural phenomena. Cultural globalization theorists have already produced concepts and metaphors to describe this, like cultural hybridity, melting pot, translation, creolization, fusion, and metissage (Vauchez, 2013). Most of these terms describe the result of mixing rather than the process. Much of the literature is also quite normative, celebrating cultural globalization while describing some of its more successful forms. In contrast to these normative-laden terms, entanglement goes to the root of the process of what exactly happens when cultural forms meet, blend, and mix. The point, which has significant bearing on how we understand globalization, is that the outcome of intersubjective entanglement is not always what Homi Bhabha (2004: 52–55) calls a "third space," a new multicultural form, but sometimes a disentanglement of the entangled elements.

Theories of cultural globalization are notoriously slippery and elastic. Most treatments favor encyclopedic descriptions that illustrate how culture is hybrid per se, and how globalization has hybridized our world even further. From the 1980s onwards, globalization studies and postmodernism created an imperative to deconstruct essentialist renditions of human society and history—including social thought. Theorists such as Fanon, Hall, Said, Bhaba, and Soja stressed the discursive power that goes into creating reified social entities like class, race, and gender. In contrast to such constructions as "the nation," "the Orient," "the tribe," and "masculinity," they counterpoise cultural hybridity. Most radically, Bhabha and Soja view all forms of culture as "continually in a process of hybridity" (Rutherford, 1998: 211). With the cultural turn in social science came an avalanche of terms that describe cultural continuums and new, budding cultural forms resulting from migration, value chains, new information technology, and the long-term effects of imperialism: the "potpourri," "the cultural hybrid" (Burke & Stets, 2009), and their underlying "logiques métisses" (Amselle, 1990). Cultural studies and postcolonial studies have been the main "factories" of hybridity theory, but migration studies, critical theory, literature, anthropology, cultural geography and sociology, and other disciplines have also chimed in.

Cultural globalization literature sometimes lacks theoretical precision and sometimes wears normative blinders when it celebrates mestizization and writes against all forms of essentialism. At the same time, it has provided a vocabulary for a particular way of looking at the social world that is today a canonized pillar of globalization studies. This pillar provides an important counterweight to economic and political studies of globalization that highlight, and sometimes reify, standardization processes. Even if multiculturalism as a political project has come under pressure in many parts of the world today, cultural hybridity continues to be a crucial aspect of globalization. The prevalence of entanglement in recent theory across academic fields testifies to the importance of accounting for it theoretically. This should also be the case when we analyze earlier instances of globalization, such as the intellectual influences that merged with Arab social theory during the "radical" era of the 1960s and 1970s.

8.3 The Lebanese Civil War as a Site for Entangled Social Theory

Some of the most influential thinkers from the Lebanese Civil War period hail from the Marxist tradition. In recent years, the works of Yasin al-Hafiz, George Tarabishi, Waddah Charara, and Hassan Hamdan, along with several other Levantine thinkers from "the long 1960s"—the period of global radicalism from the mid-1960s to the early 1980s—have been rediscovered, translated into English, and subjected to academic reevaluation. Their rediscovery is part of a new historiography of the Arab Left as a political, social, and intellectual tradition that has been overlooked and understudied. In our time of big social upheaval, scholars have begun to pay more attention to social theories of dissent and revolution in the region. Equally, Arab social scientists, many of whom participated in (or at least supported) the revolts, engaged in "archeology" of their own societies to clarify the historical experience, lessons, and trajectories of the 1960s and 1970s. Three examples of this attempt to engage with the radical past are Samer Frangie's (2015, 2016) work on Yasin al-Hafiz, Fadi Bardawil's (2020) book on Waddah Charara, and Frangie's (2012) and Hicham Safieddine's (2020) work on, and translation of, Hassan Hamdan. In all three cases, scholars born in the late 1970s reflect on the life and work of thinkers from that "other" time of dissent. I draw on their work as I develop my own analysis of the trajectory of Arab Marxism.

Lebanon is far from being the only Arab country caught up in an archeology of revolutionary thought (Haugbolle, 2020). But at the risk of being Lebanon-centric, one could say that within the larger body of literature about the Arab Left, Lebanon plays a central role. Lebanon and Beirut more than anywhere else served as a laboratory of revolutionary thought and praxis from the 1960s to the 1980s. This also included non-Lebanese dissidents who resided in Beirut and especially the Palestinian liberation movement. For young social historians and theorists today, it is imperative to work out what the proper lessons of those decades should be—both in terms of the interpretation of the civil war and its legacies and in terms of the ideological and theoretical pointers that they may take from the critical work produced in Lebanon before and during the war. When I refer to the war here, I also include the run-up to the war and the Marxist circles that al-Hafiz and Shafiq traveled in. This caveat is important because it points to a longer history of entanglement. Indeed, neither the war nor Arab Marxism introduced entangled social theory to Lebanon. It has, since the late nineteenth century, been a mainstay of Lebanese intellectual culture to mix and blend. Knowledge production in Beirut is a product of multiple traditions and influences, from the French connection that runs through Francophone cultural institutions, research centers, media, universities, and colonial networks to the anglophone links centered around the American University of Beirut, but also including a wider exposure to British and American intellectual trends through translation, publication, and cycles of migration. Add to this a natural link to other cultural and intellectual hubs in the Arab-speaking world like Jerusalem, Baghdad, Damascus, and Cairo. It is hard not to resort to worn-out metaphors when describing the city–Beirut is indeed a potpourri and a melting pot—or, qua Bhaba, a "third space" of multicultural mixing. Its social thinkers traverse multiple worlds and crossroads of East, West, global North and global South, leftism, liberalism, etc. So, too, is Lebanon and has been for at least 150 years. Social thought is naturally entangled and cross-bred there (Kassir, 2010).

Still, the 1970s provide us with a particularly interesting case of entangled social theory. During this decade, Marxism went from being a marginal trend to a widespread current with a direct political impact. Marxist ideas had been adopted through Communist parties in the region, starting in the 1920s. In the early 1960s, a wider adaptation and critical re-reading of Marx began in various milieus, including the Arab Nationalist Movement, the Syrian and Iraqi Baᶜth parties, which included Marxian milieus known as the "Baᶜth Left," and in Palestinian currents. In the mid-1960s, they had established their own journals and circles of friendships between Syria, Lebanon, Iraq, and Palestine, where a diverse, and sometimes volatile, engagement over New Left ideas took place. One of the most influential thinkers for the development of a specifically Arab Marxist tradition was the Moroccan philosopher Abdallah Laroui, who argued for the development of a historicist reading of Marx that stressed the need to adopt, appropriate, and adapt "universalist" theory to the conditions of the Middle East, including its Islamic traditions, its colonial history, and its class specificities (Hanssen, 2020).

Beirut provided a vibrant space for such an adaptation in the 1960s. An Arab New Left could develop here due to the city's political freedoms, which allowed dissidents to speak and write (more or less) as they pleased. Palestinian writers like George Habash, Fayez Sayigh, and Ghassan Kanafani found a home here and "prepared" the city for its transformation into a center for Palestinian revolutionary activity after Black September in 1970 and the forced relocation of the Palestinian Liberation Organization (PLO) from Jordan to Lebanon. Syrian dissidents like Yasin al-Hafiz, George Tarabishi, and Elias Murqus also found a home in Beirut in the late 1960s. Together, they observed the global dissent and rebellion around 1967 and 1968 which made their Marxist ideas more widely accepted. Several of them engaged directly in the political life of movements like the Popular Front for the Liberation of Palestine, the Organization for Communist Action in Lebanon, Socialist Lebanon, and smaller, short-lived *groupuscules* typical of the late 1960s moment. Inside the more nationalist Fatah, a diverse group of Maoists from across the region, known as *al-katiba at-tullabiya* (the student group), adopted a Maoist interpretation of Marxism-Leninism. Thus, in less than a decade, Marxism went from being associated with the "old" Communist parties to being a "new" and rather motley framework for revolutionary social thought and action in Lebanon.

8.4 Yasin al-Hafiz and the Road to Liberalism

On the Marxist scene of pre-war Lebanon, the general approach was to attempt to transcend the distinction between praxis and theory. Theorists were almost all members of a political movement and sought to engage the "downtrodden" that their social theory tried to make theoretically visible (Guirguis, 2020). The poor, the clients of the sectarian system, the Palestinians, the workers, and the peasants, the (Lebanese and global) South all in varying ways represented localized embodiments of Marx's notion of the proletariat. Marxist theory thus became a tool to problematize and make visible local and global inequality and power structures, but also to change them. In doing so, thinkers read and translated Marxian literature, and shared views on the foundational texts by Marx, Engels, Lenin, and later generations of Marxist thinkers. They organized reading groups and teach-ins in poor areas of Beirut, and debated Marxism vigorously at Lebanon's universities.

The Syrian political activist and intellectual Yasin al-Hafiz was one of the Arab Marxists who observed and participated in the transformation of social thought during this period between 1967 and the breakout of civil war in 1975. Like many other Arab thinkers at the time, he was obsessed with the meaning of the Arab defeat in the June War (Frangie, 2015). Al-Hafiz agreed with the Syrian philosopher Sadiq al-Azm (1934–2016) that the defeat had revealed a set of Arab political systems that had shown themselves to be neither modern nor radical or democratic enough. He went further and asked what this indictment said about radical Arab thought and its analytical parameters. As a long-time member of various political organizations, including the Syrian Baʿth Party and the Syrian

Communist Party for two years, he understood critique as an immanent practice that concerned political direction. In line with the "engaged" phase of French existentialists like Camus and Sartre of the 1960s, who heavily influenced Arab intellectuals, including al-Hafiz, he believed that critique should emerge from experience with attempts to change the social order, and that the point of such critique was to improve the ideological direction of parties and movements. After breaking with the Baʿth Party, he formed one of the New Left parties of the post-1967 turmoil, a small radical party called the Arab Revolutionary Workers Party, which included other Syrian and Lebanese intellectuals. After a stint in Paris, al-Hafiz settled down in Beirut in late 1967, where he would live until his death in 1978. Here, he published a series of books, most of them collections of essays written between 1958 and 1977, addressing various dimensions of Arab politics (al-Hafiz, 1997). As one of the first self-critical Marxists (a trend that became increasingly widespread in the 1980s and especially after the end of the Cold War), he would have a strong impact on Syrian and Lebanese leftists, especially after 1967, when he became a staunch critic of Arab radicalism.

One of the contemporary Arab scholars to have rediscovered and reevaluated al-Hafiz' work is Samer Frangie (2015, 2016). Frangie has proposed a reading of his work as an indication that we should understand the self-critique related to 1967 as a metaphor for a "much longer period of disappointment or disillusionment that saw the gradual yet irrevocable dismantling of the hopes of the postcolonial states of the 1950s and their ideologies" (Frangie, 2015: 326). Drawing on David Scott's analysis of the anti-colonial nationalist and modernist project of the 1950s and "the virtual closure of the nationalist Bandung project" that followed, Frangie (2015: 327) links Hafiz to a wider critique of Third-Worldism from the inside. Looked at this way, the defeat in 1967 merely accentuated the growing sense that this project of independence and solidarity across the non-Western world, which the Palestinian liberation movement, the New Arab Left, and Lebanon's Marxists all saw themselves as part of, had fractured from the beginning. Frangie writes:

> What would characterize the production of Arab intellectuals in the post-1967 period, or in the post-Bandung era, was the challenge to rethink their projects, politics and subjectivities in a new context, marked not only by the defeat, but by the loss, in Scott's words, of the "very coherence

of the secular–modern project—with its assurance of progressive social–economic development, with its dependence upon the organizational form of the nation-state, with its sense of privilege of representative democracy and competitive elections, and so on". (Frangie, 2015: 326)

The extended lead-up to the "fork" moment in the late 1970s also included a new sense of skepticism toward Marx's ideas as an explanatory and predictive framework of the social in the context of the Middle East that, for al-Hafiz, eventually led to his departure from Marxism as such. The disappointment of 1967 is crucial in this regard, because it cemented critique of Arab socialism as a political project including its ideological underpinning. Al-Hafiz' initial critique of the leadership in "radical" states like Egypt and Algeria—but equally applicable to Third World leaders like those in Indonesia and India–was related to the way they embraced state capitalism even while advocating a socialist Third Way between Soviet Marxism and American capitalist hegemony. In that sense, Arab socialist states became for al-Hafiz indicative of a wrong turn for the socialist Third World as such.

Intellectual historians of the Middle East tend to read the post-1967 intellectuals in a mainly regional framework related to Arab history, the struggle for Palestinian land, and liberalism vs. authoritarianism. However, thinkers like Yasin al-Hafiz were also orientated toward global questions and how global theory could explain and potentially resolve the regional predicaments. As an Arab Marxist whose mind was shaped during the 1950s, he observed the emergence of a Third Worldist project that sought to replace the previous Eurocentric theoretical apparatus for human liberation in the guise of Marx, Lenin, Luxemburg, and Gramsci. Third-Worldism gave space to indigenous theorization of the global predicament, socialism, liberation, and global order. In the words of Robert Malley (1999: 98), Third-Worldism was "a political, intellectual, even artistic effort that took as its raw material an assortment of revolutionary movements and moments, weaved them into a more or less intelligible whole, and gave us the tools to interpret not them alone, but also others yet to come."

This "assortment" of revolutionary movements and states had a shared commitment to giving agency to the non-Western world, thus continuing earlier forms of internationalism but with a much less Eurocentric emphasis. Such a vision of the future of humanity—and the future of socialism—appealed to al-Hafiz and his peers, and they initially saw the

Algerian FLN (National Liberation Front) and Egyptian President Gamal Abdel Nasser as regional lodestars for its implementation (Nash, 2002). However, as al-Hafiz became aware of from the early 1960s, Third Worldist regimes differed significantly when it came to economic policy and strategic orientation in the Cold War. These significant contradictions were inbuilt from the start, when Third-Worldism emerged as an ideological rhetoric of emancipation and resistance in the early 1950s. As work on Third-Worldism and its legacy has noted, the political reality in developmentalist states with nationalized economies such as Egypt, Indonesia, and Algeria commonly depended on a certain biopolitics, or form of governance of its citizens, that was "rooted in a regime of sovereign state control, and designed to mobilise citizens in ways favourable to capital" (Patel & McMichael, 2004: 234).

The internal critique of the local parameters of oppression and illiberalism—be they imposed by the Arab state or Arab culture—was present in New Left critique as early as the late 1950s (Takriti, 2018). It gradually matured through the decade and found its institutional form and expression after 1967. The kind of Third Worldist ideologues and militants that emerged from it dreamed of a more radical rupture than what Nasser had offered. Intellectuals like Fawwaz Traboulsi, Ghassan Kanafani, and George Habbash wanted to imagine and enact an "anticolonial translocal connectivity" which would tie liberation movements together in a more or less cohesive project globally (Sajed, 2019), based in Fanonian liberation Marxism. To do this, they veered toward solidarity movements in the West, Euro-Communism, and Maoism. We will return to the Maoist branch of the New Left later. Here, it suffices to say that al-Hafiz did not go down this road. Rather, he began to articulate the Arab predicament in broad, historicist terms influenced by Abdallah Laroui. While others on the Left in Beirut plotted for a Palestinian revolution, with its base in Lebanon, that would confront Israeli settler colonialism and American imperialism and pave the way for socialist democracy in the region, al-Hafiz published an essay in 1969 called *Munaqashat fi al-aydiyulujiyya al-falastiniyya* (A Discussion of the Palestinian Ideology), where he explicitly rejected the Cuban, Vietnamese, and Algerian path of a popular struggle in the Arab world, preferring instead the alternative of building modern conventional armies. Al-Hafiz's argumentation was based on the different conditions and needs of these cases, and the necessity to build a modern basis for the popular struggle, one that, if achieved, would be tantamount to building modern armies (Frangie,

2015: 334). This logic went directly against the logic of joining forces with other revolutionary movements, a position which the Palestinian liberation movement spearheaded in Lebanon joined by many Marxists. They advocated that Arab leftists should learn from Asian guerilla tactics and integrate into frameworks like the Tri-Continental Movement. This left al-Hafiz rather alone with his critique—a fact that may have contributed to his alienation and distancing from Marxism in the 1970s.

8.5 Mounir Shafiq: From Maoism to Islamism

Al-Hafiz represents a self-critical and historicist position in Arab Marxism that Hassan Hamdan became highly critical of and wrote against profusely. While Hamdan and others grew more certain of their argumentation during the destruction caused by the Lebanese Civil War, al-Hafiz abandoned Marx. As Frangie (2015: 339–343) shows, al-Hafiz's transformation ended in a full rejection of class analysis as the primary explanatory factor for the historical development of Arab societies. Instead, around the mid-1970s, when the war broke out, he completed a full embrace of liberalism. When he died of cancer in 1978, Lebanon had been through nearly three years of destructive civil war, and the Left had been split after the death of the Druze leader Kamal Jumblatt[1] in 1977. Al-Hafiz may have felt vindicated in his critique, even if he did not write it explicitly.

Many on the Left in Lebanon took a different turn. Some, like Kanafani and Habash, were directly involved in revolutionary movements, in their case the Popular Front for the Liberation of Palestine (PFLP). Others doubled as thinkers and militants on the Left. My analysis here turns to a small group of committed Maoists, the so-called *katiba tullabiyya*, who counted among its ranks Palestinian, Lebanese, and other Arab intellectuals who had joined the military struggle in 1975. I find them insightful and relevant for a discussion of entangled thought for being exceptionally diverse and internationally connected. At the same time, the ideological and theoretical development inside their group is telling of how social thought transformed because of wartime experiences. The *katiba* included several intellectuals who later became prominent writers and cultural producers, including the novelist Elias Khoury, the sociologist Sari Hanafi (b. 1962, see his chapter in this book), the playwriter Roger Assaf (b. 1941), the sociologist Saud al-Mawla (b. 1953), and the writer Naji ‘Alloush (b. 1935). But the group also counted future Islamist leaders like Imad Moughniya (1962–2008), Hizbollah's head of international operations who was killed in Damascus in 2008, and Tarad Hamade (b. 1957), Hizbollah politician and government minister in the late 2000s, as well as several Palestinian Maoists who became members of Palestinian Islamic Jihad after 1981. This diverse group had come together in 1974 as a meeting between a small number of Fatah members who from the beginning in the late 1960s had defended a Maoist interpretation of the revolution and a splinter group of Marxist intellectuals from the Organization of Communist Action in Lebanon. Before they formed a militia in 1976, the group had already been known as the *katiba* inside Fatah (Sing, 2011). During the war, they changed name to the Jarmaq Battalion, a tribute to the mountain in the Palestinian Galilee they could often see from their battlefield in southern Lebanon. One of its founding members, Mounir Shafiq, recounted how he did not actually primarily see the group as Maoist but rather as a revolutionary current inside Fatah that sought to maintain "the original 1960s Fatah spirit" and not the increasingly pro-Soviet and accommodationist Fatah of Arafat. Ideologically, they took certain aspects of Mao's thought, particularly the notions of a "people's war" and the "mass line"—the idea that popular struggle had to engage peasants directly and learn from them to mobilize them. In addition, learning revolution from a non-Western source—from Mao rather than Marx—appealed to their thirst for full cultural and political independence. This at least partial rejection of Marx based on his Western rather global mooring is a radical break from a universalist view of Marxism.

The *katiba* was composed of Palestinians and Lebanese from different confessional and regional backgrounds, but also counted Iraqi Communists, Maoists, and Islamists who had found refuge in Lebanon, as well as Iranians who had joined Fatah to train militarily and fight. These Iranian conscripts came from the Marxist group Fida'iyin-e Khalq (the People's Fidayin), as well as from its Islamic-Marxist counterpart Mujahidin-e Khalq (the People's Mujahidin). The *katiba* embraced the ideological syncretism of these groups. More broadly, one could say that Fatah as a nationalist movement, and the Palestinian-controlled areas as a revolutionary space, were very open to all kinds of revolutionary groups of the Left, both regionally and internationally. Maoism may not have been the largest tendency inside the Palestinian-held territory known as the Fakhani Republic in wartime Lebanon, but its followers were devoted and internationalist in orientation.

In the late 1960s and early 1970s, the Maoist approach to mobilization appealed to all who wished to reject a Western model of revolution and development. For the main leadership in Fatah, Maoism was just as over-intellectualizing as they found Marxist-Leninist theory of the Soviet strain, preferring instead a simple nationalism as the main (weak) ideological core of the liberation struggle. Arafat had his own version of the "mass line," and it was a much simpler nationalism based on his own humble background and his ability to communicate in a language that touched the lifeworld of ordinary people—what we might today call populism. Arafat aligned this ideology—which was just as much a form of charisma or mode of being—with a political pragmatism that gradually became quite devoid of Chinese romanticism. At the same time, revolution remained rhetorically important for Arafat, who maintained his Third Worldist alliances even though his political alliances gradually shifted. In contrast, Maoism offered a more uncompromising worldview that fully rejected Western models of societal transformation and instead sought political and emotional visions in Asian revolutionary philosophy and experience. This (very modernist) rejection of Western modernity opened the door to political Islam when it began its ascendance during the last part of the 1970s.

The intellectual *métisse* during this time in Lebanon also included leftists from Europe and the USA. Western members of the solidarity movement with Palestine, who mingled with the revolutionaries of Beirut, were generally attracted to Marxist-Leninist factions. They liked that their comrades spoke a common language (that of Marxism-Leninism, and that of English, mastered by the more intellectual and educated on the Left more so than regular Fatah members). They admired the theoretical sophistication of Kanafani and Habash and found much to learn from practitioners of revolution in the PFLP, DFLP (Democratic Front for the Liberation of Palestine), and Fatah. Quite a few of these foreign solidarity militants leaned toward Maoism. To give an example of how these meetings took place, we can take the experience of Norwegian Maoist Peder-Martin Lysestøl, one of the founders of a solidarity movement called the Palestine Committee in Norway.[2] As a representative of the Norwegian Left student movement, he spent time in Yugoslavia and Cairo in the late 1960s and encountered fellow Maoists and members of Fatah. These encounters pushed him toward membership of the Norwegian Maoist group AKP-ml. One of his contacts in Cairo in 1968 was a key member of the later *katiba tullabiyya*, Mounir Shafiq. Shafiq helped procure Fatah material for the Norwegians and inspired them to organize a solidarity movement. In May 1970, Lysestøl and his comrades invited Shafiq to speak in Oslo in a landmark visit that mobilized a large section of the left-wing Norwegian student movement for the Palestinian cause. He became one of the main people responsible inside Fatah for creating such links to the European Left as part of its foreign committee. Despite their ideological differences, Shafiq advised Arafat and attempted to keep him from forming a close alliance with the Soviet Union. The Norwegians approved of this line and communicated it to the Norwegian public in their magazine *Fritt Palestina*. Lysestøl and Sjue stayed in contact with Shafiq and exchanged ideas over the years, even to this day. Several times in 1970 and 1971, he visited him and other Palestinians in Jordan and Beirut, conducting long meetings to coordinate their understanding of the revolution.

As a Palestinian Communist intellectual with a Jordanian Christian background and a long life in Lebanon, Shafiq has a unique trajectory that is relevant for our analysis (Dot-Pouillard, 2008). First, he was one of the liaisons (there were many others) between the Palestinian revolution and the "world revolution" in the guise of New Left groups, student groups, solidarity groups, and liberation movements and governments across the world (Thomson et al., 2022). Second, Shafiq (1971, 1973) has produced a significant body of reflections and theoretical work about the Palestinian revolution and Marxism of the period, as well as a memoir (Shafiq, 1994) that we can draw on to analyze his changing positions (Sing, 2011). And finally, Shafiq became one of the pioneers of an Islamist interpretation of the struggle, which was to become one of the major factors in the fragmentation of the Palestinian revolution, and therefore also in the Marxist disillusionment that Yasin al-Hafiz and Sadiq al-Azm foreshadowed.

Initially, Shafiq's (1971) writings on the Palestinian revolution affirm the notion that their struggle is a vanguard and a frontline in a global war of positions. He then tries to argue for maintaining the original, internationalist, and more radical position of Fatah (Shafiq, 1973) from its inceptive period before 1970 by stressing the need for mobilization that speaks directly to the concerns of the common people, in line with Mao's idea of a "people's war." But as time wore on in the 1970s and civil war broke out, Shafiq and several of his comrades began to question their ideological position. As mentioned, the general climate in mid-1970s Lebanon gradually produced doubts about the Third Worldist project of a global South alliance against imperialism and capitalism. Shafiq (1994:

125–155) has described how doubts began to set in inside the *katiba* around the time the Two-Year War (1975–1976) had ended. Members of the *katiba* like Elias Khoury had participated in the bloody battle of the mountain in late 1976—an experience with violence that caused him and many other leftists to rethink their engagement. Syria—a Third Worldist power in the region supported by the Soviets—had intervened to put a halt to the PLO and the Lebanese Left. Shortly afterwards, in 1977, Mao Zedong died, and the new leadership prosecuted hardline Maoists in the trial of "the gang of the four." The Maoists of the *katiba tullabiyya* began to realize that the Cultural Revolution had failed. These events foreshadowed the transformation of Third-Worldism that is often associated with 1979. In Lebanon, Third Worldist combatants had lived and felt the contradictions a few years earlier. They began to ask questions about their creed. Was Marxism-Leninism, and Marxism-Maoism with it, perhaps failing as the universalizing ideology that explained their predicament and its solution, in Lebanon, in Palestine and in the region as a whole? Did it perhaps, after all, not contain the supreme social, historical, ideological, and methodological knowledge that they had thought? And was this perhaps because Marxism was in fact not a universal ideology but a set of ideas that primarily reflected European modernity? As Shafiq describes this change of heart, the Jarmaq Brigade comrades came to attribute the failure of the Cultural Revolution in China to the "European (sic!) mentality," namely the "European idea" of a "total break with the past"—the classic Marxist understanding of modernity as a force where "everything that is solid melts into air" (Sing, 2011: 31–33).

The defeats and transformations that followed the Two-Year War, the assassination of leftist leader Kamal Jumblatt, and the death of Mao in 1977 occasioned a major rethinking about the cultural specificity of a revolution as opposed to its historical materialist universality, and about how to win over the masses. When protests began in Iran in 1977 and escalated in 1978, the Maoists in Lebanon were struck by how the Iranian masses would stream into the streets of Tehran shouting "Allahu akbar" and "la ilaha illa Allah" ("God is great" and "there is no God but God"). At this point, Shafiq recounts, most of his comrades concluded that Marxism had proven to be "impractical" compared to Islamic principles that served directly as instruments for a revolution of the Palestinian and Arab masses (Sing, 2011: 36). As for his own Marxist peers in Lebanon, Shafiq concludes that their study of Marxism at Western universities had made them unreceptive to the inner transformation that was necessary to embrace of Islam—an embrace that Shafiq now saw as strategically necessary. What the masses needed, he believed, was a comprehensive Islamization of society, led by a vanguard party. It would operate on fertile soil, as the cultural roots of society were, so he now firmly thought, essentially Islamic. These radical conclusions foreshadow the emphasis on *'asala* (roots) and *turath* (tradition) that became a general trend among Arab intellectuals and leftist thinkers during the 1980s (Browers, 2009: 55–78). They also foreshadow Shafiq's own involvement in setting up the Palestinian Islamic Jihad movement. After intense studies and discussions between late 1976 and 1979, the Maoists in the *katiba* and the squad concluded that its "pivotal axis"—mass mobilization through Islam—was without any value or even unreliable if they had no deeper understanding of the core creed of Islam. The idea that there could be no revolution without belief eventually forced many of them to pull away from historical materialism.

Not all Palestinian Maoists were "converted" to political Islam. Many from the *katiba* remained Marxist or Maoist for years to come, while others abandoned ideological certainty as a reaction to the violence of the war. But the conversion of Shafiq and those who followed him is remarkable nonetheless because it was a direct reason—if not the only one—for the emergence of Palestinian Islamist movements and the further fragmentation of the Palestinian liberation movement that it produced. It is also important for the changing political language of resistance that it created. A recurrent comment in my interviews with Scandinavian solidarity activists when I ask them about the first meetings with Palestinian militants in the late 1960s and early 1970s is their joy of discovering a common language of dissent and revolution—the language of Marxism-Leninism. There is no question that the arrival of a new political language based on Islamic principles and imagery as a central force also left a mark on Fatah's vocabulary. As a case in point, take Arafat's speech on the occasion on his first visit to Khomeini's Iran:

> Khomeini is our Imam, our leader, the leader of all mujahidin, we are two peoples in one, two revolutions in one and every fida'i, every mujahid, every revolutionary Iranian will be ambassador of Palestine in Iran. We [sic] have liberated Iran, we will liberate Palestine. We will continue our efforts until the moment we have defeated imperialism and Zionism; the struggle of Iranians against the Shah is identical with the struggle of Palestinians against Israel. (Arafat quoted in Markham, 1979: 1)

The tone of this speech reflected the occasion more than a wholesale abandonment of secular nationalism on the part of Arafat. Nonetheless, the full embrace by Palestinian leaders—including George Habash—of the Iranian revolution marked a historical shift in Arab radical thinking. For Shafiq, it was not so much the Iranian people's reaction to Khomeini that struck him. Rather, it was the way the Lebanese and Palestinian masses instinctively endorsed the Imam that convinced him that the *katiba*'s gradual "conversion" to political Islam was not just vindicated but destined (Sing, 2011: 38). A "mobilized and unanimous people" would, finally, provide the iron fist of popular backing that was needed to reclaim Palestine. A new political vocabulary, amalgamated from Koranic language, would replace Marx and Mao to produce a "truly indigenous" revolutionary script.

8.6 Conclusion: Lacunas and Blind Spots in Intellectual History

This chapter analyzed two trajectories in Arab Marxism that, long before post-Marxism and leftist self-flagellation became mainstream in the 1990s, opened for self-critique and new ideological and theoretical directions. Through a contextual analysis of two thinkers and their reflections on historical events that they witnessed in the 1960s and 1970s, the chapter showed the gradual transformation of Marxist theory into Islamic and liberal registers. It analyzed them as entangled intellectual traditions that gradually, and for very contextual reasons to do with conditions during the Lebanese Civil War, came into dialogue. Islamism and liberalism were, however, not the only traditions that opened for internal critique in Arab Marxist circles. Sometimes, the critique was aimed at Marxist theory as such and its ability to describe and predict current reality. At other times, the critique was aimed more at the practice of Marxists who claimed—rightly or wrongly—to be guided by Marxist principles. In this way, other important roads out of Marxism were taken which have not yet been accounted for. The analysis here shows the extent to which theory informed ideology, and how ideology, in turn, was informed by social action and experience. Intellectual history and social theory in and of the region must still account better for these overlaps between experience, theory, and ideology.

One of the major blind spots in the historiography of the Left and in intellectual history remains feminism and the role of women generally. Alongside "the usual suspects" like Traboulsi, Hamdam, al-Hafiz, and Chararah, female militants and writers like Azza Beydoun and Dalal al-Bizri contributed to the revolutionary project and produced books, articles, and social work that remains underappreciated by scholars. Palestinian organizations like the General Union for Palestine Students had female leaders who greatly influenced the intellectual and theoretical trajectory of the Palestinian Left. In the context of Egypt, as Hanan Hammad (2016) has shown, the female Communist writer Arwa Salih produced a literary work that heavily criticizes the male-centric and misogynist practices of male Egyptian Communist Party intellectuals. These critiques and contributions should be made visible and written into the history of Arab Marxism as part of the entangled web of ideas and experiences that have produced Arab social theory.

Notes

1. Lebanese writer and political leader. From April 1975 to his assassination in March 1977, he led the Lebanese National Movement, a large coalition of Palestinian and leftist forces in the Lebanese Civil War.
2. Personal interview with Peder-Martin Lysestøl, Trondheim, March 8, 2020.

References

Amel, M. (2021). *Arab Marxism and National Liberation: Selected Writings of Mahdi Amel*. Brill.

Amselle, J.-L. (1990). *Logiques métisses. Anthropologie de l'identité en Afrique et ailleurs*. Payot.

Appadurai, A. (1996). *Modernity at Large: Cultural Dimensions of Globalization*. University of Minnesota.

Bhabha, H. K. (2004). *The Location of Culture*. Routledge.

Bardawil, F. (2020). *Revolution and Disenchantment: Arab Marxism and the Binds of Emancipation*. Duke University Press.

Browers, M. (2009). *Political Ideology in the Arab World: Accommodation and Transformation*. Cambridge University Press.

Burke, P. J., & Stets, J. E. (2009). *Identity Theory*. Oxford University Press.
Castoriadis, C. (1975). *L'Institution imaginaire de la société*. Seuil.
Dot-Pouillard, N. (2008). De Pékin à Téhéran, en regardant vers Jérusalem: la singulière conversion à l'islamisme des «Maos du Fatah», *Cahiers de L'Institut Religioscope, 2*, 1–39.
Frangie, S. (2012). Theorizing from the Periphery: The Intellectual Project of Mahdi 'Amel. *International Journal of Middle East Studies, 44*(3), 465–482.
Frangie, S. (2015). Historicism, Socialism, and Liberalism After the Defeat: On the Political Thought of Yasin al-Hafiz. *Modern Intellectual History, 12*(2), 325–352.
Frangie, S. (2016). Exiled from History: Yasin al-Hafiz's Autobiographical Preface and the Transformation of Political Critique. *Thesis Eleven, 131*(1), 38–58.
Garcia, L. G. (2019). Islamists and Communists—A History of Arab Convergenze Parallele. In L. Feliu & F. I. Brichs (Eds.), *Communist Parties in the Middle East* (pp. 241–257). Routledge.
Guirguis, L. (2020). "Dismount the Horse to Pick Some Roses". Militant Enquiry in Lebanese New Left Experiments, 1968–73. In L. Guirguis (Ed.), *The Arab Lefts: Histories and Legacies, 1950s–1970s* (pp. 187–203). Edinburgh University Press.
Al-Hafiz, Y. (1997). *Al-Aʿmal al-kamila* [Collected Works] (5 vols.). Dar al-Hasad.
Haugbolle, S. (2016). Ziad Rahbani and the Liberal Subject. In M. Hatina & C. Schumann (Eds.), *Arab Liberal Thought After 1967: Old Dilemmas, New Perceptions* (pp. 177–194). Palgrave Macmillan.
Haugbolle, S. (2020). Archival Activists and the Hybrid Archive of the Arab Left. In D. D. Ratta, K. Dickinson, & S. Haugbolle (Eds.), *The Arab Archive: Mediated Memories and Digital Flows* (pp. 7–19). Institute for Network Cultures.
Hammad, H. (2016). Arwa Salih's *The Premature*: Gendering the History of the Egyptian Left. *The Arab Studies Journal, 24*(1), 118–142.
Hanssen, J. (2020). Crisis and Critique: The Transformation of Arab Radical Tradition between the 1960s and the 1980s. In L. Guirguis (Ed.), *The Arab Lefts: Histories and Legacies, 1950s–1970s* (pp. 222–242). Edinburgh University Press.
Kassir, S. (2010). *Beirut*. University of California Press.
Khatib, L. (2022). *Quest for Democracy: Liberalism in the Arab World*. Cambridge University Press.
Malley, R. (1999). The Third Worldist Moment. *Current History, 98*(631), 359–369.
Markham, J. (1979, February 19). Arafat, in Iran, Reports Khomeini Pledges Aid for Victory Over Israel. *The New York Times, 1*.

Nash, A. (2002). Third Worldism, *African Sociological Review, 7*(1), 94–123.
Patel, J., & McMichael, P. (2004). Third Worldism and the Lineages of Global Fascism: The Regrouping of the Global South in the Neoliberal Era. *Third World Quarterly, 25*(1), 231–254.
Rutherford, J. (1998). The Third Space. Interview with Homi Bhabha. In J. Rutherford (Ed.), *Identity: Community, Culture, Difference* (pp. 207–221). Lawrence & Wishart.
Safieddine, H. (2020). *Arab Marxism and National Liberation: Selected Writings of Mahdi Amel*. Brill.
Sajed, A. (2019). Re-remembering Third Worldism: An Affirmative Critique of National Liberation in Algeria. *Middle East Critique, 28*(3), 243–260.
Shafiq, M. (1971). *Ḥawla al-tanaquḍ wa-l-mumarasa fi l-thawra al-filasṭiniyya* [About the Contraction and the Practice of the Palestinian Revolution]. Dar al-Tali'a.
Shafiq, M. (1973). *al-Thawra al-filastiniyya bayn al-naqd wa-l-tahtim* [The Palestinian Revolution between Critique and Destruction]. Dar al-Tali'a.
Shafiq, M. (1994). *Shuhada' wa-masira. Abu Hasan wa-Hamadi wa-ikhwanuhuma* [Martyrs and Protest. Abu Hasan and Hamadi and their Brothers]. Muʾassasat al-Wafa'.
Sing, M. (2011). Brothers in Arms: How Palestinian Maoists Turned Jihadists. *Die Welt Des Islams, 51*(1), 1–41.
Takriti, A. R. (2018). Political Praxis in the Gulf: Ahmad al-Khatib and the Movement of Arab Nationalists, 1948–1969. In J. Hanssen & M. Weiss (Eds.), *Arabic Thought Against the Authoritarian Age: Towards an Intellectual History of the Present* (pp. 86–112). Cambridge University Press.
Thomson, S., Olsen, P., & Haugbolle, S. (2022). Palestine Solidarity Conferences in the Global Sixties. *Journal of Palestine Studies, 51*(1), 27–49.
Tsing, A. (2000). The Global Situation. *Cultural Anthropology, 15*(3), 327–360.
Vauchez, A. (2013). Le prisme circulatoire. Retour Sur Un Leitmotiv Académique. *Critique InternatioNale, 59*, 9–16.
Safieddine, H. (2020). *Arab Marxism and National Liberation: Selected Writings of Mahdi Amel*. Brill.

CHAPTER 9

Arabic Social Theory in Japanese and Indonesian: Transregional Ideoscapes of the Long 1960s

Claudia Derichs

9.1 Introduction

Linking up with Sune Haugbolle (in this volume) and his use of the work of Cornelius Castoriadis (1975), I would also like to "develop the idea that social thought is not just (individual) thinking about the social at a particular moment, but equally (collective) thought resulting from social experience over time" (Haugbolle, Abstract). With this conception, I intend to consider the social less in terms of pure theory and more in terms of lived experiences and practices that were inspired by theoretical reflection yet translated into empirical reality and praxis—or vice versa at times. I illustrate and discuss this by way of two empirical examples of transregional connectivities: the revolutionary movement of Japanese–Palestinian solidarity and the faith-based relations between

C. Derichs (✉)
Humboldt University, Berlin, Germany
e-mail: claudia.derichs@hu-berlin.de

D. Jung and F. Zemmin (eds.), *Postcolonialism and Social Theory in Arabic*, The Modern Muslim World,
https://doi.org/10.1007/978-3-031-63649-3_9

Muslim Southeast Asia and the Middle East in the so-called "long 1960s." The former is a crucial element of the Third-Worldism of the 1970s and 1980s, whereas the latter rests on religious affinities that allowed actors in the said period to mobilize followers in the pursuit of social and political Islamization. Both movements formed transregional ideoscapes in Arjun Appadurai's (1996) sense of the term, and represented what I have elsewhere called emotional geographies (Derichs, 2017). Moreover, and more relevant for our discussion at hand, is the fact that both movements bestowed a "center status" to the Middle East, meaning that:

a. Palestine as an imagery formed the center for the ideological identification with Third-Worldist liberation struggles in general and the Palestinian liberation struggle in particular; and
b. the Middle East represented the center of the Muslim world which activists from the periphery (in Southeast Asia) looked up to.

The gist of my argument in this chapter is, hence, to show that the Arab world formed a rallying point for unfolding ideological thought and practice over several decades, implying that Europe, or the West, was no more than the antipodal point of reference for legitimating this thought and practice. The argument is developed in three steps. Section 9.2 relates to the broader ideological landscape of the decades from the 1960s onwards, embedding what we may call "the Arab world" in the mental map of Third-Worldism and its ideological features. Sections 9.3 and 9.4 are devoted to the empirical cases of Japanese–Palestinian ties and Indonesian–Middle East ties respectively. The concluding section, Section 9.5, opens the view to research to come, particularly with regard to the relevance of discussing alternative bodies of literature and thought from the "Global South."

9.2 The Arab World in the "Long 1960s": Mental Maps and Ideological Appeal

My two empirical cases below date back to a time period that is often referred to as the "long 1960s," indicating that developments and events in the 1960s were not restricted to that decade but lasted well into the 1970s and even the 1980s. What was put in motion in the sixties had repercussions for the decades that followed, particularly so in the field of revolutionary thought and activism, and in religious-political struggles.

In the case of Japanese–Palestinian solidarity, it was radicalized groups of Japan's New Left in the late 1960s who subscribed to a theory of "international operations bases" and who left Japan for exactly this purpose. The first batch of activists highjacked a Japan Airlines (JAL) plane in March 1971 and forced its pilots to take them to North Korea. The second batch of activists relocated in/to Lebanon, where they joined forces with the Popular Front for the Liberation of Palestine (PFLP). Kidnappings and hijackings by the group, who operated first under the name of the Arab Red Army and later the Japanese Red Army, followed until late into the 1980s. In Japan and the Middle East alike, the group's action aroused sympathy and admiration among a whole generation of youth and young adults, leading to the pilgrimage-like visits of Japanese artists, students, political activists, and others to the Middle East. Fans of the Japanese Red Army (JRA) became completely bewitched (魅せられた), as contemporary witness Maki Tahara puts it (Tahara, 2022). A number of social theoretical treatises by intellectuals as well as followers of the JRA tried to explain the Japanese fascination with the Arabic revolutionary lifestyle (Esashi, 2022; Himori, 2005; Wakō, 2010). Others emphasized the embrace of cultural diversity in the Arab world (Shiomi, 2010). It is this group that the subsequent discussion will concentrate on as one case study demarcating the mental map of a transregional "Middle East Asia" ideoscape.

The second case study focuses on the intensifying relationship in the long 1960s of Southeast Asian Muslim youth and scholar activists with adherents of the Muslim Brotherhood in and beyond the Middle East. The theoretical reflections of the prominent Muslim Brotherhood figures al-Banna (1906–1949) and Qutb (1906–1966) formed the basis for Indonesian students' thinking about an ideal Islamic Indonesian society. While their activities were semi-legal if not illegal during most of the authoritarian rule of President Suharto (1967–1998), their legal presence became possible in the late 1980s and led to the formation of the political party PKS (Partai Keadilan Sejahtera or Prosperous Justice Party), which is a consolidated player in today's Indonesian political and societal landscape. PKS offers a conceptualization of state and society that (still) looks to the Arab world as a center.[1] The orientation of PKS stands in quite strong contrast to the other big players in the Indonesian sociopolitical landscape, i.e. the mass movements Nahdlatul Ulama (NU) and Muhammadiyah together with their aligned political parties. These movements emphasize a Southeast Asian (Indonesian) Islam that distances itself from the alleged Arabic center—*Islam nusantara* (Islam of the archipelago) and *Islam berkemajuan* (progressive Islam) respectively. The mental maps of the two different currents—one subscribing to the Arab world as the center of Islam (PKS) and the other promoting the de-centering of Islam—reflect the dynamics within the transregional ideoscape of Southeast Asia–Middle East. My case discussion in Section 9.4 relates to the precursor of PKS, i.e. the Jemaah Tarbiyah movement, which emerged out of the semi-legal/illegal Islamist student circles of 1970s Indonesia.

The appeal of "the Arab" shimmers through both the Japanese and the Indonesian accounts of activism in the long 1960s. The two cases will be (briefly) discussed against the backdrop of the social theoretical ideas and political ideologies that rendered "the Arab" so appealing to Third-Worldist, sociopolitical (South-)East Asian activists of the 1970s and 1980s. To set the stage, I sketch the *espiritu del tiempo* in the Arab region.

What marked the current affairs and events of the long 1960s in the Arab world? What was the political activist landscape of the time, and how can it be positioned within the wider ideological framework of those years? Hanssen and Weiss drew this picture:

> Indeed, Communists and other leftist forces across the Arab world found themselves pinched between the Scylla of post-populist authoritarian regimes and the Charybdis of political-Islamist opposition groups such as the Muslim Brotherhood and other avatars of the so-called Islamic revival. Meanwhile, secular as well as religious elements from the liberal center all the way to the extreme right embraced varieties of "nation-state nationalism" in order to carve out positions of influence in a matrix of post-colonial rule that preserved little space for independent political activity. (Hanssen & Weiss, 2018: 10)

In view of the global intellectual scenery, the authors state that "by the early 1970s the Palestinian cause was fast becoming a broad-based *cause célèbre* within global anti-colonial and anti-imperialist circles" (Hanssen & Weiss, 2018: 10–11; emphasis in original). In this climate, Japanese radical leftist activists, too, turned toward the Palestinian cause. In

Indonesia, the Afro-Asian solidarity of the President Sukarno era (1945–1967)— symbolized by the Bandung conferences of 1955 and 1965—was crushed by General Suharto in the 1965 massacre. The Indonesian Left never fully recovered from this genocide; into its vacuum slipped faith-based activists who gradually developed and fostered relationships with fellow activists from the Middle East (especially from the Muslim Brotherhood) and promoted purist ideas of Muslimness. While the liberation of Palestine was not that strong a motivation for the Indonesian Islamist activism of the 1970s, it was nonetheless conceived of as a struggle of fellow Muslims.

9.3 Japanese–Palestinian Ties

The first tentative contacts between members of the Japanese radical Left and Arab activists date back to the late 1960s. It was at a time when the student movement in Japan was breaking apart and splitting into small local groups. One of these groups formed in the city of Kyoto, with members referring to themselves as the Kyoto Partisans. Among their ideological heads was Tsuyoshi Okudaira. In the capital city Tokyo, the Red Army Faction had formed, led by Takaya Shiomi, a philosophy student who was arrested in 1970. In the domestic Red Army (hereinafter: Sekigun) circles was the female activist Fusako Shigenobu, who would become the leader of the Japanese Red Army (Nihon Sekigun; conventional acronym: JRA) in Lebanon. The sociologist Patricia Steinhoff describes in an interview how the Japanese touched base with the PFLP:

> [T]he Kyoto Partisans had little groups around and they were doing little stuff. Okudaira – it's not clear how much there was leadership in these things – but he was a fairly high-level person, and he had established some connection to the PFLP. He had already started learning Arabic. So he was interested in going to Lebanon, and there was some interest in other groups. There were people from Japan who were going to work in the Palestinian refugee camps as volunteers, like doctors and nurses and people with skills – going to volunteer in the camps. It was in the air. People knew about it – that you could go and that you would be making a revolutionary contribution. In that context, Shigenobu hooked up with Okudaira. (Steinhoff, 2007)

Shigenobu and Okudaira went to Beirut in 1971, where they linked up with PFLP cadres and prepared the ground for numbers of other followers from Japan to join their struggle. Sociologist Kei Takata relates that those who went to the Middle East "had developed trust networks with the Arab revolutionaries through their enthusiasm for revolution and for the numerous perilous actions which they [later] dedicated their lives to for the Palestinian struggle" (Takata, 2020: 86). Such devoted submission to the Palestinian cause speaks for more than the temporary revolutionary mood of just one or two persons. The notion of Third-Worldism gradually became theorized through connecting the "Third World inside Japan" to the Palestine liberation struggle. Sekigun pondered Japan's identity as an advanced Asian nation critically. Unlike the anti-Vietnam war movement in Japan, which frequently appeared as a "support group" for North Vietnamese communists, Sekigun's activism was based in Marxist thought and, in the early years, followed its top theorist Shiomi. According to Till Knaudt, Sekigun believed in orthodox Marxism. Instead of reflecting the relationship between colonizers and colonized, Shiomi emphasized the relationship between capitalists and proletarians (Knaudt, 2016: 148–149). This changed after 1972, when the attack at Tel Aviv's Lod airport by three Japanese militants, including Okudaira, engendered a remarkable shift in perspective and a deconstruction of Marxist ideas.[2]

In the airport attack of March 30, 1972, three members of the Lebanon-based Japanese group opened fire on Tel Aviv's Lod airport (today's Ben Gurion airport), which caused the death of twenty-six people and dozens of injured. Of the three Japanese militants, two were killed. One of them was Okudaira. One of the three, Kozo Okamoto, survived and became a celebrated figure in Arabic militant circles. The incident itself became known as the Lod attack and was for a long time considered the first suicide attack in the struggle for the liberation of Palestine.[3]

While Okudaira subscribed to guerilla warfare from quite early on, Shigenobu's pathway into the Palestine liberation struggle commenced from Shiomi's "international operations bases" theory—although Shiomi never pointed out Palestine explicitly. As a leading Sekigun cadre in the group's International Affairs Committee, Shigenobu's task had been to establish international contacts that would lead to the formation of a support network for Sekigun outside Japan. After the Lod attack and Okudaira's death, Shigenobu remained the only original Sekigun member from Japan known to be staying in Lebanon.[4] However, as she was working in the PFLP press bureau, she had nothing directly to do with the planning and execution of the Lod attack. Evidence suggests that Lod was a joint operation of the PFLP and the Kyoto Partisans led in Lebanon by Okudaira (Steinhoff, 1996: 314).[5]

According to Steinhoff, Shigenobu, in her early years in Lebanon, "continued to write about Middle East issues for publications in Japan and interacted with top leaders in the Middle East, including PLO head Yasser Arafat, Muammar Al Khadafi of Libya, and Saddam Hussein of Iraq, as well as with Europeans and other foreigners affiliated with PFLP" (Steinhoff, 2016: 176–77). Shigenobu's 1982 book publication recalls a summer in Beirut and a passionate campaign for Arab revolutionary life in the field (Shigenobu, 1984). A retrospect of the living conditions in the Arab world appeared in 2001, one year before her arrest in Tokyo (Shigenobu, 2001). The book is addressed to her daughter Mei, but can be read as an individual reflection on concepts of family, women, and social cohesion in Arab society that is meant to reach out to the wider Japanese public. It raises awareness for various traits of Arab societies that mainstream Japanese society lacks because of particular cultural legacies and constraining normative frameworks. In later years, too, her books appeared on the shelves of Japanese bookstores. In a compilation of 2012, written while in jail, she summarized some twenty years of life in the social and ideological surroundings of the "Palestinian battleground" (Shigenobu, 2012). Theorist Shiomi himself picked up Shigenobu's thoughts and published his insights from them in an article entitled "Arab Culture has a high tolerance for differences" (Shiomi, 2010). It was a contribution to an edited volume on how the JRA made a global career (Koarashi, 2010).

Japanese intellectuals referred to the peculiarities and legacies of "1968" in and for Japan, studying the publications of "activist thinkers" (for lack of a better term), including those in and around Sekigun. One of the most prominent Japanese sociologists on the sixties Eiji Oguma wrote two heavy volumes on Japan's 1968, a substantially summarized version of which was published in the English language (Oguma, 2018). For Oguma, 1968 in the global perspective "was a product of the resonance of unrelated phenomena throughout the world," triggered and enhanced by larger trends such as media development and the dislocation of the Cold War Order, in the meta-theoretical framework of modernization (Oguma, 2009, 2018). The JRA was born from these contemporaneous developments, and it intentionally related *seemingly* unrelated phenomena throughout the world, managing to present a sharp rebellion against the existing world order in general and the defining tropes of Japanese social order in particular. Elements of Arabic culture and society played a prominent role in their argumentation.

Efforts at theorization in the mood of Third-Worldism came to fruition in that decade. The phrase "Third World inside Japan," which had started to be used in Japanese leftist discourse from the late 1960s to describe the areas and people who were exploited and suppressed by the "First World" in Japan, gained particular purchase after 1972. In that year, a domestic current of the Red Army that had merged with another militant group to form the United Red Army (Rengô Sekigun or Renseki) committed the incredible act of torture and murder of fourteen of its own members. When the bodies were discovered by the police in February, the Japanese public was shocked, and the radical Left became almost totally discredited. The incident is known in Japan as the *Renseki jiken* (Renseki incident) and considered a critical juncture in the history of the country's New Left.[6]

The Lod attack of March 1972 can partly be read as a reaction to the *Renseki jiken* (Derichs, 2006). In the aftermath of both incidents, which shook the ideational architecture of the Japanese radical Left to its foundations, new thought of the previously mentioned type "Third World inside Japan" emerged. The notion related to areas such as the southern island group of Okinawa or the poor urban neighborhoods known as *Yoseba*, where day laborers gather. In the later phase of the 1960s movement, radical activists, including JRA members, showed concern over these suppressed areas and strove to assimilate with the "Third World inside Japan" by engaging in volunteer activities and mobilizing protests. The Lod attack and the *Renseki jiken* inspired ex-Sekigun member Tsuneo Umenai in Japan to construct a critical theorization of its own, going beyond Japan in the conceptions of "First" and "Third" world.[7] In the summer of 1972, following the *Renseki jiken* and the Lod attack, a critique was published by Umenai. This critique embodied the renunciation of the "old" Left's Marxism; it marked a strong break with the strategies and concepts of the preceding generation of old and new leftists.

Umenai's theoretical reflections are reminiscent of the famous *dependencia* theory that originated in Latin America, which sees postcolonial global development as relying on a structure of dependence: The natural resources of the poor states are exploited and extracted for the development of the rich states, i.e. the former become further impoverished while the latter's economies flourish.[8] Umenai's complex theoretical thought and argumentation resonated within the Japanese New Left. It offered no less than an ideological reorientation for a widely shattered Left movement. The rationale of Umenai served the formation of a new current of activists who became known for numerous bomb attacks. Their action can best be called terrorist; it was the most devastating form of political violence that postwar Japan had hitherto seen.[9]

Umenai's relationship with Sekigun goes back to the late 1960s. Until November 1969, when the police raided a Sekigun training camp, he had been responsible for building bombs. He went underground after the raid and remained in hiding for decades.[10] But he made his ideas visible through his publications. In July 1972, his piece "All Those Who Aspire for the Overthrow of the Japanese Empire" appeared in the journal *Eiga hihyō* (Film Criticism). It was a flaming call to restart the engine of resistance (Andrews, 2019).[11] According to William Andrews, Umenai's quest for a radical change of the entire New Left was influenced by the theoretical ideas of former Trotskyist Ryû Ôta:

> Rather than the conventional Marxist dialectic tracing the class struggle, Umenai examines history through the framework of colonialism and highlights oppressed groups neglected by traditional leftist thought as the worthy conveyors of revolution (Andrews, 2019: 6).

Umenai attacked the ideology of the Japanese New Left at large and its adherence to Marxism. Drawing from the real life of day laborers and other impoverished sections of society, he proposed the "precariat" as the real revolutionary force in the world. In contrast to Marxism, it is not the working class that forms the stratum on which capitalism-critical theory is oriented, but the sections of the population that live in constant poverty and sense their unsurmountable marginalization:

> The precariat consisted of marginal groups both inside Japan and in the Third World. The Marxist focus on the national proletariat in the advanced nations simply was wrong. The working class in the imperialist homelands had made their own compromise with their national imperialisms. This working class acted more like capitalist small businessmen who participated in the oppression of the colonies. They oppressed their wives and children as well (Coogan & Derichs, 2022: 171).

Umenai's theory was based on the logic that economic contradictions in the relations of production—the struggle for surplus value—no longer took place in the advanced nations, but that the plundering of the colonial world nurtured the global system. In fact, the system had always functioned in this way, i.e. this reality had already been obvious at the beginning of capitalist development. Marx had only concealed it. Colonial exploitation had weakened the class conflict in England and allowed wages to rise successively. Umenai drew an analogy from this to postwar Japan. Japan's economic expansion into Asia followed the pattern of colonial exploitation. The "reparations" paid for Japan's aggression in World War II had in fact been used to pave the way for economic expansion in Asia. Umenai thus considered Marxism to be a reactionary, outdated, and obsolete framework of thought. He compared Japan's role in China to the Holocaust, the former being worse than the latter in terms of the number of people murdered. Compared to Japan's aggression in Asia during World War II, the suffering inflicted on the Japanese nation by the atomic bombing of Hiroshima and Nagasaki was minor. Umenai's "Third-Worldism" embodied the consistent break with Marxist reasoning and articulated the radical demand that Japan must be destroyed as a nation, must cease to exist as a national entity:

> [Besides Japanese,] many Korean and other non-Japanese people were also killed in the A-bomb attacks. Nor were Japanese farmers, citizens, or students viable substitute social models for the "industrial proletariat"; they too were the enemies of the Third World. Umenai demanded that Japan as a national entity cease to exist. Even a "Japanese Socialist Republic" would only mimic the Soviet Union and Communist China. The Japanese must be made a homeless "vagabond people." Only then would the Third World precariat finally be free (Coogan & Derichs, 2022: 172).

Knaudt, who studied Umenai's texts extensively, attests an apocalyptic note to them that bordered on the genocidal. Because he was hiding since late 1969, his texts conveyed an almost mystical aura. They were both ephemeral and revelatory in opening up a new "anti-Japanese" turn inside fragments of the Japanese New Left (Knaudt, 2016: 265–75).

The Middle East in general and Palestine in particular were incorporated into Umenai's reasoning. Looking to the impoverished masses in Asia (East, South, and Southeast Asia) and the Middle East, especially Palestine, he proposed that Japanese militarism would reassert itself to take control of natural resources there. Middle East oil was a resource of major interest. To counter this trend in the global economy, new urban guerrillas would emerge in Japan. They would attack public building projects as well as military bases, and they would carry out targeted assassinations against the exploiters, i.e. those who head the companies and business dynasties. One group in particular subscribed to Umenai's vision, the East Asia Anti-Japan Armed Front. It soon became the most dangerous postwar militant group inside Japan in the mid-1970s.

In contrast to Umenai, Shigenobu engendered a different yet equally internationalist focus on the Middle East and Palestine through her activism (Yui, 2011). This may have been influenced by her connection to radical artist circles in Japan. Film critic Masao Matsuda and filmmakers such as Koji Wakamatsu and Masao Adachi were well known to her. They ran a radical cinema network. Adachi produced a famous documentary in Lebanon's training camps, and Matsuda was part of a collective (1968 to 1972) that published two revolutionary news journals.[12] It may be said that the information that was channeled through these journals also transported a considerable amount of revolutionary thought from the Tricontinental Conference of Havanna (1966) into the Japanese New Left.

A most illustrative incident that the JRA's time in Lebanon left indelibly imprinted on Japanese militants occurred on March 30, 2002, in Tokyo, when Takao Himori burned himself to death in Tokyo's Hibiya Park. Decades earlier, Himori had lived in Beirut, where he had helped recruit volunteers for the PFLP. After an unnamed Japanese activist training with the PFLP died in a swimming accident, Himori brought the corpse back to Japan and never returned to Beirut. He was in Japan when the Lod attack happened, was arrested a few weeks later, and served a short jail sentence. He then went underground for some fourteen years before contacting his family. He continued to be one of the JRA's leading public supporters and a critic of Japan's commitment to capitalism and affiliation to the West. Himori left a message saying he killed himself to protest against the plight of the Palestinians.[13]

The case of the Japanese Red Army/Nihon, Sekigun allows us to address the interplay between intellectual life, social movements, and political mobilizations in the long 1960s. Admittedly, its impact on Asian or Arabic social theoretical thought is rather weak. But it is a useful heuristic element for centering on a specific transregional figuration of radical political thought in Japan that drew extensively from the empirical case of Palestine in the Middle East. Moreover, it demonstrates how ideological deconstruction and construction tapped substantially from the Japanese activists' lived experience in and with the Arab world.

9.4 Indonesia and the Muslim Brotherhood

The setting in this section is different from the previous one. Here, social theoretical thinking *of* and *by* Arabic actors has shaped the reflection and performance of Asian activists and movements. Activism is informed by faith-based argumentation instead of "secular" codes of action legitimation. A commonality may, however, be seen in that actors in both regions relate to ideas that counter the narrative of the powers that be. We shift the gaze toward Indonesia and its connections to the Middle East (Egypt and Saudi Arabia in particular) in the long 1960s and concentrate on the interaction among Islamist social and political movements from a contemporaneous perspective. We focus on the roles and contributions of Southeast Asian Muslims in the increasing diversification of "global Islam" (Green, 2020), as began in the late 1960s and continuing until today. Studying the connections and relations between faith-based political movements in Southeast Asia and the Middle East requires a rethinking of the boundaries that form the frames of reference for movement organizations and mobilizing actors such as those affiliated to various (international) branches of the Muslim Brotherhood. In what follows, I deliberately downplay the distinction between state and non-state activism and embrace the collectively shared ideas and goals of faith-based activism in the spirit of liberation struggle—looking at how Islamist activism of the time informed Third-Worldism. The focus on Southeast Asia–Middle East relations (Indonesia, Egypt, and Saudi Arabia as cases in point) once more pushes the discussion of the long 1960s away from the Eurocentric lens; it makes sense of and expands the concept of the long 1960s with and from emic Asian and Arabic perspectives. The concrete phenomena at hand are Islamist movements of the late 1960s to late 1980s in Indonesia which connected to activists of the Egyptian Muslim Brotherhood. This empirical case is instructive for the tracking of transregional connectivity as well as the construction of an "Islamized" social theory. The centrality of the "Arab" in parts of Asia figures strongly, too, but in the particular shape of the Middle East as the perceived center of Islam.

The relationship between Southeast Asia and the Middle East dates back centuries and is particularly significant in light of the growth of

Islam's importance in the region around the Bay of Bengal.[14] The mobility of Muslim merchants following the monsoon winds around the Indian Ocean enabled countless Muslim religious scholars, thinkers, and artisans to migrate from the perceived heart of Islam (i.e. the Hijaz) to new horizons of Muslim trade and commerce, including Southeast Asia, forming a thriving and inter-connected network of Muslim community (Sheriff & Ho, 2014). This mobility influenced the form of Islam that emerged at the new frontier. In Southeast Asia, Islam is commonly regarded as a fusion of elements from Middle Eastern religious sources and local cultures. While research on the pre- and early modern Southeast Asia–Middle East connection has been relatively well established, little appears to have been studied on the ideoscapes that formed between the two regions during the long 1960s. Emancipation from colonial powers, as well as advances in communication and transportation, accelerated the circulation of ideas and Muslim internationalism in this period.

Egypt's defeat in the "Arab Cold War" followed by Gamal Abdel Nasser's death in 1970 created the conditions for the shift of influence in the Islamic world to state (Saudi Arabia, Iran) and non-state actors alike, fostering the prominence of political Islam in the latter half of the twentieth century. Saudi Arabia, bolstered by its oil resources, hosted an international Islamic conference in Mecca in 1962 and established the Muslim World League, an institution intended to balance the weight of Nasserist and Baathist regimes and forge transnational Islamic solidarity beyond the Arab world, inclusive of Southeast Asia (Aydin, 2017). This initiative resulted in the expansion of Saudi influence, as well as Saudi Arabian charity initiatives and sponsorship of Muslims from Indonesia and Malaysia to study Islam in the kingdom rather than in traditional locations such as Al-Azhar in Egypt or Tarim in Yemen. It also exported a particular Saudi-Salafiyya worldview while discarding foreign ideologies deemed unfavorable to Islam, such as Arabic socialism, liberalism, and communism in the Muslim world. In Southeast Asia, Malaysia and Indonesia were prime destinations for Saudi Arabia's endeavors. While Malaysia's government from the mid-1970s and throughout the 1980s cultivated and actively promoted an intellectual movement under the label of "Islamization of Knowledge" (on which I have elaborated in detail elsewhere [Derichs, 2017] and which is addressed in Sari Hanafi's chapter in this volume), Indonesia's political regime heavily discouraged such activities. Malaysia quickly established official transnational links with Saudi Arabia through the Saudi-based Muslim World League and the World

Assembly of Muslim Youth. In Indonesia, Saudi Arabian interpretations of Islam were perpetuated not by a single organizational structure but by a range of individuals who employed various methods to promote the ideology within a given location (Hassan, 2022). Until today, the Institute for the Knowledge of Islam and Arabic (LIPIA) in Indonesia's capital Jakarta, supported by Saudi Arabia, embraces traditional Islamic studies and is inclined toward this line of thought as reflected in its curricula (Jahroni, 2013). LIPIA graduates, along with returning Indonesians who studied in Saudi Arabia, eventually become agents for communicating Saudi Arabian Islamic ideology throughout Indonesia, improving Saudi Arabia's standing in Indonesia by forming extensive networks of support communities across the archipelago (Hassan, 2022; Jahroni, 2020).

Three years after the Saudi-organized Islamic conference of 1962, Indonesia's President Sukarno convened the inaugural Afro-Asian Islamic Conference in 1965 in Bandung, where he stated that Islam had been oppressed for generations and called for colonialism to be resisted through Islam. Another five years later, the death of Nasser allowed the relaxation of restrictions on and the reemergence of Islamic movements in Egypt such as the Muslim Brotherhood, which had been banned under Nasser's administration. Capitalizing on the opportunities for political and intellectual reorientation that opened up after Nasser's death, these movements transformed the concept of "Islam" from a religious expression to a political philosophy. Particular comprehensions of justice deriving from selected principles of *sharî'a* and *fiqh*, for instance, were proposed as answers to Muslim aspirations for liberation from whatever they felt was oppressing them. The downfall of Muslim societies was blamed on Nasser's secular vision of pan-Arabism. Deconstructing this vision and substituting secular statehood by Islamic governance became envisaged as a remedy. The Muslim Brotherhood's appeal circulated widely throughout the Muslim world. The suppression of the Brotherhood during Nasser's presidency had compelled many of its members to leave Egypt and seek asylum in Saudi Arabia and Western countries, which ultimately contributed to the movement's international outreach. In Indonesia, several works by Sayyid Qutb and Hassan al-Banna were translated and consumed among Islamic circles at universities (particularly at secular universities), inspiring the mobilization of revival movements such as *Jemaah Tarbiyah* (Machmudi, 2008). Mohammad Natsir, then the founder of the Indonesian Islamic Propagation Council (DDII), was instrumental in engaging with Arab leaders and securing scholarships for

Indonesians to study in the Middle East, especially in Egypt and Saudi Arabia. These students eventually played a crucial part in the dynamics of Islamic activism in Indonesia and the way Middle Eastern Islamist ideology impacted on Indonesia, be it in the context of political Islam or interpretations imported from Saudi Arabia.

The 1979 Iranian Revolution marked a watershed moment in Muslim Southeast Asia, leaving a far-reaching impact on political Islam. Iran demonstrated that establishing an Islamic regime over a secular state was feasible. Certain ideologies from the Islamic Republic of Iran were exported and inspired Islamic movements in South and Southeast Asia. The appeal of the Iranian Revolution was also reflected in the selective yet principally embracing attitude of pan-Islamism from Muslim Brotherhood figures like al-Banna and Qutb toward it (Tammam, 2011; Ünal, 2016). Alliances formed between Sunni Islamists and Shiite Iranian revolutionaries (Abdelnasser, 1997) until, in the mid-1980s, dissent grew among Sunni Islamic movements about Khomeini's *wilâyat al-faqîh* philosophy. Indonesia was relatively accommodating of Shiite currents and the ideology associated with the Iranian Revolution. Books authored by Iranian intellectuals such as Ali Shariati and Khomeini were enormously popular and were translated into Indonesian, igniting discussion about political Islam throughout the country (Mujiburrahman, 2018). A Shiite school of thought was founded in the country. While the utilization of religious inclinations for political goals was inhibited until the latter half of the 1980s, Islamic explanations of political and social affairs permeated the intellectual and cultural lives of Indonesia's middle class. A defining characteristic of this period was the motivation within Indonesian society to move beyond religious fanaticism and shortsighted views on small religious concerns in favor of an open and non-sectarian approach to Islam (Assegaf, 2015; Feener, 2007). These efforts can be read as attempts to immerse faith and piety into concepts of social cohesion that subscribe to Indonesia's national motto of *bhinneka tunggal ika* (unity through diversity). They are also a trait of political Islam generally, which is concerned with social and political organization more than with doctrines of faith.

Cold War anti-communism provided an explicitly favorable platform for outmaneuvering Afro-Asian solidarity in the long 1960s and replacing it with Muslim solidarity. The first Afro-Asian Islamic conference (KIAA, Konferensi Islam Afrika-Asia) in Bandung in 1965 has not been the subject of much study, but it is a symbolic event for the subsequent framing of the concept of Third World solidarity in Islamic terminology.[15]

The KIAA symbolically illustrated the Afro-Asian solidarity of the time on the basis of a shared faith (Chisaan, 2012). But although this conference had the potential to carry the Afro-Asian spirit further on an explicitly Islamic platform, the connecting threads were mostly cut in the wake of the Indonesian anti-communist genocide of 1965. Individual activists sustained by the transnational connections that had been developed before the genocide resumed their networking efforts only in the late 1970s. The rhetorical framing, however, was then no longer that of Afro-Asian solidarity. The envisaged goals were the establishment of an Islamic state—a concern that confirms Hanssen and Weiss's notion of "nation-state nationalism" mentioned above—and the implementation of *sharî'a* laws. For this purpose, Indonesians linking up with fellow activists abroad was an obvious endeavor, and Muslim Brotherhood activists were an equally obvious sparring partner.[16] Initiating such cooperation, however, very much depended on individual efforts. It was difficult for Indonesian students to openly meet Brotherhood members in Egypt, since their operations were suppressed there. Given this, contacts largely occurred in Saudi Arabia (Machmudi, 2008: 170–190). Saudi Arabia and Malaysia both became important transit sites for Indonesian activists and ideological documents (books etc.). The *suluk al-ma'thurat* (a collection of prayers) of Hassan al-Banna became particularly popular in Indonesia. Through the channel of Saudi Arabia, Indonesian promoters of the Brothers' ideology, such as Hilmi Aminuddin and Abu Ridha, spread ideas and information without having to directly meet Brotherhood activists in Egypt.

The Muslim Brotherhood's influence was diffused in study circles at secular universities in the 1980s, promoted by the abovementioned Jemaah Tarbiyah movement. It is worth quoting Yon Machmudi at some length to illustrate this:

> The Jemaah Tarbiyah focuses its activities on Islamic predication through *tarbiyah* activities. *Tarbiyah* refers to a practice of spiritual supervision carried out by a spiritual leader of a Sufi group, the *murshid*. *Tarbiyah* aims to cultivate and enhance the spiritual quality of pupils under the guidance of their teacher. This term was adopted by Hasan al-Banna not only for spiritual enhancement, but also as a way to transfer Islamic knowledge and other skills needed by his followers. *Tarbiyah* was manifested in small religious circles, or *usrah*, which al-Banna considered to be an essential tool in guiding Muslims to live better in accordance with the teachings of Islam.

> That is why, from the beginning, Jemaah Tarbiyah focused its programs on cultivating theology (*tawhid*), moral issues (*akhlaq*), and thought (*fikrah*) in the process of gaining popularity among students who had become disillusioned with the politics of their times (Machmudi, 2008: 134).

The campus circles Machmudi speaks of conceived of themselves as contributors to the Islamization of Indonesian society by strengthening individual morality and achieving an ideal family life, as well as by creating a strong community based on functional institutions that reconcile faith and social order through Islamic teachings. The spiritual leadership of the supreme guide (*al-murshid al- ʿamm*) in Egypt was acknowledged yet translated into guidance for domestic requirements. Similar to the previous example of the JRA, there were only a few individuals who acted as connectors between Indonesia and the Middle East, but their holistic approach spread the ideological spirit more intensively than huge mass demonstrations. Again from Machmudi:

> The interaction of Indonesian students with ideas of the Muslim Brothers in Saudi Arabia persuaded them of the importance of a multi-dimensional struggle for Islam [which can be read as a pendant to the struggle for Palestine liberation in the previous case; C.D.]. Islam was not confined within a practice nor narrowed into political activism. It encompasses all political, economic, social and cultural dimensions of the human being (Machmudi, 2008: 152).

The multidimensionality of the ideological manifestations embedded in these linkages via Islam/faith in the Indonesian case and solidarity in the Japanese case illustrates the dynamic of counterhegemonic "ideas from below" from the 1960s throughout the 1980s. Be it transregional Third-Worldism, pan-Islamic solidarity, progressive Islamism, or the implementation of Islamic governance, fundamental issues of the postcolonial period such as the political and cultural questions that emerged, how the relevant actors thought about and reacted to challenges in the (religio-)political and social settings, and the circumstances of linking up across national and regional borders are still understudied.

9.5 Concluding Remarks

Re-visiting the pan-Islamic thought that emerged in both (South-)East Asia and the Middle East alongside the leftist movements during the so-called long 1960s is a useful exercise in order to broaden the analysis of the relationship between both regions. But there is work ahead. There is a void in the transregional mental map that is yearning to be filled, and the interpretation of this period from an Arabic point of view and through Arabic sources goes a long way toward filling in the missing picture. This is what I would like to associate with the notion of writing social theory in Arabic. Moreover, the relation between social and ideological thought and social theory may be pondered more intensively—perhaps by drawing from the rich empirical material that can be expected to lie stored in archives across the Arab world. Discursive, intellectual, and religious traditions are inevitably bound to the tide of (global) political developments. They can become appropriated for political goals, as the shift from African–African solidarity to an authority-defined "cultural Islam" in Indonesia demonstrates.

According to the editors of the *Routledge Handbook of the Global Sixties*, "[…] the very concept of the global sixties is also an inevitable by-product of the trend toward global history that has captured the profession in recent years, especially for those doing contemporary history" (Klimke & Nolan, 2018: 3). This concept admittedly recognizes that the movements of the sixties were subject to differing local inflections and depended on distinct political conditions and circumstances. Yet "they often drew on a readily available, globally circulating arsenal of intellectual reference points, protest techniques, and other cultural practices that lend their voices a forceful mode of expression" (Klimke & Nolan, 2018: 9). While secular traits of Third-Worldism such as those in Japan are acknowledged, the importance of the Palestinian liberation struggle for this ideological current is hitherto underestimated. Moreover, Islam as an intellectual reference point is often missing in the compilations of the global sixties—or if it is extant, primarily under the rubric of an Islamic Left. Faith-based social theorizing is relegated to the realm of religious studies rather than being conceptualized as an analytical tool for examining a Zeitgeist phenomenon such as the global sixties from historical, philosophical, and social science perspectives.

These observations count, I assume, for the majority of studies in English on the decade of the 1960s and the subsequent years. While the long 1960s are often "nostalgically celebrated as a revolutionary heyday and lamented as a failed political project," a weak point in the literature is "that long-held evaluations of this tumultuous decade have too often remained parochially centred on European and North American experiences in a handful of cities" (Maasri et al., 2022: 2). Decentering the West as the main locus of sixties' events and broadening the geographic view is, to my understanding, a task for writing social theory in Arabic and broadening the mental map. Apart from contributing to epistemic decolonization, such work would also contribute to a linguistic democratization in global knowledge production.

Writing social theory from lived experiences and movement activism rather than intellectual traditions and ideas allows us, as discussed above, to trace transregional people-to-people imaginations of community, belonging, solidarity, liberation, and, in more recent terminology, "the good life." It relates the reflection on social theory to notions of self-fulfillment and assertion of the self, to self-submission to a shared cause, and to putting the social into a bottom-up perspective (or a perspective "from below"). In the ideological landscape of transregional connectivities, "the Arab world" formed a major center and the rallying point for movement mobilization during much of the Cold War period. A task ahead is to research how this centrality is spelled out *in* Arabic and *from* an Arab point of view—if it is acknowledged or rejected, and what kind of sources and references could be made productive for the dissemination of this point of view.

Notes

1. As at the time of writing, a PKS candidate is co-contesting in Indonesia's upcoming presidential election (February 2024); the stance toward the Arab world has been watered down to some extent due to the strong and popular impact of ideas of a domestic Islam (mentioned subsequently) which challenge PKS views.
2. The other two Japanese militants had not been Sekigun members in Japan. For more details on the Lod airport attack, see Coogan and Derichs (2022), Chapter 15.
3. For more details, see Derichs (2006). For an analysis of the Lod attack and its survivor Okamoto, see Steinhoff (1976).

4. Shigenobu was not the only Japanese woman volunteer for the Palestinian cause in the early 1970s, but she became the most charismatic and long-term female leader of the JRA in Lebanon.
5. Andrews (2016) reports that Okudaira was already in Lebanon when Shigenobu finally arrived in Beirut for good on March 1, 1971.
6. The tragedy was that these young people were forced to die through the hands of their own comrades, the alleged wrongdoing being their inability to commit proper "communization." For more details see Coogan and Derichs (2022), Chapter 16. Koji Wakamatsu's film "United Red Army" (2007) is a visual account of the tragedy.
7. Umenai developed his thought from the writings of another famous figure, theorist and activist of the New Left Ryû Ôta, and likeminded people around him. Ôta's notion of a "revolution of the dispossessed" had a strong impact on Umenai. In combination with the tragic events of early 1972, he came up with what can in retrospect be called a Japanese contribution to postcolonial theory. See also Andrews (2019).
8. For *dependencia* theory, see Frank (1966). A standard work in Spanish was published in 1971, written by Eduardo Galeano. For comparative theoretical reflections on Third World politics, see Smith (2013).
9. The East Asia Anti-Japan Armed Front (Higashi Ajia Hannichi Busō Sensen) was infamous for carrying out a devastating bomb attack in August 1974 against the giant Mitsubishi corporation, killing eight people and injuring up to 400. Other bomb attacks followed suit.
10. The discussion of Umenai draws mainly on Knaudt (2016: 265–274).
11. Andrews (2019). A month earlier, he published a text in the journal *Sashō* (visa) on the Red Army. See Knaudt (2016: 265).
12. They were called *News from the World Revolutionary Movement* (*Sekai kakumei undō jōhō*) and its related Society of Revolt (Reboruto-ha). For Matsuda's network, see Knaudt (2016: 67–73). Besides Matsuda, the collective included anarchists Masakuni Ōta, Kenji Yamaguchi, and Shōji Sasaki, the older brother of Norio Sasaki, one of the founders of the terrorist group the East Asian

Anti-Japan Armed Front in the early 1970s. The publications glorified Che Guevara and republished works by the Spanish Civil War veteran Alberto Bayo y Giroud as *Handbook of Guerrilla War*. It further ran texts by Franz Fanon and articles on Black Power and the political situation in South Korea.

13. For Himori's traumatic experience and attempts to cope with it, see Himori (2005).
14. I am grateful to Ariff Hafizi bin Mohd Radzi for substantial collaboration in the formulation of the following paragraphs.
15. A very valuable study on the KIAA is Chisaan (2012).
16. For details on this relationship, see Machmudi (2008), Chapter 5.

References

Abdelnasser, W. M. (1997). Islamic Organizations in Egypt and The Iranian Revolution of 1979: The Experience of The First Few Years. *Arab Studies Quarterly, 19*(2), 25–39.

Andrews, W. (2016). *Dissenting Japan: A History of Japanese Radicalism and Counterculture, from 1945 to Fukushima*. Hurst & Company.

Andrews, W. (2019). *Pan-Asianism and the Post-War Japanese Radical Left: Some Movements and Tendencies*. https://throwoutyourbooks.wordpress.com/2019/12/10/panasianism-post-war-japanese-radical-left-movements/. Last accessed on January 12, 2022.

Appadurai, A. (1996). *Modernity at Large: Cultural Dimensions of Globalization*. University of Minnesota Press.

Assegaf, U. F. (2015). Aspects of Shi'ism in Contemporary Indonesia. In C. Formichi & M. R. Feener (Eds.), *Shi'ism in Southeast Asia: 'Alid Piety and Sectarian Constructions* (pp. 249–268). Oxford University Press.

Aydin, C. (2017). *The Idea of the Muslim World: A Global Intellectual History*. Harvard University Press.

Castoriadis, C. (1975). *L'Institution imaginaire de la société*. Seuil.

Chisaan, C. (2012). In Search of an Indonesian Islamic Cultural Identity, 1956–1965. In J. Lindsay & Maya H. T. Liem (Eds.), *Heirs to World Culture: Being Indonesian 1950–1965* (pp. 283–314). KITLV Press

Coogan, K., & Derichs, C. (2022). *Tracing Japanese Leftist Political Activism (1957–2017)*. Routledge.

Derichs, C. (2006). Die Japanische Rote Armee [The Japanese Red Army]. In W. Kraushaar (Ed.), *Die RAF und der linke Terrorismus* [The RAF and Left Terrorism] (Vol. 2, pp. 809–827). Hamburger Edition.

Derichs, C. (2017). *Knowledge Production*. Routledge.

Esashi, A. (2022). *Watashi datta kamo shirenai. Aru Sekigun josei heishi no 25nen* [It Could Have Been Me. 25 Years of a Female Sekigun Soldier]. Inpakuto shuppansha.

Feener, M. R. (2007). *Muslim Legal Thought in Modern Indonesia*. Cambridge University Press.

Frank, A. G. (1966). *The Development of Underdevelopment*. New England Free Press.

Galeano, D. (1971). *Las venas abiertas de América Latina* [Open Veins of Latin America]. Siglo Veintiuno.

Green, N. (2020): *Global Islam: A Very Short Introduction* (1st edn.). Oxford University Press.

Hanssen, J., & Weiss, M. (Eds.) (2018). *Arabic Thought Against the Authoritarian Age: Towards an Intellectual History of the Present*. Cambridge University Press.

Hassan, N. (2022). Salafism, Education, and Youth: Saudi Arabia's Campaign for Wahhabism in Indonesia. In P. Mandaville (Ed.), *Wahhabism and the World: Understanding Saudi Arabia's Global Influence on Islam* (pp. 135–157). Oxford University Press.

Himori, T. (2005). *Suiheisen no mukō ni* [Beyond the Horizon]. Fūjinsha.

Jahroni, J. (2013). The Political Economy of Knowledge: Shari'ah and Saudi Scholarship in Indonesia. *Journal of Indonesian Islam, 7*(1), 165–186. https://doi.org/10.15642/jiis.2013.7.1.165-186. Last accessed on June 3, 2022.

Jahroni, J. (2020). Saudi Arabia Charity and the Institutionalization of Indonesian Salafism. *Al-Jami'ah: Journal of Islamic Studies, 58*(1), 35–62.

Koarashi, K. (Ed.) (2010). *Nihon Sekigun. Sekai wo shissô shita gunzô* [The Japanese Red Army: The Group that Careered Through the World]. Tosho shinbun.

Klimke, M., & Nolan, M., et al. (2018). Introduction: The Globalization of the Sixties. In C. Jian (Ed.), *The Routledge Handbook of the Global Sixties* (pp. 1–9). Routledge.

Knaudt, T. (2016). *Von Revolution zu Befreiung: Studentenbewegung, Antiimperialismus und Terrorismus in Japan (1968–1973)* [From Revolution to Liberation: Student Movement, Anti-Imperialism, and Terrorism in Japan (1968–1973)]. Campus.

Maasri, Z., Bergin, C., & Burke, F. (2022). Introduction: Transnational Solidarity in the Long Sixties. In Z. Maasri, C. Bergin, & F. Burke (Eds.), *Transnational Solidarity: Anticolonialism in the Global Sixties* (pp. 1–26). Manchester University Press.

Machmudi, Y. (2008). *Islamising Indonesia: The Rise of Jemaah Tarbiyah and the Prosperous Justice Party*. ANU Press.

Mujiburrahman. (2018). Indonesian Translation and Appropriation of the Works of Shariati and Hanafi in the New Order's Islamic Discourses. *Studia Islamika, 25*(2), 279–308.

Oguma, E. (2009). *1968: Hanran no shûen to sono isan* [1968: The End of the Revolution and the Legacy it Left Behind]. Shinyôsha.

Oguma, E. (2018). What Was and Is "1968"?: Japanese Experience in Global Perspective. *The Asia Pacific Journal, 16*(11), 6. https://apjjf.org/2018/11/Oguma.html. Last accessed on September 12, 2022.

Sheriff, A., & Ho, E. (2014). *The Indian Ocean: Oceanic Connections and the Creation of New Societies.* Hurst

Shigenobu, F. (1984): *Beirûto 1982 natsu* [The Beirut Summer of 1982]. Hanashi no tokushû.

Shigenobu, F. (2001). *Ringo no ki no shita de anata o umô to kimeta* [Deciding to Give Birth to you Under an Apple Tree]. Gentôsha.

Shigenobu, F. (2012). *Kakumei no kisetsu. Paresuchina no senjo kara* [Seasons of Revolution. View from the Palestinian Battleground]. Gentôsha.

Shiomi, Takaya (2010): Arabu no seikatsu bunka ha ishitsu-na mono nimo atatatakai [Arab Culture has a High Tolerance for Differences]. In K. Koarashi (Ed.), *Nihon Sekigun. Sekai wo shissô shita gunzô* [The Japanese Red Army: The Group that Careered Through the World] (pp. 167–227). Tosho shinbun.

Smith, B. C. (2013). *Understanding Third World Politics: Theories of Political Change and Development.* Palgrave Macmillan.

Steinhoff, P. (1976). Portrait of a Terrorist: An Interview with Kozo Okamoto. *Asian Survey, 16*(9), 830–845.

Steinhoff, P. (1996). Three Women Who Loved the Left: Radical Woman Leaders in the Japanese Red Army Movement. In A. Imamura (Ed.), *Re-imagining Japanese Women* (pp. 301–322). University of California Press.

Steinhoff, P. (2007, September 9): Interview: Dr. Patricia Steinhoff 1, in W. David Marx. *neojaponisme* (blog). https://neojaponisme.com/2007/09/09/steinhoffpartone/ Last accessed on October 12, 2022.

Steinhoff, P. (2016). Transnational Ties of the Japanese Armed Left: Shared Revolutionary Ideas and Direct Personal Contacts. In A. M. Àlvarez & E. R. Tristán (Eds.), *Revolutionary Violence and the New Left: Transnational Perspectives* (pp. 163–181). Routledge.

Tahara, M. (2022). "Shitô" Shigenobu Fusako to Nihon Sekigun [The Shigenobu Fusako "clique" and the Japanese Red Army]. *Bungei Shunju, 8*, 130–140.

Takata, K. (2020). Connecting with the First or the Third World?: Two Paths Toward the Transnational Network Building in the Japanese Global Sixties. *Moving the Social, 63*, 65–90. https://doi.org/10.13154/mts.63.2020.65-90.

Tammam, H. (2011). *The Salafization of Muslim Brothers: The Erosion of the Fundamental Hypothesis and the Rising of Salafism within the Muslim Brotherhood: The Paths and the Repercussions of Change* (transl. from the Arabic text Tasalluf al-iḫwān: taʾākul al-uṭrūḥa al-iḫwānīya wa-ṣuʿūd as-salafiya fī Jamāʿat al-Iḫwān al-Muslimīn). A Scholarly Peer-Reviewed Pamphlet, Bibliotheca Alexandrina.

Ünal, Y. (2016). Sayyid Quṭb in Iran: Translating the Islamist Ideologue in the Islamic Republic. *Journal of Islamic and Muslim Studies, 1*(2), 35–60.

Wakō, H. (2010). *Nihon Sekigun to ha nan datta no ka: Sono sôseki wo megutte* [What was the Japanese Red Army? On the Early Days]. Seiryûsha.

Yui, R. (2011): *Shigenobu Fusako ga ita jidai* [When Shigenobu Fusako was There]. Sekai shoin.

Printed in the United States
by Baker & Taylor Publisher Services